The
Shape of the
Signifier

1967
to the End of
History

WALTER BENN MICHAELS

Princeton University Press   Princeton and Oxford

Copyright © 2004 by Princeton University Press
Published by Princeton University Press, 41 William Street,
Princeton, New Jersey 08540
In the United Kingdom: Princeton University Press,
3 Market Place, Woodstock, Oxfordshire OX20 1SY

Second printing, and first paperback printing, 2007
Paperback ISBN-13: 978-0-691-12618-0
Paperback ISBN-10: 0-691-12618-6

The Library of Congress has cataloged the cloth edition of this book as follows

Michaels, Walter Benn.
The shape of the signifier : 1967 to the end
of history / Walter Benn Michaels.
p.   cm.
Includes bibliographical references (p.) and index.
ISBN 0-691-11872-8 (alk. paper)
1. American literature—History and criticism—Theory, etc.
2. American literature—20th century—History and criticism.
3. American literature—21st century—History and criticism.
4. Signification (Logic) in literature.   5. Literary form.   I. Title.
PS25.M53 2004
801'.95'0904—dc22   2003055640

British Library Cataloging-in-Publication Data is available

This book has been composed in Dante

Printed on acid-free paper. ∞

press.princeton.edu

Printed in the United States of America

3   5   7   9   10   8   6   4

Contents

Contents

Acknowledgments

My debt to the work of Frances Ferguson, Stanley Fish, Michael Fried, and Steven Knapp will be obvious to any reader of this book, and I am grateful for the opportunity to acknowledge it here. Michael Fried also read and criticized an earlier version of *The Shape of the Signifier*, as did Jed Esty, Ruth Leys, Mark Maslan, Sean McCann, and a couple of anonymous readers, and I am grateful for their many helpful suggestions. Even when I could not follow them, I saw their justice. Many others have made important contributions to my thinking about the subjects of this book. I want especially to thank Paul Anderson, Jennifer Ashton, Nicholas Brown, Michael Clune, Jamie Daniel, Winfried Fluck, Jason Gladstone, Reichii Miura, Lisa Siraganian, Martin Stone, and Vershawn Young. Finally, I want to thank the editors of *Critical Inquiry*, *Narrative*, *New Literary History*, *Radical History Review*, and *Transition* for permission to reprint material published, in earlier versions, in their journals.

The Blank Page

The *Autobiography* of the Puritan minister Thomas Shepard, Susan Howe says in *The Birth-mark*, was originally written in "one half of a small leather-bound pocket notebook"; if you turn the notebook over and upside down, you find what Howe calls "another narrative by the same author," one that she characterizes as "more improvisational" and that Shepard's editors call "notes."[1] In between the *Autobiography* and the "notes" are "eighty-six blank manuscript pages" (58). In both the major editions of the *Autobiography*, selections from the "notes" are included after the text of the *Autobiography* proper. "Neither editor," Howe says, "saw fit to point out the fact that Shepard left two manuscripts in one book separated by many pages and positioned so that to read one you must turn the other upside down" (60). Neither editor, of course, included the eighty-six blank pages between the *Autobiography* and the notes. The reader of the manuscript "reads"—in addition to or as part of the *Autobiography*— eighty-six pages of "empty paper"; the reader of either edition does not. Are they reading the same text? Are the eighty-six blank pages part of the text? What do you have to think reading is to think that when you run your eyes over blank pages you are reading them? Or what do you have to think a text is to think that pages without any writing are part of it?

Deleting blank pages isn't by any means the only or the most controversial of the editorial decisions that concern Howe in the essays that
make up *The Birth-mark*, all of which she describes as "the direct and
indirect results" of her "encounters" with Ralph Franklin's facsimile editions of *The Manuscript Books of Emily Dickinson* and *The Master Letters of
Emily Dickinson*, encounters which demonstrated to her that what Dickinson wrote had been destroyed rather than reproduced by Thomas
Johnson's edition of her poems. Where Howe believes, for example, that
the irregular spacing between words and even letters is "a part of the
meaning" of the poems, Johnson regularized the spacing and thus, she
thinks, altered the meaning. Examining the facsimiles, Howe came to
think of Dickinson as an antinomian in the tradition of Anne Hutchin-
son. She imagines Dickinson's preference for leaving her poems unpub-
lished as a form of rebellion, an expression of her commitment to a
"covenant of grace" (1), and she imagines the "reordering and revision"
of her manuscripts by Johnson and, to a lesser extent, by Franklin as an
expression of their commitment to a "covenant of works" (2) in which
the "production of meaning [is] brought under the control of social authority" (140). Thus editorial activities like arranging the poems in stanzas and editorial decisions like ignoring "stray marks" (132) seem to
Howe to limit Dickinson's meanings by "repress[ing] the physical immediacy" (146) of the poems.

But the alignment of Dickinson's "meaning" with grace rather than
works and, even more fundamentally, the commitment to meaning itself
can only stand in a somewhat vexed relation to Howe's objections to the
Johnson edition and to her objections to editorial practice more generally. For *The Birth-mark*'s worry about the social control of meaning is
complicated by its investment in the "physical immediacy" of Dickinson's texts, in its investment, that is, in aspects of Dickinson's texts that
Howe herself thinks of as meaningless, in the "blots" and "dashes" (8)
that she calls "marks" and that she identifies with "nonsense" (7) and
"gibberish" (2). It's one thing to object to editors who alter the meaning
of the text; it's not quite the same thing to object to editors who take
out blank pages and stray marks, marks that seem to them, and to Howe
too, not to have any meaning, to belong rather to what she calls "the
other of meaning" (148). In fact, from this perspective, Howe looks more

hostile to antinomianism than Dickinson's editors do, since she's the one defending the letter—of the poem, if not the law. But it is also this defense of the literal, not only of the letter but of the "smudged letter" and not only of the mark but of the "space," that leads *The Birth-mark* into its most original speculations about the ontology of the Dickinson text.

Howe's earlier book *My Emily Dickinson* had made no criticism of the Johnson edition and, without manifesting much interest in its blots and marks, had expressed regret that so few readers would have access to the Franklin facsimile only because it was "necessary for a clearer under-standing of her writing process."[2] In *The Birth-mark*, however, readers of the Johnson edition instead of the Franklin facsimile are no longer thought to be reading Dickinson at all. For, insofar as the Dickinson text is now to be understood as a "material object," insofar, that is, as "the print on the page . . ., the shapes of the words . . ., the space of the paper itself" (157) are now understood as essential elements of the work, not even a corrected version of the Johnson could ever be adequate to it. Indeed, what must be wrong with any Dickinson edition, from Howe's perspective, is the very idea of Dickinson's poems as a text to be edited. Howe is interested here in features that "no printed version could match" (152) (like the way Dickinson "crosses her t's"), which is to say that she is interested in the ways in which the poems, becoming "drawing," cease to be text. This is the point of the redescription of text as "material object" (60). For the very idea of textuality depends upon the discrepancy between the text and its materiality, which is why two different copies of a book (two different material objects) may be said to be the same text. The text is understood to consist in certain crucial features (e.g., [and minimally] certain words in a certain order), and any object that reproduces those features (whatever they are thought to be) will repro-duce the text.[3] One way to criticize an edition, then, is to criticize it for failing to recognize and reproduce the crucial features, and some of Howe's criticisms of Johnson take this form. But her sense of Dickinson's poems as drawings and her commitment to the "physical immediacy" of them as objects involve a more radical critique, since insofar as the text is made identical to the "material object," it ceases to be something that could be edited and thus ceases to be a text at all.

This is what it means for Howe to turn the written word into the mark and to value "blots, dashes, smudged letters, gaps" under the sign of "gibberish." Blots and smudged letters cannot be edited; they can only be reproduced. Hence the only possible edition of the Dickinson text is the "facsimile," an edition that is a reproduction instead of an edition. Because the text is disconnected from its meaning, no attempt to identify those features that are crucial to its meaning is possible—there are no such features. Or, to turn the point around, the fact that no features can be identified as crucial means that every feature is. For if it doesn't make sense to think that the way Dickinson crossed her t's matters to the meaning of her work—a *t* is a *t* no matter how it's crossed—the point of the redescription of the letter as mark is to make it matter. The printed *t* and the handwritten (or "smudged") *t* are the same letter but not the same mark, which is to say, they don't have the same shape. And, of course, the same is true of all the features to which Howe points: the spaces between the words and letters, the quality of the paper, and so forth; to alter any of these is to change the text, not because you've changed its meaning but because you've changed what Paul de Man, in an essay written in the year before Howe began work on what would become *The Birth-mark* ("Phenomenality and Materiality in Kant" [1983]), calls its "sensory appearance."[4] And it is this appearance that the facsimile reproduces—the facsimile shows you what the letters look like and how far apart they are from each other. Its point is not just to convey the meaning of the text to the reader but also to reproduce the experience of its physical features.

But even transforming the poem (a text to be edited) into a drawing (to be reproduced instead of edited) does not produce a complete equation of the work of art with the "material object." For the reproducibility even of the drawing depends on some notion of what is essential to it, some notion of what makes the drawing the drawing it is. (Indeed, thinking about what must be reproduced in order for the work of art to have been reproduced is just a device for thinking about what it is that makes the work of art the work of art it is.) And any such notion will involve distinguishing between the material object that is the drawing and the material object as such. The reproduction, for instance, will never be on the same piece of paper the drawing is on—does that mean it isn't the same drawing? We might want to call two prints of a photograph the same photograph, but the fact that they are the same photograph does not make them the same object. Even a facsimile of Dickinson's poems will reproduce only the shapes of the marks she made; it won't duplicate the ink she made them with. In this sense, the facsimile is no more committed to the material object than is the Johnson edition; it just has a different set of criteria for determining which aspects of that object count as the work of art. To be truly committed to the materiality of the object would be to suspend all such criteria. If we think of Dickinson as making poems, we will think that getting the right words in the right order is what matters; if we think of her as making drawings, then we will think that getting the right shapes in the right places will matter. But if we want the same object, then everything matters. We no longer care whether Dickinson was writing poems or making drawings.

Indeed, despite the fact that our interest in the text's materiality was provoked first by an interest in Dickinson's intention, we can no longer have any principled interest in Dickinson at all. Even though she played a no doubt crucial causal role in producing the object, our interest in its materiality requires our attention to every feature of the text, regardless of Dickinson's involvement. Thus the most radical form of Howe's commitment to Dickinson produces a certain indifference to Dickinson—for the things Dickinson didn't care about (say, the kind of ink) must matter just as much as the things she did care about (say, the shapes of the letters). So to see the material object just as a material object is to make no distinction between what Dickinson cared about and what she didn't. A thoroughgoing materialism needn't deny that the object has been made by someone but must nevertheless treat it as if it had been made by no one. That's why, in the essays on Kant at the heart of *Aesthetic Ideology*, de Man emphasizes those moments where Kant insisted on the importance of what de Man calls the "nonteleological." The "wild man" who "sees a house of which he does not know the use" (81) counts as an exemplary instance of someone engaged in what de Man calls "material vision" precisely because, seeing the house "entirely severed from any purpose or use" (88), he sees only its "sensory appearance." He sees things the way they appear "to the eye and not to the mind" (82), which is to say, he sees the house the way someone who did not know what

books were, or even what words were, would see Dickinson's poems or
Shepard's *Autobiography.*

The eighty-six blank pages count here as part of the object (de Man
mentions "the blank" between the two stanzas of Wordsworth's "A
Slumber Did My Spirit Seal" as an example of the "pure materiality" he's
talking about) not because they are important to the "purpose" of the
object's maker but because—insofar as they are part of the object's "sensuous appearance"—they are part of what the reader "reads" or "sees"
without reference to the maker's purpose. The purely material, in other
words, is everything that can be seen by the reader. The question of
which part of what the reader sees counts as part of the work of art (the
question, say, of whether the eighty-six blank pages should be included
in an edition of the *Autobiography*) is not so much answered as it is set
aside. After all, the blank pages are part of what the reader sees whether
or not they are understood to be part of the work of art. So the question
of what's in the work of art (a question about the object) is replaced by
the question of what the reader sees (a question about the subject).

De Man's insistence on what he calls "a *material* vision" (82) thus produces—inevitably, which is to say, necessarily—a replacement of the idea
of the text's meaning (and of the project of interpreting that meaning)
with the idea of the reader's experience and with a certain indifference
to or, more radically, repudiation of meaning and interpretation both.
For what "material vision" sees (it is the very mark of its materiality) is,
as one of de Man's commentators puts it, "completely emptied out of
its meaning,"[5] or, as de Man himself puts it: "the eye, left to itself, entirely
ignores understanding" (127). Objects of understanding are objects not
yet "severed from any purpose or use"; if we think of Shepard's *Autobiography* as such an object, we will decide whether to reproduce the eighty-
six blank pages by trying to decide whether we think they were meant
to serve some purpose. An argument about whether to reproduce them
would follow the same lines as the argument Howe conducts with Dickinson's editor, Ralph Franklin, about whether an edition of her poems
should reproduce the line breaks in the manuscripts. Franklin thinks they
shouldn't; in Howe's formulation, he thinks that where the lines end in
the manuscripts is a function of physical features like the size of the
paper and of Dickinson's handwriting, and that an editor of Dickinson's

poems should follow the "form" of the poems "rather than accidents of physical line breaks on paper" (145). Howe, in response, insists that Dickinson was not "careless about line breaks" and that, "in the precinct of Poetry, a word, the space around a word, each letter, every mark, silence, or sound volatizes an inner law of form." She insists, in other words, that the line breaks in the fascicles are *not* "accidents," that they "represent an athematic compositional intention" (139), and the debate between her and Franklin is thus a debate about what is or isn't accidental, what is or isn't intentional.

From the standpoint of de Man's "material vision," however, this debate misses the point—which is not to decide what was done on purpose and what was done by accident but to treat the object as if nothing were done on purpose, as if everything were accidental. Marks and spaces produced by accident are not objects of "understanding"; the question of what Dickinson intended is made irrelevant by the materialist indifference to what she meant. Thus, de Man will, in his most radical moments, describe hard-to-interpret speech acts (speech acts that seem to suggest *many* possible meanings) as speech acts that have no meaning at all, as uninterpretable "noise."[6] And thus, as we have already seen, in her most radical moments, Howe too—insisting that Shepard's eighty-six blank pages be reproduced and that every aspect (not just spelling and punctuation but stray marks, the space between the words and letters, random drops of ink) of the Dickinson text be reproduced—will be led to identify poetry not with what can be understood but with what can't: with "nonsense" and "gibberish."

But if this commitment to the meaningless is, as I have been suggesting, the most radical form of the commitment to the material object, it is by no means the only, or even the most common. Quoting Poe's remark that "nonsense" is "the essential sense of the Marginal Note (7)," Howe distinguishes between what she calls "works" and what she calls "marginal notes"; unlike works, "marks in the margin are immediate reflections" (15). Marks that are not works—like birthmarks—are signs of the writer's presence. When Russell Cheney finds a shopping list on the back of a letter sent him by F. O. Matthiessen, the shopping list, not the letter, produces the "actual scene" of Matthiessen's life: "It sort of took my breath it was so real—as though I'd reached out and touched you" (14). The power of the shopping list here derives not from its meaning but from its physical connection to Matthiessen; it affects Cheney not, in other words, as a representation of what Matthiessen meant (it might just as well be "stray" marks) but as evidence of his physical presence, as a trace of where he was.[7] If the impossibility of understanding the mark sometimes looks like a kind of skepticism—you can't know what the text means—here that skepticism about meaning is turned into an opportunity for experience; instead of understanding Mattheissen's text, Cheney feels like he's touching his body. It's when the mark becomes meaningless that it becomes most "real."

By far the most usual form taken by the transformation of text into material object, however, involves the emergence of the reader as what Howe (quoting Richard Sieburth) calls an "active participant" in rather than a "passive consumer" (19) of the meaning of the text. Here, of course, it's the multiplicity of meaning rather than its absence that seems crucial; what's being celebrated (or, sometimes, deplored) is the different meanings the same text can have for different readers in different situations. But it isn't hard to see that the interest in the reader's participation renders the text's meaning as irrelevant as de Manian material vision does. Once we become interested in what we see, in what the text makes us think of, we become in principle as indifferent to the question of what the text means as de Man could wish. Indeed, it is hard to say whether de Man's rigorous and even ascetic critique of interpretation is the deep truth of the sentimental celebration of different readers reading differently or whether their sentimentality is the deep truth of de Man's asceticism. In any case, the claim that the text means nothing will turn out to have exactly the same cash value as the claim that it means different things to different people. Readers for whom the same text can have different meanings are not readers who have different beliefs about what the text means; they are readers who have different responses to the text, whatever it means. They do not, that is, have different interpretations of the text; they have different *experiences* of the text.[8]

The difference between interpreting a text and experiencing it is articulated by de Man as the difference between an encounter with "language" in its "cognitive" mode and an encounter with language as it "frees itself of its constraints and discovers within itself a power no longer dependent on the restrictions of cognition" (79). The "language of cognition" (133) is language you understand—or misunderstand; you know (or think you know) what it means. But your relation to what de Man calls the "language of power" is one of "pure affect rather than cognition" (89). Indeed, that's the point of calling it the language of power or, what de Man also calls it, of "force" (122); to understand a text is one thing, to feel its force is another. Language as force "has the materiality of something that actually happens, that actually occurs" (134). Like Howe's material object (like the eighty-six blank pages "the reader reads"), de Man's material event (say, "the blank between stanzas 1 and 2 of the Lucy poem 'A slumber did my spirit seal' " [89]), "leaves a trace on the world." But where Howe sometimes justifies her commitment to these traces on the grounds that they are intentional (not "careless") and sometimes despite the fact that they are not intentional (even the "random" or "stray" mark must be preserved as trace of the author's presence), de Man's materialism is more thoroughgoing—it has nothing to do with what the author intended or what the reader believes, with the text's meaning or with the reader's interpretation of that meaning.

Indeed, the central point of those essays collected under the title *Aesthetic Ideology* is to identify that ideology—to identify ideology itself—with what from the standpoint of de Man's materialism counts as the "illusion of meaning" and to identify the alternative to that illusion (what "actually happens") with what he calls "history." "History is . . . the emergence of a language of power out of a language of cognition" (133). So what the "materiality of the letter" is to knowledge, the "materiality of actual history" (11) is to ideology, and what *Aesthetic Ideology* calls for is thus a turn away from ideology and toward history. By the time *Aesthetic Ideology* got published, however (in 1996), what de Man had characterized as the emergence of history everyone else was characterizing as the end of history. For if, on Francis Fukuyama's account, the end of the Cold War did not mean the end of ideology, it did mean what Fukuyama called the "end" of "mankind's ideological evolution,"[9] and it thus made ideology as irrelevant to action as de Man's materialism had. In the posthistorical world, the struggle between socialism and liberalism would be replaced by "the endless solving of technical problems" and "the satisfaction of sophisticated consumer demands" (25). Replacing the question of what people believe with the question of what they want, Fukuyama's posthistoricism repeated the de Manian replacement of the cognitive with the affective. And this turn to affect at the end of history produced the same result as the turn to affect at the beginning of history: the primacy of the subject. Liberals and socialists have different beliefs about the world, and the disagreement between them necessarily transcends their subject positions, which is just to say that if the liberals are right, then the socialists must be wrong. But once what people believe is replaced (as Fukuyama says) by what they want or (as de Man says) by what they see, the difference between them requires no disagreement. The difference between what you want and what I want is just a difference between you and me; the difference between what you see and what I see is just the difference between where you're standing and where I'm standing—literally, a difference in subject position.[10]

THIS MOVEMENT from questions about the ontology of the text to an insistence on the primacy of the subject makes a single argument out of what I have in my own writing treated as two separate arguments and two separate projects. One, most fully articulated in the "Against Theory" essays (written in collaboration with Steven Knapp), is an argument that texts can mean only what their authors intend them to mean. The other, set out in my book *Our America* (1995), is an argument against identity and, what's particularly relevant to the present book, against the idea that the things you do and the beliefs you hold can be justified by a description of who you are. The reason, of course, that that way of putting the point is relevant to the present project is that the appeal to who you are has for many years been central to certain kinds of literary theoretical arguments, explicit in claims that the reader plays a role in determining the meaning of texts and implicit (at least, so *The Shape of the Signifier* will argue) in claims that the meaning of the text is determined by the syntactic and semantic rules of the language in which it is written. So, although I did not in writing it understand *Our America's* critique of identity to be in any significant way connected to the defense of intention in "Against Theory," the argument of the current book is not only that they are connected but that each claim entails the other. If you think that differences in belief cannot be described as differences in identity, you must also think that texts mean what their authors intend.

This argument is rehearsed in the preceding pages of this introduction but in the opposite direction and on the opposite side. The effort here has been to think through the question not only of what a text means but, even more fundamentally, of what the text is—of what is in it and what isn't, what counts as part of it and what doesn't—without the appeal to the author's intention. And the point is that if you do this, you find yourself committed not only to the materiality of the text but also, by way of that materiality, to the subject position of the reader. You find yourself committed to the materiality of the text because, if you don't think it matters whether the author of the text did or didn't intend the eighty-six blank pages to count as part of it, the mere fact that they are there must be dispositive. And you find yourself committed to the primacy of the subject position because the question about what's there will always turn out to be (this argument is made at length later) a question about what's there to you, a question about what you see. Once, in other words, the eighty-six pages count not because some author meant them to count but because they are there, in front of you, then everything that is there must also count—the table the pages are on, the room the table is in, the way the pages, the table, and the room make you feel. Why? Because all these things are part of your experience of the pages, and once we abjure interest in what the author intended (once we no longer care whether or not the author intended us to count the room the work of art is in as part of the work of art), we have no principled reason not to count everything that's part of our experience as part of the work. And, of course, while our experiences will often be very similar, they will always be a little different—where you stand will be a little different from where I stand, what you feel will be different from what I feel, who you are is not who I am.

So the argument, in miniature, is that if you think the intention of the author is what counts, then you don't think the subject position of the reader matters, but if you don't think the intention of the author is what counts, then the subject position of the reader will be the only thing that matters. This is a theoretical argument, not a historical one, and, of course, "Against Theory" was an entirely theoretical essay. But *Our*

America was meant not only as a critique of identity but also as a history of at least a certain crucial episode in its invention and deployment, and *The Shape of the Signifier* is meant to have a historical dimension as well. One way to put this would be to say that I am here interested in the historical simultaneity of (as well as the theoretical link between) the modern interest in the ontology of the text and the rise of what I characterized in *Our America* as a distinctively modern notion of identity. If, in other words, modernism is defined by its interest in the work of art as an object and by its preoccupation with the relation between that work of art and its reader or beholder, these aesthetic concerns are themselves produced in relation to the accompanying invention of racial identity and then of its transformation both into the pluralized form of cultural identity and into the privileging of the subject position as such. *Our America* was about what has turned out to be a relatively early moment in that history; *The Shape of the Signifier* is about a more recent one.

One name for this more recent moment is postmodernism. And one reason that *The Shape of the Signifier* is subtitled *1967 to the End of History* is that 1967 was the year in which Michael Fried published "Art and Objecthood," which for many writers marks the event that put the "post" in postmodernism; Fried's is "a work of mourning," as Craig Owens put it in 1982, and what it mourns is "the death of modernism."[11] In this sense, the two times in my subtitle might be said to mark not a beginning and an end but two ends—first of modernism, then of history. But the announcement of the end of ideological dispute has not ended ideological dispute; it has instead defined our period as one in which the question of dispute—are our clashes ideological, cultural, economic?—has become central.[12] And the declaration of the end of modernism, coinciding as it did with an outpouring of remarkable painting and sculpture fundamentally concerned to decide what modernism was, served above all to mark the continuing urgency of modernism's ontological preoccupations. Or, rather, a new urgency. Just as, in politics, the decline of a socialist alternative to capitalism has given the question of identity a whole new valence, in art, the rise of theory—which may be said, in the United States, to have begun with the invention of technologies designed to explain modernism and to have turned into technologies designed to produce postmodernism—has made essential the question of what kinds of subjects are entailed by what kinds of objects.

That question can, of course, be asked as well as answered in different ways, as a question about the object or as a question about the subject.[13] In *The Birth-mark*, as we have seen, it's about the object—the mark—and in this form the same question is obviously central to debates about deconstruction in literary theory or about Minimalism in the art theory of the 1960s and 1970s. But is it also, in a slightly different form, just as central to the postpsychoanalytic interest in trauma or to the science fiction understanding of language on the model of the computer virus and of the person on the model of the computer. In literary theory, what Howe is interested in was often called the materiality of the signifier, and one way to put what I am arguing here is just to say that the commitment to the materiality of the signifier—the commitment to the idea that the text consists essentially of its physical features—was fundamental not only to the very few people who understood themselves actually to have made that commitment but also to the larger number of people who were critical of the materiality of the signifier and also to a great many people who had never even heard of the materiality of the signifier.

Another more controversial way to put it would be to say that this view of the ontology of the text carries with it—entails—a parallel or complementary view of the position of the reader. I am arguing that anyone who thinks the text consists of its physical features (of what Derrida calls its marks) will be required also to think that the meaning of the text is crucially determined by the experience of its readers, and so the question of who the reader is—and the commitment to the primacy of identity as such—is built into the commitment to the materiality of the signifier. What this means is that figures whose deepest commitments are to categories of racial or cultural difference (e.g., the political scientist Samuel B. Huntington and the novelist Toni Morrison) belong to the same formation as someone like de Man, who couldn't have cared less about culture. To put the point in an implausible (but nonetheless, I will try to show, accurate) form, it means that if you hold, say, Judith Butler's views on resignification, you will also be required to hold, say, George W. Bush's views on terrorism—and, scarier still, if you hold

Bush's views on terrorism, you must hold Butler's view of resignification. The position, then, that you take about whether those eighty-six
blank pages should count as part of the text will generate other positions—not only on terrorism but also on more obviously literary questions like whether texts have more than one meaning, as well as on
more generally social questions like whether it is important that we
should (or whether it is true that we can) remember historical events
like slavery and the Holocaust. And, to turn things around, the position
you hold on the significance of the Holocaust will generate a position
on whether the eighty-six blank pages must count as part of Thomas
Shepard's *Autobiography.*

   Of course, I do not claim that very many people actually hold all the
positions that I do claim would follow from holding just one. This aspect
of my argument is very much more theoretical than historical, since it
involves describing what people ought, if they were consistent, to believe
and to want in addition to (and sometimes instead of) describing what
they actually do believe and want. For this reason, I originally thought
to configure this book in purely theoretical terms, confining my discussion to theoretical arguments about theoretical texts. But it quickly became clear that these confines were too narrow. On the one hand, it's
true that the difference, as I describe it, between, for example, the interpretation of a text (the beliefs we have about its meaning) and the experience of a text (how it looks to us, how it makes us feel) is obviously
not a historical phenomenon; the experience of a speech act and the
interpretation of it have always been and will always be overlapping but
not identical entities. On the other hand, the privileging of the experience, which is to say the widespread effort to redescribe the interpretation as the experience and, in effect (as I will argue), to get rid of the
notion of interpretation altogether *is* a historical phenomenon. And the
fact that this theoretical argument (or, as it seems to me, mistake) has
been accompanied by a proliferation of novels (like Morrison's *Beloved*
or Leslie Marmon Silko's *Almanac of the Dead*) that not only repeat the
privileging of experience over belief but seek to extend it to the possibility
of our experiencing (rather than learning about) things that never actually happened to us is also a historical phenomenon. So, although I
haven't exactly tried to produce enough accounts of enough works to

write what might plausibly count as a real history of recent American aesthetic and theoretical production, I have tried to give some suggestion of what that history might look like. I have tried, in other words, to lay out what is meant as a kind of grid on which not only the works I discuss but a great many other works could be located and in terms of which that history can be at least imagined.

The grid, the book, is arranged in three chapters. The first, "Posthistoricism," centers on the years just before and just after the end of the Cold War and examines some of the technologies (e.g., multiculturalism) for reconfiguring ideological difference (i.e., disagreement) as cultural, linguistic, or even just geographical difference. It seeks also to demonstrate the reliance of such technologies on what I argue is a powerful but incoherently reductive materialism, deployed simultaneously in an array of interesting and ambitious novels (by Kathy Acker, Octavia Butler, Bret Easton Ellis, and Kim Stanley Robinson) and in the theoretical writings not only of Fukuyama and Huntington but of Judith Butler, Donna Haraway, and, especially, Richard Rorty.

The second chapter is called, is called "Prehistoricism," both because it provides the actual prehistory of the primacy of the subject position and because it shows how that primacy is based on a characteristically unacknowledged appeal to nature. The chapter deals primarily with a set of theoretical issues raised in the late 1960s and through the 1970s, both in art theory (here Michael Fried and Robert Smithson—who in 1968 described "pre and post-history" as part of the same "consciousness"[14] —are the central protagonists) and in literary theory (here de Man is the central figure, but the argument is extended in passing to one of the major texts of Jacques Derrida). Some of the photographs of Cindy Sherman and James Welling are offered as examples of what was at stake for a certain art practice in the debate about meaning and representation, and the chapter concludes with a discussion of deep ecology and its affinity with the deconstructive critique of representation.

The third chapter, "Historicism," begins with a discussion of what might be called the historicist novel—the novel not only about history but about the presence of the historical past—and moves on to what might then be called the antihistoricist novel. Morrison, Silko, Art Spiegelman, and Stephen Greenblatt are the main historicists; Ellis and Samuel Delany, the antihistoricists. If the historicism involves what are by now familiar commitments to cultural identity and cultural heritage, and to events that are experienced and transmitted rather than represented and known, the antihistoricism turns out to involve a commitment to classes rather than cultures and to a simultaneously demonized and eroticized version both of liberal capitalism and of the principle—freedom of contract—that animates it. The chapter ends with a discussion of some of the arguments for and against the deeply historicist project of securing reparations for slavery and with an argument that seeks to disarticulate present justice from past injustice.

The book concludes with a coda, "Empires of the Senseless." The central text here is Hardt and Negri's *Empire*, and the central topic is the effort to imagine a political program without any political beliefs. The war on terrorism and weapons of mass destruction is one manifestation of this effort, but the coda's primary interest is in the (re)emergence of the biopolitical as a synonym for and legitimation of what is also called the postpolitical. The differences between (and within) bodies may here be understood as underwriting the insistence on all the nonideological differences—or, more precisely, the insistence on the importance of difference as such—with which *The Shape of the Signifier* is concerned, including Howe's and de Man's materialisms. It is, in other words, those differences that have nothing to do with differences in belief—racial difference, sexual difference, linguistic difference, even (and, in a certain sense, especially) cultural difference—that emerge as foundational. None of these differences is, in the de Manian sense, "cognitive"; people with different bodies don't thereby have different beliefs. And even people with different beliefs can be understood as not disagreeing with each other as long as their beliefs are understood to constitute a culture rather than an ideology; hence the extraordinary recent prestige of the notion of culture, and of the dramas of inclusion and exclusion, assimilation and extinction that accompany it. We don't worry when people who have what seem to us false beliefs stop believing them (i.e., when false beliefs disappear); we do worry when cultures disappear. Culture, in other words, has become a primary technology for disarticulating difference from disagreement.

It has also become a primary technology for disarticulating difference from inequality. Elaborating on Alain Badiou's remark that the term "worker" seems to have been largely replaced by the term "immigrant" in recent political discourse, Slavoj Žižek has usefully pointed out that "in this way, the *class* problematic of workers' exploitation is transformed into the *multiculturalist* problematic of racism, intolerance, etc."[15] The difference between these problematics is, as we used to say, essential, since insofar as exploitation is at the core of class difference, class difference is ineluctably linked to inequality, where cultural difference, of course, is not. Cultures, in theory if not always in practice, are equal; classes, in theory and in practice, are not. From this standpoint, the rise of culture, or of the so-called new social movements, or of the problem of identities and identification, or—most generally—of the problem of the subject has functioned as the Left's way of learning to live with inequality.[16] Or, as Žižek says, of learning to live with "the advent of the global liberal democratic order," which is what, as Žižek notes, Fukuyama called the end of history.[17] There are other names for it; some of the more recent political ones, as we have already begun to note, have included the clash of civilizations, the rise of Empire, and the war on terror. But the effort to imagine a world organized by subject positions instead of beliefs and divided into identities instead of classes has of course, under general rubrics like postmodernism or poststructuralism or posthistoricism, been widespread.

That effort, the construction of that world, is the subject of this book, and not exactly its deconstruction but something more like the dismantling of its theoretical framework is the book's project. And although much of what follows will be concerned with questions of political and cultural theory, even more will be focused on a set of commitments that often find their most powerful expression in attempts like Susan Howe's both to exemplify and to explain her theory of the text. Indeed, it's not only the intensity of her engagement with the text as material object but also the lability of her explanations of that engagement that produce *The Birth-mark*'s power. Sometime Howe understands the mark or blank as a form of signification—the expression of an "athematic compositional intention"; sometimes she turns the mark into a "trace" that records or reflects a body rather than representing a meaning; and sometimes, when the mark becomes "gibberish," even what it reflects is rendered irrelevant. In contrast to this lability, it is the single-mindedness of de Man's commitment to the mark instead of the sign—to the "purely material" as the "purely formal," "devoid of any semantic depth"—that distinguishes *Aesthetic Ideology*. Indeed, the replacement of the sign by the mark articulated in (although by no means unique to) *Aesthetic Ideology* is foundational for and constitutive of the aesthetics of posthistoricism just as the emergence of the subject produced by the same process is—once the subject has thoroughly grasped itself as a structure of identification—constitutive of its politics.

ONE

Posthistoricism

The End of History

Wㅤhat ended when, in 1989 in Moscow, history ended? One answer—at least in part, the right answer—is that the Cold War ended. But even those most elated by the "victory" of the United States over the USSR didn't think that the end of the Cold War meant the end of history, and for Francis Fukuyama, the rapid decline and (as it turned out) fall of the Soviet Union was only symptomatic of the real victory, which had already taken place at least by 1988 and which he noticed when he read a speech by Mikhail Gorbachev describing "the essence of socialism" as "competition."[1] If the essence of socialism was now being described as competition, then socialism, at least according to its leaders, was turning into capitalism. So it was not the end of the Soviet Union's challenge to the United States that ended history; it was the end of socialism's challenge to liberal capitalism. What ended when history ended, according to Fukuyama, was fundamental disagreement over the ideal mode of social organization. The "triumph of the West," Fukuyama argued, was the triumph of "the Western *idea*" (1), liberal democracy; insofar as the failure of communism left no plausible alternatives to liberal democracy as an *idea*, insofar, that is, as it might

be imagined that no one was any longer arguing for the theoretical superiority of socialism to capitalism, what might properly be called ideological conflict was over. And, although Fukuyama's thesis was met with
instantaneous and overwhelming skepticism, and although it is perfectly
obvious that conflict (both in the United States and abroad) hardly ended
when history did (indeed, the attack on the World Trade Center and the
subsequent war on terrorism brought conflict home to the United States
in a way that the Cold War never did), there is an obvious sense also in
which both the skepticism and the conflict have tended to be understood
in ways that confirm Fukuyama's thesis.

Terrorism, after all, is not an ideology, it's a tactic, and to declare war
against it rather than against the beliefs that might be understood to
motivate it is thus to discount in principle their ideological significance.[2]
They are relevant only as the causes of the terror they produce (in the
same way that, for example, poverty is sometimes understood as the
cause of crime). And I will argue later that the discourse of the war on
terrorism not only makes the beliefs of the terrorists irrelevant but also
makes it possible to imagine that both they and their victims don't actually have any. More generally, the emergence of "globalization" provides
an all-inclusive grid for conflict in a world that writers from Agamben
to Žižek agree in describing, à la Fukuyama, as that of "post politics."
This is in part because globalization is itself just another name for the
triumph of capitalism and in part because translating that triumph from
ideology into topography has made it easier to detach both the phenomenon itself and especially the opposition to it (as, once again, I will argue
later) from any political ideas and to attach them instead to an array of
more or less attractively consenting or resisting bodies—the ones that a
suprisingly wide array of writers will urge us to "put on the line."[3]

But we didn't need globalization or the war on terrorism to make
Americans aware of the perils of the postideological. As early as 1991,
while maintaining that the "fading away of the cold war" had not, "as
forecast, brought an end to history," the historian Arthur Schlesinger
Jr. was not only agreeing that it had eliminated "ideological conflict"
but insisting that because the "disappearance of ideological competition
in the third world removes superpower restraints on national and tribal
confrontations," the world was now a "more dangerous" place than it

had been during the Cold War.[4] The primary point of *The Disuniting of America* was not, however, that the superpowers no longer policed the third world—Schlesinger had almost no interest in the third world. His point was, rather, that the ideological victory of the West had made possible "confrontations" that were no longer themselves ideological and that were just as likely to take place in the first and second worlds as they were in the third. Without communism to hold it together, such confrontations had destroyed the Soviet Union; what *The Disuniting of America* worried about was what, without capitalism (since everybody was a capitalist now), would hold the United States together. And if it was only because communism had ceased to be a problem that multiculturalism, as Schlesinger saw it, had become one, it was only because communism had also ceased to be a solution that multiculturalism could take its place and become that, too. Both Schlesinger and his opponents, that is, shared Fukuyama's sense of the new irrelevance of ideological struggle; in Leslie Marmon Silko's enthusiastically multiculturalist *Almanac of the Dead* (published, like *The Disuniting of America*, in 1991 and representing that disuniting literally as a revolution of "the indigenous peoples of the Americas" against their European conquerors), the revolution is led by Indians who explicitly dissociate it from any "political party" or marxist "ideology."[5] ("The Indians couldn't care less about international Marxism" [326].) In fact, in as dramatic a repudiation of the ideal of communism as Fukuyama could have imagined, Silko's Indians execute the Cuban Marxist who has been sent to help them organize. Tired of being instructed in Marxist doctrine and tired, in particular, of hearing Comrade Bartolomeo criticize their own "tribalism" as " 'the whore of nationalism and the dupe of capitalism' " (526), they hang him.

Fukuyama called such nonideological conflicts "post-historical." They could, as Schlesinger feared and Silko hoped, pose a threat to the United States, but they posed no threat to liberal capitalism. Only Marxism could do this because only Marxism challenged liberal capitalism's status as an ideal, its understanding of itself as a social system without "fundamental" contradictions and so immune in principle to the supersession that had overtaken previous social systems. According to Marx, insofar as capitalism was based on a class structure, it necessarily produced inequality and

conflict, and thus contained within itself the seeds of its own transformation into something else—communism. So capitalism's ability to outlast
communism proved, Fukuyama wrote, that Marx was wrong; there is
no "fundamental contradiction" in capitalism, "the class issue has been
successfully resolved" (11), and, in fact, "the egalitarianism of modern
America"—precisely because it "represents the essential achievement of
the classless society envisioned by Marx"—represents the end of contradiction, which is the end of history.

The crucial claim here was that "the class issue" had been "resolved"
because it is only if that claim was true that the Marxist critique of
capitalism could be dismissed. Marx argued that capitalism itself was
inevitably producing the contradiction that would destroy it, and this is
what Fukuyama denied. In denying it, he didn't need to say that actually
existing capitalism had solved the problem of economic inequality—and
indeed he didn't say it: he does not say that "there are not rich people
and poor people in the United States, or that the gap between them has
not grown in recent years." What he does say is that "the root causes
of economic inequality do not have to do with the underlying legal and
social structure of our society." In actually existing capitalism, in other
words, there are inequalities, but capitalism does not in principle require
such inequalities and does not itself cause them. At the end of history,
there should be no such inequalities; insofar as we have already arrived
at the end of history, their persistence must thus be understood not
as "the inherent product of liberalism" but as "the historical legacy of
premodern conditions."

What this means is that Marxism was wrong in describing capitalism
as a class system, and that what look to the Marxist like class differences
produced by capitalism are in fact differences between "groups" inherited from essentially precapitalist and preliberal stages of history. Thus,
for example, "black poverty in the United States is not the inherent product of liberalism, but is rather the 'legacy of slavery and racism' which
persisted long after the formal abolition of slavery." Blacks, on this analysis, do not belong to an economic class whose exploitation is a function
of "the social structure of our society" (if they did, then Marx would be
right, and liberal capitalism, as historically dominant as it has become,
would not be the culmination of history); they belong instead to a

"group" whose "cultural and social characteristics" are a "historical legacy."[6] And the principles of capitalism will eventually make those characteristics—and the inequalities they produce—disappear.

The defeat of Marxism, then, is only incidentally the defeat of actually
existing socialism and the triumph of actually existing liberalism; it is
essentially the defeat of the idea of Marxism, and what this means in
Fukuyama is the defeat of the Marxist idea of the class struggle and,
indeed, of the Marxist idea of class. Whatever Fukuyama's "groups" are,
his point is that they aren't classes, and when, in Silko, "the people"
execute the Cuban Marxist Bartolomeo, they are not a class either. Indeed, it is precisely because the Cuban keeps treating them as if they
were a class, insisting on the primacy of economic analysis and refusing
to acknowledge the relevance of the Indians' historical struggles (he
won't listen to their five-hundred-year chronology of European oppression and Indian resistance) that the revolutionaries feel compelled to get
rid of him. "Comrade Bartolomeo . . . has no use for indigenous history.
Comrade Bartolomeo denies the holocaust of indigenous Americans"
(531). What Silko calls "crimes against history" are crimes against the
"people" because, in Silko, the "people" are as little a product of the
economy and as much a product of history as Fukuyama's "groups,"
which is to say that both Silko and Fukuyama are anti-Marxist insofar as
they both regard present inequalities as a function not of contemporary
liberal capitalism but of events that are themselves historical. But where
Fukuyama wants to get rid of the historical legacy, Silko wants to reclaim
it. In Fukuyama, it is history, not capitalism, that victimizes blacks—
hence Marx was wrong; in Silko, it is history, not socialism, that will
redeem the Indians—hence Comrade Bartolomeo must die.

But if, in liberalism, the "people" are neither an ideological entity nor
an economic one, what are they? They cannot be an ideological entity
because, with the defeat of Marxism, one people cannot be distinguished
from another people on the basis of ideology—properly ideological differences no longer exist. They cannot be an economic entity because,
with the defeat of Marxism, the Marxist characterization of liberal capitalism's constituent element as the class has been discredited—the differences that matter are only incidentally economic. It might then be imagined that the triumph of liberalism makes the differences between

peoples irrelevant; this is the view that Michael Lind, in a book called *The Next American Nation* (1995), attributed to those whom he called "democratic universalists," among whom he would have counted Fukuyama himself.[7] But Lind insisted that Americans were "a single people" (260), different as a people from other peoples, and, as Schlesinger and Silko make clear, the real effect of the end of history had not been to get rid of difference but to transform it, to replace the differences between what people think (ideology) and the differences between what people own (class) with the differences between what people are (identity).[8] Only at the end of history could all politics become identity politics.

So although in *Almanac of the Dead*, "communists" are replaced by "tribal people" (481), Silko's revolutionary Indian heroine is as vehement in her admiration for Marx "the man" as she is in her denunciation of Marxism the ideology: "Marxism is one thing! Marx *the man* is another" (519). Marx the man is a "tribal man"—"Marx of the Jews, tribal people of the desert" (520). Marx the Marxist taught that men belonged to classes; Marx "the tribal Jew" himself belongs to a race.[9] Preferring Marx to Marxism, Silko prefers race and the appreciation of ethnic difference to class and the elimination of economic difference.[10] That's why the revolution she envisions involves not the workers of the world casting off their chains but its "indigenous people" taking back their "ancestral land." Although "indigenous" is as much a geographical as it is a biological term, the very idea of the struggle between the indigenous armies of the Americas and those whom Silko calls the "Europeans" suggests its racial implications; after all, none of the Europeans was actually born in Europe. And when the "all-tribal people's army" makes plans to offer deserters from the U.S. Army "safe conduct to Oslo or Stockholm" (590–91), "indigenous" emerges in its completely racialized form; only if indigenousness is genetic can some people born in the Americas count as native and other people born in the Americas count as Nordic.

Silko, then, is committed to a more or less straightforward ethnonationalism. But such a position is hardly available to a writer like Schlesinger (for whom "tribal" is a pejorative epithet) or to a writer like Lind (who explicitly looks forward to the elimination of racial difference through miscegenation). Schlesinger and Lind are nationalists, not ethnonationalists; indeed, what Lind calls "liberal nationalism" is defined by its difference from and opposition to ethnonationalism: "Liberal national-ism," Lind writes, rejects "race as the basis of nationality" (286). And, defending his own idea of "a unique American identity" (19), Schlesinger explicitly separates that identity from race and appeals instead to Gunnar Myrdal's formulation of "the American Creed," to "the ideals of the essen-tial dignity and equality of all human beings, of inalienable rights to free-dom, justice, and opportunity," ideals held "in common," as Myrdal put it, by Americans "of all national origins, regions, creeds, and colors" (27).

Whatever the ultimate value of the American Creed may be, however, it is obviously inadequate for the purpose of establishing "a unique Amer-ican identity," since, in turning away from race and toward "ideals," it escapes ethnonationalism but only at the price of escaping nationalism as well. For even if we were to imagine that the ideals of the essential dignity and equality of all human beings had originated in America or were more prevalent in America, we would still not have any reason to think that there was something distinctively American about either the ideals or the belief in them. The ideals themselves are obviously univer-salist; more important, the belief in them is also universalist, which is to say, the very characterization of them as ideals is universalist. To believe in these ideas is to believe that they are true for everyone and that every-one should believe them—since Russians, like Americans, *have* inalien-able rights to dignity and equality, Russians, like Americans, should be-lieve in those rights. In fact, insofar as the end of the Cold War (at least as Fukuyama understands it) means that the Russians *have* come to be-lieve in them (and the end of history means that *everyone* has come to believe in them), the distinctiveness (the Americanness) of the American Creed has disappeared. With respect to the question of American iden-tity, the Creed can now be seen for what it really is—an ideology, not a source of identity at all.

This is why Lind's "new nationalism" will have nothing to do with notions like that of the American Creed and why he argues that "the very notion of a country based on an idea is absurd" (3). It's absurd not (or, at least, not only) for psychological reasons but for logical ones: "What if two countries are founded on the same idea?" Lind asks. "Does that mean they are the same country?" (5). Dismissing the "democratic universalism" underlying the view that American identity might be anchored in a set of ideas like the American Creed, Lind realizes that what is required is a conception of identity that, if it is not biological, is not ideological either. And he finds this where Schlesinger too eventually finds it. For if Schlesinger begins *The Disuniting of* America by announcing his allegiance to the ideals of the American Creed, he ends it by transforming those ideals, altering not their content but their status, their ideality. In the wake of "the conflict of ideologies," the crucial thing about people, as we have already seen, is not what they believe but who they are. Thus the crucial thing about America is that it is "a transformative nation with an identity all its own" (16)—the posthistorical struggle is to maintain this identity. The new conflict is not, in other words, between the American Creed (what Americans believe) and some other creed (what other people believe) but between American national identity and other identities, between what Schlesinger now calls "our own culture" and "other cultures" (136). Creed becomes culture; the "real American nation," as Lind puts it, is "the cultural nation."

Political Science Fictions

Even beyond the American context, the posthistoricist allure of a world organized by cultures can hardly be overstated. "The great divisions among mankind and the dominating source of conflict" in the twenty-first century, the political scientist Samuel Huntington predicted in "The Clash of Civilizations?" in 1993, "will be cultural." "A civilization," he says, is "the highest cultural grouping of people and the broadest level of cultural identity people have, short of that which distinguishes humans from other species."[11] Huntington, of course, is not interested in what distinguishes humans from other species; what made this essay well known was its claim that "world politics is entering a new phase" (67), the phase in which, as I have already noted, "cultural" difference will be the primary source of conflict. But the wording of his definition of "civilization," with its suggestion that not only the differences between humans but also the differences between humans and "other species" are essentially cultural, suggests both the importance of culture as the source of conflict and, more generally, its importance as the site of difference. Huntington divides the world into "seven or eight major civilizations" ("Western, Confucian, Japanese, Islamic," etc.). But even in texts devoted to imagining "others" a good deal more other than Huntington's Confucians and Muslims, even, that is, in those texts where the other *is* imagined as belonging to a different species, the idea that otherness is essentially cultural has seemed increasingly persuasive. In the *Ender Quartet* (by Orson Scott Card), for example, the new xenologers who have replaced the old anthropologists still do work the anthropologists would have recognized as their own: they study the "culture" of three-foot-tall aliens who look a little like pigs with hands until they metamorphose at maturity into trees.[12] And while they're studying "piggy culture," the xenologers worry about whether the very act of studying the culture will "contaminate" it. Understood, then, as the study of culture rather than as the study of man, anthropology is unaltered by its transformation into xenology. But, of course, the idea that the differences between humans and others can now be thought on the model of the differences between humans and humans means that many other things *are* altered. Which is only to say that, whether or not Huntington is right about the details, about how many cultures there are and about how to describe them, once creatures who look like pigs and turn into trees are understood above all as *culturally* different from humans, then what Huntington calls a "new world" definitely is being created.

Science fiction, of course, is relevant here because science fiction would seem to be almost generically committed to noncultural (i.e., physical) difference. The otherness of the alien is the otherness of its body, and, in fact, this insistence on the physical difference between human and alien may be deployed not only against the Huntington-style idea that differences are essentially cultural but also against the idea that the differences between humans—insofar as what matters is physical difference—are in any way important. In Octavia Butler's *Xenogenesis* trilogy, human beings of different races are forcefully reminded of the irrelevance of their phenotypical differences by the fact that they are being asked to breed with aliens who look like sea slugs with limbs and tentacles. The difference between black and white skin looks pretty insignificant compared with the difference between humans and walking mollusks. Butler herself is African-American, as is Lilith, the chief human character of the trilogy, but from this perspective it might be argued that one of the points of the trilogy is to render racial difference irrelevant or, more generally, by dramatizing the difference between humans and aliens, to render all differences between humans irrelevant. Perhaps we could say that in science fiction the choice between imagining aliens as physically different from humans and imagining them as culturally differ- ent from humans should be understood as a choice between ways of imagining not the difference between humans and aliens but the differ- ence between humans. To insist that the difference between humans and aliens is physical is to insist on the insignificance of differences between humans (they all look more or less the same); to insist that the difference between humans and aliens is cultural is to insist on the importance of differences between humans (they don't all act the same). The primacy of culture in Card might thus be identified with a commitment to diver- sity; the indifference to culture in Butler might be identified with indiffer- ence to diversity.

But if not only in science fiction and anthropology but in almost all recent discussions of essentialist versus social constructionist theoriza- tions of difference, the relevant alternative to cultural difference is physi- cal difference, in Huntington the alternative to culture is not bodies but ideologies. When "The Clash of Civilizations?" was published in *Foreign Affairs* in 1993, it drew a greater response, as Huntington himself happily remarks, than any essay that journal had published since George Ken- nan's anonymous article of 1947. And, of course, the reference to Kennan is relevant in ways that go beyond the merely self-congratulatory, since, if Kennan may be said to have announced the beginning of what would come to be the Cold War, "The Clash of Civilizations?" was one of the series of essays ("The End of History?" was the prototype) that pro- claimed its end. In fact, it is the end of the Cold War that makes Hunting- ton's "new phase" new. Kennan had insisted on "the innate antagonism between capitalism and Socialism" as a concept essential to the Soviet Union's hostility to the United States;[13] in posthistoricist discourse, as we have already seen, the disappearance of the Soviet Union marks the end of that antagonism, which is to say, the end not merely of the antagonism between two countries but of the antagonism between two social ideals. "With the Cold War over," Huntington says, "cultural commonalities increasingly overcome ideological differences," and the differences that remain are precisely not ideological; "the fundamental source of conflict in this new world will not be primarily ideological. . . . The great divisions among humankind and the dominating source of conflict will be cultural" (67). It is not the replacement of *physical* by cultural difference but rather the replacement of *ideological* by cultural difference that marks the coming of the new world.

From this perspective, the question of whether differences are physical or cultural—a question that has, as I have noted, been at the center of recent debates between essentialist and antiessentialist accounts of identity—begins to look secondary. Huntington, in fact, tends to treat the cultural as if it were physical, as if the "characteristics" of one's culture were like the "characteristics" of one's body, "less mutable" than one's "politics and economics": "In class and ideological conflicts, the key question was 'Which side are you on?' and people could and did choose sides and change sides. In conflicts between civilizations, the question is 'What are you?' That is a given that can't be changed" (71). The idea that what you are is "a given that can't be changed" would, of course, be anathema to those antiessentialists who insist that identity ("what you are") is performative—the whole point of its being performative is that it can be changed. At the same time, however, it would be a mistake to imagine that Huntington's opposition between the cultural and the ideological would be undone by the recognition that the relative fixity of the cultural is only relative, that cultural identities are, as we say, more "mobile" than he recognizes. For the difference between what can and can't (so easily) be changed is only symptomatic of a more powerful difference, the difference between ideology and identity. And the commitment to the idea that identities are not fixed in no way undermines this difference; the debate over whether identities are fixed, like the debate over whether differences are cultural or physical, should be understood instead as a way of propping it up, as a way of insisting on the primacy of identity—physical or cultural, fixed or mobile—over ideology. To choose between physical and cultural, fixed or mobile (or, we might add in anticipation, between pure and hybrid), is to choose between two different accounts of identity. And to choose between two different accounts of identity is already to have chosen identity itself.

This choice involves what I have begun to describe as the disarticulation of difference from disagreement. From the posthistoricist perspective, what looks distinctive about the Cold War is precisely that it linked difference to disagreement. Indeed, the early and continuous characterization of the enmity between the United States and the Soviet Union as predominantly "ideological," as something more than and different from the enmity of two great powers, insists on the importance of disagreement.[14] Insofar as the differences between the United States and the USSR were understood not simply as the differences between powers but as the differences between social systems (as a disagreement over the relative merits of capitalism and communism), the question of whether or not you were a communist (the question of what your political beliefs were) could function independently of the question of whether you were an American (the question of what your identity was). The Cold War, in other words, could be understood to make identity irrelevant—what mattered (in Huntington's terms) was never who you were but only which side you were on. When Huntington describes the middle of the twentieth century (from the end of World War I to the end of the Cold War) as a period in which "the conflict of nations yielded to the conflict of ideologies" (68), he identifies not only a political but also a theoretical shift: conflicting nations assert the importance of their interests; conflicting ideologies assert the truth of their views.

It is in this sense that the Cold War may be (and often was) described as universalizing, as involving every part of the world and potentially every part of the universe. The point is not merely the geopolitical one that the two countries involved were so powerful that their spheres of influence more or less blanketed the world. The point is rather the logical one that the question as to which of two social systems is *better* is intrinsically universal: the belief that private ownership of property is unjust has no particular geographical application; to prefer communism (or capitalism) is to prefer it everywhere for everyone. A notion like sphere of influence, by contrast, can only be local (even if the locale is very large) and hence strategic; the United States didn't dispute the (former) USSR's predominance in the countries that bordered it precisely because they bordered it. Conflicts where ideology seems irrelevant—conflicts that can be explained by appeal to differing interests instead of differing ideologies—

need make no appeal to anything beyond strategy. But, in the context of ideological dispute, this strategic suspension of the question of which is the superior social system is *only* strategic—if capitalism is superior to communism, it is just as superior in (and hence desirable for) Poland (and Poles) as it is in the United States for Americans.

Ideological conflicts are universal, in other words, precisely because, unlike conflicts of interest, they involve disagreement, and it is the mere possibility of disagreement that is universalizing. We do not disagree about what we want—we just want different things; we disagree about what is true, regardless of what we want. Indeed, it is only the idea that something that is true must be true for everyone that makes disagreement between anyone make sense. Posthistoricist thinkers often criticize the appeal to universality as an attempt to compel agreement, and they remind us of the "ethnocentric biases" that such appeals conceal; after all, "standards of universality" are themselves only local.[15] But, of course, the fact that people have locally different views about what is universally true in no way counts as a criticism of the universality of the true. Just the opposite; the reason that we cannot appeal to universal truths as grounds for adjudicating our disagreements is just because the idea of truth's universality is nothing but a consequence of our disagreement. The universal does not compel our agreement, it is implied by our disagreement; and we invoke the universal not to resolve our disagreement but to explain the fact that we disagree.[16]

The alternative to difference of opinion is difference in point of view (or perspective or subject position). The point of the appeal to perspective is that it eliminates disagreement—to see things differently because we see from different perspectives (through different eyes, from different places) is to see the same thing differently but without contradiction; if I see something from the front and think that it looks black, and you think it looks white from the back, we do not disagree. More radically, if we understand different perspectives not merely as seeing the same thing from different points of view but as constituting different objects, as seeing different things, then there is still no disagreement—I see a white thing and you see a (different) black thing. This was the point of Stanley Fish's insistence in *Is There a Text in This Class?* that readers who found themselves with very different interpretations of a poem like *Lycidas* might begin to think that they "could not possibly be reading the same poem" and that they would be "right": "each . . . would be reading the poem he had made."[17] The difference between interpretations here becomes a difference between the objects of interpretation, and the difference between the objects of interpretation is accounted for by reference to the difference between the subjects who are doing the interpreting. So just as difference as disagreement makes the subject position of the observer irrelevant (since to disagree with someone is to produce a judgment that, if it is true is true also for the person with whom you disagree—that's why we think of ourselves as disagreeing), difference without disagreement makes the subject position essential (since to differ without disagreeing is nothing more than to occupy a different position).

And this essentializing of the subject position does not depend on any account of that position which might be called essentialist. It has nothing to do with the question of what determines the subject position (race, culture, sex, gender); it has to do only with the relevance of the subject position, however determined. You don't, in other words, need to belong to a race or a sex for your subject position to be crucial—two opposing players in any game differ without disagreeing. In chess, for example, the person playing white doesn't think the person playing black is mistaken; the conflict between them is not about who is right but about who will win: what matters in a game is not what you believe to be true but which side you're on.[18] Indeed, the model of the game undoes Huntington's opposition between the question of which side you're on and the question of what you are. If, on the Cold War model, the question of which side you're on is answered by what you think is true (that socialism is more just than capitalism), on the posthistoricist model, the question of which side you're on can only be a question about what you are (to play the white pieces is not to have the beliefs appropriate to them—there are no such beliefs—but to *be* white). The whole point of posthistoricism (the whole point, that is, of the commitment to difference) is to understand all differences as differences in what we are and thus to make it seem that the fundamental question—the question that separates the postideological Left from the postideological Right—is the question of our attitude toward difference: the Left wants to insist on it, the Right wants to eliminate it.

Wherever we locate ourselves on this axis, however (and it is by now no doubt obvious that the point of this argument is to attack the axis, not to argue for one or another position along it), we can see that the movement from the clash of ideologies to the clash of civilizations should be understood as a movement from the universalist logic of conflict as difference of opinion to the posthistoricist logic of conflict as difference in subject position. From this perspective, the rise in the United States of racial and cultural difference as emblems of difference *as such* might be understood as a rehearsal for the end of ideological difference. And science fiction, which (with its reconfiguration of the racial other as the alien other) undermines racial difference as an empirical phenomenon, must nevertheless be understood to assert its priority as a theoretical model. Thus on the one hand, as we have already noted, the contrast with the alien makes the differences between humans look absolutely trivial. The heroine of *Xenogenesis* is African-American, and its cast of human characters (Asian, Latino, white) meets most current standards of diversity, but the differences in human skin colors and hair textures may be rendered insignificant (made to look like differences in, say, height and weight) when the humans are juxtaposed with talking, tentacled sea slugs.[19] In this sense, the confrontation between human and alien seems designed to dispel the notion that the physical differences between humans—the difference between races—could be crucial. On the other hand, the contrast with the alien makes physical difference uniquely relevant, since the defining difference between humans and aliens is the difference in their bodies. Thus although Butler's *Xenogenesis* is *relatively* uninterested in both the categories of difference (racial and cultural) that have tended to dominate the field of posthistoricist conflict, it is *absolutely* uninterested in the categories of ideological difference that dominated the Cold War—capitalist and communist, liberal and Marxist.

In fact, although it is set in a period after humanity has almost completely destroyed itself in a nuclear war and thus invokes the most characteristic of Cold War fantasies, *Xenogenesis* blames that war not on political struggle but on human nature, or, more precisely, on the fact that "human bodies" are "fatally flawed" because they have "a mismatched pair of genetic characteristics" that makes the species simultaneously "intelligent" and "hierarchical" and hence, as Butler describes it, doomed to commit "humanicide."[20] The point here is not Fukuyama's and Huntington's (that the end of the Cold War brought about the end of ideological struggle) but rather that there never was any ideological struggle in the first place. The conflict between capitalism and communism was really just a conflict over who would rise to the top of the hierarchy; the disagreement about the merits of private property was really just a competition over who could get the most of it. If the postmodern critique of the universal turns Fukuyama's and Huntington's historical account of the end of disagreement into a theoretical account of the impossibility of disagreement, science fiction like Butler's turns their history into biology.

In texts like *Xenogenesis* and *Xenocide*, then, the fundamental differences are between humans and aliens, and the fundamental questions are not about how society should be organized but about whether the different species (or, alternatively and inconsequentially, different cultures) can survive.[21] Indeed, one might say that the replacement of ideology by bodies and cultures makes it inevitable that the only relevant question be the question of survival, which is why texts like *Xenogenesis* and *Xenocide* are called *Xenogenesis* and *Xenocide*. Because the transformation of ideological differences into cultural differences makes the differences themselves valuable, the politics of a world divided into cultures (a world where difference is understood as cultural) must be the politics of survival—a politics, in other words, where the worst thing that can happen will be a culture's death. Victory over the enemy on the Cold War model may be understood as the victory of right over wrong—this is what the victory of the humans over the insectlike aliens called "buggers" looks like at the end of *Ender's Game*, the first volume of Card's series. But insofar as the enemy is redescribed not as people who disagree with us about how society should be organized (communists) but as people who occupy different subject positions (aliens), the happy ending of their destruction must be redescribed, too. By the beginning of the second novel in the *Ender* series (*Speaker for the Dead*), the very thing that made Ender a hero (destroying the enemy) has made him a villain (destroying an entire species). The ideological enemy has been rewritten as the physiocultural other; all conflict has been reimagined on the model of the conflict between self and other.

And this is true whether the texts in question understand difference as essentially physical or as essentially cultural. It is for this reason that the essentialist-antiessentialist debate in contemporary theory is so fundamental—not because the disagreements between the two positions are so fundamental but because their agreement is. What they agree on is the value of difference itself, a value created by turning disagreement into otherness. The dispute, in other words, between essentialism and antiessentialism is only secondarily the expression of a dispute about whether difference is physical or cultural; it is primarily the expression of a consensus about the desirability of maintaining difference, of making sure that differences survive. If difference is physical, then what must survive are different species; if difference is cultural, then it's cultural survival that matters. The point of both stories is that the happy end cannot be the victory of one species or culture over another.

The idea here is not merely that survival as such—whether it's the survival of the species or the survival of the culture—is valued. What the interchangeability of species and culture makes clear is rather the value of identities—it's identities that must survive—which is to say that it's not death but extinction that must be avoided. On Earth, this distinction is made vivid in contemporary imaginations of what are, in effect, nonviolent genocides, as in, for example, the idea that current rates of intermarriage and assimilation doom American Jewry to destruction and thus constitute a second Holocaust. Intermarriage poses no threat to the people who intermarry, which is just to say that when someone like Alan Dershowitz worries about the vanishing American Jew, he is worried not about people who are Jewish but about the identity that is their Jewishness. It is the identity, not the people, that is in danger of disappearing.[22] *Xenogenesis* dramatizes this distinction by inverting its terms: where Dershowitz's Jews are living happily ever after while their identity languishes, Butler's human "resisters" are risking their lives to make sure that their identity survives. In *Xenogenesis*, those humans who mate and reproduce with aliens are rendered virtually immortal by alien biotechnology, whereas the "resisters"—who hide from the aliens and struggle to reproduce on their own—are crippled by disease and the threat of a very high rate of mortality. Because identity itself is imagined as valuable, the resisters are willing to die in order for their identity to live.

But the resisters are not the true heroes of *Xenogenesis*; in fact, the human desire to "stay human" may be more plausibly described as the object of the novel's critique than of its appreciation. "Human beings fear difference," a human mother tells her half-human, half-alien son. But if the son has inherited the human fear of difference, he has inherited just the opposite from his alien ancestors: the Oankali, his mother tells him, "crave difference." In his own life, she predicts, he will experience some conflict between these emotions; when he does, she advises him, "try to go the Oankali way. Embrace difference."[23] *Xenogenesis* not only insists that all differences be understood as differences in subject position, as differences between what people want rather than what they believe; it makes difference itself the object of affect—the thing that is feared or craved, that is or isn't wanted. Huntington replaces the conflict between ideologies with the difference between identities; Butler seeks to replace the conflict between identities with the conflict between identity and difference.

"Butler's fiction," Donna Haraway says, "is about resistance to the imperative to recreate the sacred image of the same."[24] Insofar as the "question of 'differences,' " she writes in "The Biopolitics of Postmodern Bodies," "has destabilized humanist discourses of liberation based on a politics of identity and substantive unity" (211), her idea is to replace the politics of identity with a politics of difference. In *Xenogenesis*, the difference between these politics is expressed in the debate over miscegenation. The "humanist" discourse is the discourse of those humans who fear difference and who thus refuse to mate with aliens; its replacement is the discourse of those humans who embrace difference by embracing aliens. Hence, not only does Butler insist on miscegenation as the privileged form of sexual activity, she makes incest the only alternative to it. The human children of human parents are crippled and disfigured by genetic disorders represented as the effects of inbreeding; the hybrid "constructs" produced by humans who mate with aliens are unimaginably healthy and beautiful. If the emergence of the alien—with different bodies rather than different ideas—eliminates ideology as the source of conflict, it replaces ideology with the differences between those bodies, between identities, between races or cultures, between aliens and humans. But while Huntington imagines that such differences make identitarian conflict inevitable, Butler's goal is to make it impossible. So in

Xenogenesis it is not difference itself that is the source of conflict, it is one's attitude toward difference. *Xenogenesis* makes sex with humans a way of expressing the desire for the same; it makes sleeping with aliens an expression of the desire for difference.

At the same time, however, it has a hard time keeping these desires apart. For if the resisters' desire to "stay human" expresses their fear of difference, it obviously also expresses their desire for difference (difference, that is, from the aliens). Insofar as identity and difference are complementary rather than oppositional terms, the human desire to stay human is simultaneously (and without contradiction) the desire to stay the same and the desire to be different. And the commitment to difference embodied in the commitment to miscegenation produces the same effect from the opposite direction. In a thoroughly miscegenated world, the traits of particular races or species would, of course, disappear— everybody would be the same. That's why in *The Next American Nation,* Lind calls for increased intermarriage among Americans of different races and approvingly cites the conservative columnist Morton Kondracke's remark that Americans would be better off if "each of us were related to someone of another color and if, eventually, we were all one color" (291). If miscegenation is an expression of the appreciation of difference, it is also a technology for the elimination of difference. (This is the point of my earlier equation of miscegenation with assimilation.)

The discourse of hybridity is thus a form of rather than an alternative to the discourse of identity, and the politics of difference is a form of rather than an alternative to the politics of "identity and substantive unity."[25] Dismayed by what they regarded as the co-optation of the radical potential of a "cultural politics of difference" by a liberal "multiculturalism," many writers of the mid-1990s insisted on the primacy of subject positions that could not be "unified," that could not be turned into identities suitable for appreciation in high school classrooms. What Norma Alarcon (in her contribution to *Mapping Multiculturalism,* an essay called "Conjugating Subjects") called the "bi- or multiethnicized, raced and gendered subject-in-process" would be "called upon to take up diverse subject positions," and the "paradoxes and contradictions" between these positions would "move the subject to recognize, reorganize, reconstruct, and exploit difference through political resistance and cultural productions" that would "reflect" not an identity but a *"provisional"* identity, not a subject but "a subject-in-process" (138). But precisely insofar as Alarcon's "contradictions" are understood to "reflect" the subject, they are, of course, deprived of their bite—it's only beliefs that can be contradictory, and beliefs don't reflect the subject, they transcend it. That's what it means for the relevant thing about beliefs to be that they are true or false rather than yours or mine. Hence the characteristically poststructuralist internalization of difference (the insistence on difference within as well as between) counts as a refinement rather than a repudiation of the commitment to the subject position. When, for example, the coauthors of *Contingency, Hegemony, Universality* (2000) agree on "the failure of any claim to identity to achieve final or full determination" (2) (when, in other words, they prefer identification to identity), the terms of their preference are located entirely within the discourse of the subject. Against the theoretical naïveté of identity politics (with its assumption that we simply are what we are), they assert the importance of recognizing that we can never just be what we are, that "subject-formation" is, as Judith Butler puts it, always "incomplete." But the question of whether the subject's beliefs are true or false has nothing to do with the question of whether he or she is finished yet. And the problem with identity politics is not just its account of identity.

In this light, what I described earlier as a consensus about the value of difference should instead be described as a consensus about the value of the opposition between difference and sameness, the other and the self. It doesn't matter whether what's valorized is the other or the same; what matters is only that, whatever's valorized, it's valorized *as* the other or the same. Actually, it doesn't even matter whether either one is valorized. "It's not a matter of doing away with the discourse of the other," Alarcon usefully remarks, " 'because the other is in each case present in the activity that eliminates [it].' " So the crucial thing—the thing that produces the primacy of the subject position—is just the complete saturation of the field of conflict by self and other, by sameness and difference, by identity and identification. And if, as I have suggested, the science fiction encounter with the alien provides an exemplary opportunity for the emergence of these terms, the completeness of that saturation is made even more visible in the work of those writers whose generic commitments make it impossible to produce the other as alien but whose commitments to identity remain in no way compromised.

It's because the only choice is between the different and the same that the desire for "something different" (as opposed, say, to something better) can count as the utopian point of Martian colonization in Kim Stanley Robinson's Mars trilogy: "not to make another Earth" and therefore "to think harder than ever before about what it means to be Martian."[26] But where Butler imagines the new and strange as the alien, there are no aliens in Robinson. Hence the desire for difference cannot take the form of a commitment to miscegenation, and hence, if the theorization of conflict cannot rely on Cold War–style political disagreement (since the Mars trilogy, like *Xenogenesis*, takes place after that war's end), it cannot rely either on the competition between species through which Butler imagines Huntington's clash of civilizations.[27] The problem for the Mars trilogy, then, is to imagine the distinctiveness—which is to say, the difference from Earth—of a Mars inhabited entirely by people who are not distinctive, who are (except for being taller and thinner) in no way different from the people of Earth. If, in Butler, the alien is the site of biocultural difference, the absence of the alien in Robinson requires a difference that will rely as little on bodies and cultures as it does on beliefs. The challenge for the Martian "natives" is how to redescribe the sons and daughters of Terrans as "the indigenous people of Mars" (*Blue Mars*, 360).

On Earth, of course, they couldn't; on Earth, as we have already seen in Silko's *Almanac of the Dead*, "indigenous" is a racialized term. The year 1992, when the Mars trilogy was begun, was also the five hundredth anniversary of Columbus's arrival in the Americas, and at least one response to that anniversary, the response of indigenous peoples themselves, was to insist on indigenousness as an inherited rather than an acquired characteristic. Thus the "celebration" of Columbus's voyage and its "effect on native peoples" would be countered by the declaration of 1993 as the International Year of the World's Indigenous People, "those of us who have lived on the lands of our ancestors since the beginning of history."[28] It's only because they are descended from people who lived on Manhattan at "the beginning of history" that members of the Native American Council of New York City can distinguish between themselves and other New Yorkers at the end of history. But Martians at the end of history must be able to identify themselves as Martians without the genealogical appeal. They must, in other words, be able to produce an account of "what it means to be Martian," but they must do it not only without any distinctive culture but also without any help from their ancestors. Hence in the Mars trilogy, the category of the indigenous people of Mars is articulated entirely in geographical, virtually geological terms. Which is to say, in the absence of any political difference from Earth and despite the absence of any biological difference between Martians and Terrans, the indigenous peoples of Mars assert an entirely geographical and geological identity: "Our bodies are made of atoms that until recently were part of the regolith," a Martian leader announces. "We are Martian through and through. We are living pieces of Mars" (*Blue Mars*, 590). Not only do you not need different ideologies, you don't need different races or species, you don't need different cultures—all you need is different places.

This identification of the person with the place both literalizes and perfects the commitment to identity by reducing it to—what it always was—the commitment to the subject position. It doesn't matter, in other words, whether you think of difference as physical, cultural, or regional, whether you think of it as the difference between nations or the difference between corporations. In the effort to rescue difference from disagreement (which is to say, in the effort to rescue difference from the universalism implied by the mere possibility of disagreement), even the difference between someone who is here (Mars) and someone who is there (Earth) can do the trick. Someone who is here sees things one way; someone who is there sees things another way. For posthistoricist identitarianism, this difference—between here and there, between Mars and Earth—does all the work that the antiessentialist (so-called) difference between cultures does or that the essentialist (so-called) difference between bodies does.

Huntington thinks that in "ideological conflicts," the "key question" is, "Which side are you on?" In such conflicts, the question of which side you're on is a question about what you believe, a question that cannot be answered by a statement about your identity. In the New World, where civilizations, not ideologies, clash, the question is not which side you're on but, "What are you?" The difference between these two questions, Huntington thinks, is a difference between things that can and cannot "be changed." You can change your beliefs; you can not change what you are. But if, as I began to suggest earlier, the science fiction reduction of what you are to where you are undoes this opposition, it does so only to the extent that the opposition really is founded on the question of what can and cannot be changed. The function of the opposition, in other words, is to assert that what matters is the question of whether your position can be changed. And this is just as true for all those on the cultural Left—insisting on mobility and the performative—as it is for those, like Huntington, on the cultural Right. Indeed, one way of describing the difference between the cultural Left and the cultural Right is precisely in terms of this difference over the nature of subject positions, over whether they are fixed and stable or mobile and unstable. But, as Butler's imagination of the alien and Robinson's imagination of the native enable us to see, it doesn't matter whether your subject position is fixed or mobile—what matters is just that it *is* a subject position, an identity rather than an ideology. The emergence of the debate over whether identities are mobile or fixed is, in other words, really the emergence of a consensus about the primacy of identity.

Partez au vert/Go on the green

It is for this reason that even those—like Schlesinger and Lind—who understand themselves to oppose the appeal to identity nonetheless find themselves required to make it. Because the difference between one cultural nation and another, between "our own culture" and "other cultures," cannot be understood on the model of the difference between ideologies, their defense of American culture cannot hinge on its superiority (in the way that, for instance, capitalism might have been thought superior to communism) but must insist instead on its suitability for those whose culture it is. "We don't have to believe that our values are absolutely better than the next fellow's or the next country's," Schlesinger says, "but we have no doubt that they are better *for us*" (137). Or, as Lind puts it, "One should cherish one's nation, as one should cherish one's family, not because it is the best in the world, but because, with all its flaws, it is one's own" (10). Rather than America being valued as a place where certain beliefs are held, the beliefs Americans hold will be valued because they are American. So not only do we not have to believe that American values are really better than the next country's, we are required to believe that they are *not* better. For if we believe that they're better, then, as we have already begun to see, their function as a mark of our distinctiveness is jeopardized; other peoples, recognizing the superiority of our beliefs, might be convinced by them and come to share them. The idea that some values are better than others is, in other words, intrinsically universalist; the idea that those values which seem to us good are only good *"for us"* is intrinsically identitarian. The whole point, then, of the transformation of creed into culture is to enable us to secure our identity by giving up our superiority.

Lind's invocation of the family as a model for the "cultural nation," which is to say, for the nation as an object of affection rather than admiration, is a familiar one. The nation as family has been a recurring motif in American nativism at least since Charles W. Gould's *America, A Family Matter* (1922). But where, in the 1920s, the invocation of the family was explicitly racist, in Lind, the family is not meant to have anything to do with "blood." It is intended only as an example of what it means to prefer some things to others without thinking that the things one prefers are in fact preferable—you don't have to think that your sister is, by some universal standard, lovable, in order to love her; you only have to think that, with all her "flaws," she's yours. But to put the point this way is, of course, immediately to recognize the limits of the family as a model of a truly cultural—that is, nonracial—nationalism. The thing that makes your sister your sister is the fact that she's related to you—it's the blood that makes the family a family and that exempts our preference for it from the need of further justification.[29] The only nation the family can plausibly model is the ethnonation, which is the nation that "liberal nationalists" like Lind and Schlesinger seek to oppose.

"Liberal nationalists" like Lind, then, cannot rely on the family as the exemplary national institution; instead, they "believe that language and culture—not biology—define nationality" (261). The point here is not just that language (rather than family) is connected to culture but that language can be called upon to do for culture what the family failed to do—it is linguistic diversity that will provide the exemplary insistence of the nonbiological and nonideological pluralism that liberal nationalism requires. Because the particular language we speak is not determined biologically—people of different races can speak the same language—linguistic diversity can be deployed against racial diversity. But because, at the same time, there's no reason to think that any one language is superior to any other—there's no reason, that is, for all people to aspire to any one language—linguistic diversity can be deployed also against ideological unanimity. If culture is like language, both the multicultur-alists (who are ethnonationalists) and the democratic universalists (who aren't any kind of nationalists) are wrong—the American people are one people, not many, and they really are a people, not just the advance guard of democratic universalism.

Liberal nationalists, then, have a culture in the same way that they have a language; they believe what they believe and they do what they do for the same reason that they speak the language they speak—because it's theirs. So just as we do not think that English is true and French false, we must not think that what Americans believe is true and what Americans do is right while what the French believe is false and what they do is wrong—not because this would be ethnocentric but, just the opposite, because it would make the ethnos irrelevant, it would be uni-versalist. Which is why liberal nationalists must be committed to the view that the differences between, say, what Richard Rorty calls the "moral vocabulary" of Saint Paul and the "moral vocabulary" of Freud should be understood precisely as differences in vocabulary.[30] We shouldn't—indeed, according to the principles of liberal nationalism, we cannot—think of Saint Paul and Freud as holding competing "descrip-tions of the world," for then we should be moved to think of one of them as right and the other as wrong. Instead, we must think of them as playing what (following Wittgenstein) Rorty calls "alternative language games," in which case saying that Freud's beliefs are more true than Saint Paul's makes as little sense as saying that German is more true than Hebrew.

Rorty's antifoundationalism thus provides the philosophical basis for Schlesinger's and Lind's cultural nationalism. Rorty wishes to replace the search for beliefs that, if they are true, are true for everyone (what he calls the commitment to "universal validity" [67]) with the willingness to acknowledge that Freud's beliefs are true for Freud and Saint Paul's are true for Saint Paul (what he calls the "willingness to live with plurality"). And this purely epistemological critique of the universality of truth finds its necessary social expression in a commitment to the primacy of those groups whose particularity makes the critique of universality possible. If some things are true for the Hebrews and some things are true for the Austrians, then the only way to know what is true for you is to know whether you are a Hebrew or an Austrian. On the one hand, cultural nationalism is impossible without antifoundationalism; on the other hand, antifoundationalism is impossible without identitarianism (whether or not Rorty means to commit himself to the primacy of identity).

Thus, although Rorty is less interested than Schlesinger or Silko in what he apparently understands as the merely sociological question of who we today in the United States actually are, the requirement that we be somebody and that we be able to say who we are is as crucial to *Contingency, irony, and solidarity* (1989) as it is to *The Disuniting of America* or *Almanac of the Dead*. It's Rorty's "irony" (we know that our beliefs, no matter how strongly we hold them, are not "universally valid") that produces his commitment to "solidarity" (the fact that our beliefs are not "universally valid" doesn't mean they aren't valid for us). And when it comes to acting on our beliefs, solidarity trumps irony. "We don't have to believe that our values are absolutely better than the next fellow's or the next country's, but we have no doubt that they are better *for us*," we have already heard Schlesinger say, and he goes on to add, "and are worth living by and dying for." What Rorty calls the "fundamental premise" of his philosophy is another version of Schlesinger's call to arms: "A belief can still regulate action, can still be thought worth dying for, among people who are quite aware that this belief is caused by nothing deeper than contingent historical circumstance" (189). So if we cannot justify our "moral vocabulary" any more than we can justify speaking Hebrew or being Austrian, we don't need to worry because, of course, the fact that we speak Hebrew or are Austrian doesn't need justification. Which is to say that, on Rorty's account, it cannot make sense to die for a belief because you think it's true; it can only make sense to die for a belief because it's yours. Indeed, the antifoundationalist hero who is prepared first to "face up" to the contingency of his beliefs and then die for them is facing up to nothing other than the primacy of his own identity. It is insofar as he has come to believe what he believes in the same way that he has come to speak the language he speaks (through "contingent historical circumstance") and insofar as he can justify what he believes only by saying who he is (another "contingent historical circumstance"), that he is heroic. Contingency is identity; anti-foundationalism is identitarianism.

The fact that Rorty and Schlesinger are more willing to give their lives for their beliefs than they are to maintain the truth of those beliefs may seem odd, but it is actually an essential characteristic of nationalist logic. Quoting a Ukrainian writer who insists that "a nation can exist only where there are people who are prepared to die for it," Walker Connor, a distinguished scholar of ethnonationalism, remarks that the "dichotomy between the realm of national identity and that of reason has proven vexing to students of nationalism."[31] But the Ukrainian's sense that the Ukraine needs dead bodies more than it does good reasons is a consequence rather than a violation of rationality. It is only because a belief that is held in the same way that a language is spoken cannot be the sort of thing you argue for that it must be the sort of thing you die for. The virtue of the linguistic analogy is that if, on the one hand, you cannot give good reasons for speaking the language you speak, on the other hand, you don't need to. So your inability to justify your insistence on speaking German instead of Hebrew is inevitably matched by your inter-locutor's inability to justify his insistence that you speak Hebrew instead of German. The only justifiable attitude toward different vocabularies is, as Rorty suggests, tolerance. And the only acceptable response to intolerance is, as he also suggests, force.

What justifies both the tolerance and the violent response to intoler-ance is the absence of any intrinsic conflict between vocabularies; He-brew and German do not contradict each other, and insofar as Saint Paul's and Freud's moral vocabularies are like Hebrew and German, they don't contradict each other either. But if, then, the great advantage of the linguistic model of culture is that it provides difference without con-tradiction (as long as we don't see any conflict between our beliefs and "the other fellow's," we don't need to think of ours as being better or worse than his), its great disadvantage is that it makes contradiction inconceivable (if Paul says that Jesus is God and Freud says he isn't, they aren't disagreeing, they're just speaking different languages). Fukuyama imagines a world where, with the triumph of liberalism, no one any longer disagrees; Rorty, turning an event into an epistemology, imagines a world where not only have people stopped disagreeing but it has become in principle impossible to disagree. The advantage is that once different ideas are turned into different languages, it makes no sense—and, indeed, it seems wrong—for anyone to want to get rid of them. The disadvantage is that once different ideas are turned into different languages, it makes no sense for anyone to want to protect them either. If "we're concerned with identity," as Charles Taylor has put it in his well-known (if guarded) defense of multiculturalism, "then what is more legitimate than one's aspiration that it never be lost?"[32] But the real question should be, if we're concerned with identity, how can we possibly care whether it gets lost?

To see the problem here, we have only to ask ourselves what we wish to protect when we wish to protect what another defender of cultural diversity, Will Kymlicka, calls our culture's "distinct existence and identity."[33] One answer—perhaps the most obvious one—is that we wish to protect our beliefs and practices. But as Kymlicka and others have pointed out, this answer won't work. What we seek to protect is more precisely our identity, and our identity cannot be conceived simply or primarily in terms of "shared values"[34] because if we think of cultures as shared values, it becomes impossible to commit ourselves in principle to respecting other cultures. Why should we respect values that are different from ours, which is to say, values that (insofar as they are different) we must find mistaken and that we may even find repugnant? We don't think, to take a relatively uncontroversial example, that by describing people who believe in apartheid as people who participate in a culture of apartheid, we have earned their beliefs a right to recognition and survival. Multiculturalists are not, in other words, committed to the idea that systems of belief that seem to them deeply wrong and even repugnant can be made defensible simply by redescribing them as cultures. Multiculturalists do not and need not think that calling the commitment to white supremacy a culture earns that commitment the respect that multiculturalists do think cultures require.

But if it is not some set of values that must be respected when cultures are respected, what is it? We know that the concept of culture has been closely (and problematically) linked to the descent-based concepts of race and ethnicity, but even if we ignore the problems—even if we accept the primacy of descent—we have no way of connecting difference in descent with anything we might call cultural difference. No one, for instance, thinks that the language people speak is genetically determined. Indeed, it's precisely because we do *not* believe that the language we speak is determined by our genetic makeup that we may become so determined to defend it when we attempt to protect our culture. If, to take an example crucial to both Taylor and Kymlicka, the Quebecois somehow *did* believe that their children were genetically encoded to speak French, they would not worry about bilingualism and the proliferation of English in Quebec—they would not worry, that is, that their children might grow up speaking English. But because, of course, they know perfectly well that their children are not genetically so encoded, they do worry about what language their children will speak, and the survival of French in Quebec has become a central feature of Canadian multiculturalism.

So multiculturalism doesn't commit us to defending differences in values (we don't think it's important to nurture values we find repugnant), and it also doesn't commit us to protecting racial or ethnic difference, if only because the differences we do want to protect—like linguistic differences—cannot be derived from race or ethnicity. Of course, we might still want to protect racial or ethnic difference, but this would be a very different sort of undertaking, one that would replace laws like those prohibiting the public use of English with laws prohibiting intermarriage between people of French Canadian and Anglo-Canadian descent.[35] Which is only to say that if we cannot understand the cultures multiculturalism wishes to protect as sets of beliefs, we cannot understand them as gene pools either. And which is why, as I noted previously, linguistic (rather than ideological or physiological) difference plays such a central role in the multiculturalist conception of culture. For if it is true that the language we speak is not a function of our genetic makeup, it is equally true that it is not a social value or belief in the way, say, that a commitment to or against apartheid is.

To say that the language we speak is not something we believe is just to say, as we have already seen Rorty say, that we don't think of our language—or of any language—as being true or false. And to say that our language is not a value we hold is just to say that we don't think of any language as being better or worse than any other language: "no language," John Edwards has written, "can be described as better or worse than another on purely linguistic grounds," by which he means that all "languages are always sufficient for the needs of their speakers."[36] This is why it makes sense to respect linguistic difference. Because my language cannot be truer or better than yours, it cannot be right for me to compel you to speak my language rather than yours, and, absent some clear evidence of convenience, it cannot even make sense for me to exhort you (much less compel you) to speak my language instead of yours. What reasons, except reasons of convenience, could I possibly give you? To recognize that our language—or, more generally, our culture—is not a set of beliefs or values is, as we have already seen, to rule out the possibility of there being any good arguments for or against linguistic or cultural practice; all we need to say in justification of our language is that it is our language.

But, just as the fact that our language isn't a set of beliefs makes sense of our desire to fight (rather than argue) for it, the fact that it isn't a value makes nonsense of our desire to preserve it, of what Taylor calls our "aspiration that it never be lost." It is, in other words, just because we do not need to justify our culture that we cannot wish for it to survive. Why should anyone care if a culture survives? Insofar as a culture might be understood to consist in a set of beliefs or values, of course, it is easy to see why one might care. The commitment, say, to liberal democracy is incoherent except as a commitment to the idea that liberal democracy is a superior form of government, and what it means to think that it's superior is to think that it's superior for everyone everywhere, hence not only for people elsewhere but for people later. But, as we have seen, the whole point of the idea of culture—the reason our language emerges as the exemplary practice of our culture—is that, if we are multi-culturalists, we cannot think of our culture as a set of beliefs or values. We do not think of our culture as an ideology, superior to the ideology of others; if we did, then it would make no sense for us to think that cultures other than our own should survive. Which is just to say that we do not want beliefs that seem to us mistaken and unjust to survive.

But if our culture does not ultimately consist in a set of values, why should we want even our own to survive? Why should we care if the language we speak will continue to be spoken? Because we do not think of our language as a value (we don't think of it as better or worse than other people's languages), we do feel it would be unjust for others to penalize us for speaking our language, or for us to penalize others for speaking their language. Does it then make sense for us to want our language to survive?[37] If we are required to live in a world in which we will not be able to speak our language, we will be the victims of an injustice; who will be the victims of injustice in a world where our language does not survive, which is to say, in a world where no one speaks our language?

The answer is obvious: no one. If we speak French, it makes sense for us to wish to live in a society where French is spoken, but it cannot make sense for us to wish that French continue to be spoken—it cannot make sense for us to care one way or the other about what language will come to be spoken. If our children—exposed to TV and to books, to road signs and newspapers, in English—become bilingual in French and English, and their children barely speak French, and their children don't speak French at all, no one has been the victim of any injustice (or even inconvenience). Everyone is always speaking his or her language; it's just that the language our great-grandchildren speak is different from the language we speak. The only victim is the language itself—but how can a language be a victim? And if cultural extinction is a truly victimless crime, how can it be a crime at all?

So whether or not the "aspiration" that "identity" "never be lost" is, as Taylor says, "legitimate," it's hard to see why it's an aspiration that anyone can actually have. It's hard, in other words, to see how it can make sense for anyone to want an identity to survive. It may well make sense for us to want practices that we think of as good to survive, but the point for multiculturalists is not that we should seek to perpetuate those practices we approve of but rather that we should seek to perpetuate those practices we understand to constitute our identity. This is what distinguishes the commitment to diversity as such (i.e., to multicultur-

alism) from an instrumentalist tolerance (on the model, say, of the marketplace of ideas). The idea of tolerating and even encouraging lots of
different practices on the model of the marketplace of ideas involves the
sense that promoting such diversity will help us find the best practices.
But since the practices to which multiculturalism is committed are the
practices that constitute an identity, their value is intrinsic, which is to
say that we are not interested in creating a world in which the best
of them survive—as multiculturalists, we are committed to all of them
surviving. In fact, it is in terms of its commitment to "cultural equality"
(80) or "cultural parity" (86) that the advocates of what they sometimes
call "true" or "strong" multiculturalism distinguish it from liberal "assim-
ilationism."[38] Assimilationist multiculturalism, Avery Gordon and Christopher Newfield argue in *Mapping Multiculturalism*, accepts cultural pluralism only if diversity is organized around a common "core" (91). Strong
multiculturalism denies the primacy of the core and insists not only on
the differences between cultures but on "cultural parity" rather than
"implicit hierarchy" "among these different cultures" (86).

But as long as we, like the strong multiculturalist, are concerned with
cultural equality (with practices that seem to us different but do not
seem to us better or worse), as long, in other words, as we are concerned
with practices that seem to us valuable only insofar as they constitute
an identity—why should we care if any of them survive? If we are socialists, we will, of course, want socialism to survive. But that's because
socialists do not (indeed cannot) believe that socialism is on a plane of
equality with capitalism; we do not believe in socialism (or, for that matter, capitalism) the way we speak English. We speak English not because
it's better or worse than any other language but because it's ours, and if
the point of multiculturalism is to insist on cultural equality, then we
participate in our culture in precisely the same way that we speak our
language. But if all cultures are as equal as all languages are, then we
can't possibly be any more concerned about which cultures will survive
than we can be about which languages will. Our great-grandchildren
will all speak *some* language—why should we care which one it is? Our
descendants will all have some culture—as long as we know in principle
that it can't possibly be better or worse than ours, why should we care
which one it is?[39] The commitment to cultural diversity makes sense as

long as the practices it asks us to value are those practices that seem to us neither better nor worse, neither true nor false—as long as they involve or constitute an identity. It seems right, in other words, that people who speak French should not be forced to speak English. But, precisely because those practices seem to us neither better nor worse, it makes no sense for us to care about whether they survive. Because I care that people who speak French should be able to speak French, I can't possibly care if anyone actually does speak French.

The Shape of the Signifier

Nevertheless, in posthistoricism, the question of what language is being spoken characteristically trumps the question of what is being said, and questions about what something is will characteristically be understood as questions about what it calls itself. On Kim Stanley Robinson's Mars, "The question is, what is Mars's own name for itself?" (*Green Mars*, 54). The question gets asked in the second volume of his Mars trilogy, *Green Mars*; the context in which it's asked is what Robinson calls an "areophany," a ritual in which the first colonists on Mars recite the names for Mars in as many languages as they can: English, Arabic, Japanese, and so forth. The answer to the question, Robinson tells us about two hundred pages later, is "Ka." But this is an answer that in an important sense only deepens the question. "Ka" is a sound that is included in "a whole lot of Earth names for Mars" (*Green Mars*, 64), Robinson says. But it's hard to see why the fact that the Arabs call Mars "Qahira" and the Japanese call it "Kasei" should mean that "Ka" is "Mars's own name for itself." "Ka" is also the name used by those whom Robinson describes as the "little red people on Mars." But the little red people in Robinson don't actually exist; they are presented as a kind of myth invented by humans. Indeed, one of the ways in which Robinson's Mars trilogy (and much recent Mars fiction, like Ben Bova's *Mars* and Greg Bear's *Moving Mars*) differs from some other recent ambitious works of science fiction (say, Octavia Butler's *Xenogenesis* series or Orson Scott Card's *Ender Quartet*) is in its apparent indifference to the question of the alien. Robinson's Mars is a lifeless planet before colonization. So if the question about Mars's own name for itself cannot be a question about what humans call

it, it cannot exactly be a question about what Martians call it either. In
the Mars trilogy, there are no Martians.

And yet it's a little misleading to say that in the Mars trilogy there are
no Martians, for although everybody in the trilogy is human, there are
people by the trilogy's end who not only call themselves Martians but
describe themselves as "the indigenous people of Mars" (*Blue Mars*, 360).
And this concern with Mars's indigenous population appears also in Ben
Bova's recent Mars book, which, like the Mars trilogy, contains no Martians but which, also like the Mars trilogy, is interested in the question of
what it would mean for there to be—or, in Bova's Mars—for there to
have been Martians. Bova's *Mars* begins with its hero wondering, as he
and his companions first set foot on the Martian surface, if there are
"Martians hidden among the rocks . . . watching them the way red men
had watched the first whites step ashore . . . centuries ago."[40] Of course,
there aren't, but Bova's *Mars* was published in 1992, and, transforming
Robinson's mythical red people into the (equally, but differently, mythical)
red men of the New World, Bova not only insists on the parallel between
the two landings but enforces the parallel between the two peoples: what
Bova's hero, Jamie Waterman, will discover is that there once were red
men on Mars. And although Bova is less explicitly interested than Robinson in what they might have called Mars or themselves, he does provide
some information about what their language might have been.

For Jamie himself is what Bova calls a "red man," the son of a white
woman and of a Navajo who "has turned himself into an Anglo," and he,
like his putative Martian predecessors, has been in danger of vanishing, if
only through assimilation into the white world. It's not until his Navajo
grandfather takes him to the Anasazi ruins at Mesa Verde (where the Cliff
Palace, made of "reddish brown sandstone," is said to be "almost the
same color as Mars") and reminds him of who he is that he feels the full
force of his Indian identity. "Your ancestors built that village five hundred
years before Columbus was born," the grandfather says. So later, when
Jamie discovers "a rock formation" on Mars—in a cleft "like the cleft at
Mesa Verde"—he realizes that he's looking at "buildings," constructed,
he imagines, by "the ancestors of his ancestors." And so the red people
of Mars really are like the red men of New Mexico, and the fact that
Jamie's first words on Mars—"Ya'aa'tey"—are spoken in "the language of

[his] ancestors" means he is speaking a tongue that indigenous Martians could have understood: if Mars's own name for itself is the name Martians call it, Ben Bova imagines that name will be a Navajo one.[41]

Bova's *Mars* is thus not only a narrative of New World exploration, it's also a kind of *Roots* for Martians. Which, of course, somewhat complicates the parallel to Columbus's arrival in the Americas, since for Columbus to be like Jamie, the Indians he discovered would have to turn out to be his long-lost cousins, and it's hard to see how redescribing the European conquest of the Americas as a family reunion can count as a protest against the European exploitation of the indigenous peoples of the Americas. But then it's even harder to see how Navajo Jamie can count as a Martian Anasazi. For even if the Martians were the ancestors of the Anasazi, the Anasazi weren't the ancestors of the Navajo—the Navajo arrived in New Mexico after the Anasazi had already disappeared. And if the Navajo are not exactly native to New Mexico, the Anasazi weren't either: the Paleo-Indians from whom they descended "were not indigenous to North America";[42] which is just to say that basically all the peoples of the Southwest seem to have arrived there from somewhere else—their indigenousness is more acquired than inherited. And while this process is obscured by Bova's appeal to the red man—it seems that he wants to protect the indigenous people against their invaders by making everyone, *including* the invader, indigenous—it is rendered rather dramatically visible on Robinson's Mars, where those who call themselves native Martians are just the children and grandchildren of the first colonists from Earth. We are "becoming indigenous to the land" (*Blue Mars*, 369), says one of Robinson's Martians. It's as if the descendants of the European conquerors (of Cortez and Columbus and William Bradford and John Smith) had declared themselves Native Americans—which, of course, in the various nativist narrativists that made places like Mesa Verde symbols of American identity, they did.

But the prestige of the indigenous for Robinson is linked to something more than the claims of prior habitation, and to something more, even, than the claims to cultural identity that, in the classic American literature of the 1920s, so frequently accompanied the appeal to the American Indian and even to Mesa Verde.[43] In Robinson, as in a wide range of more recent texts, indigenous cultures are valued not (or not only) for the fact that they resist assimilation to other cultures—it's the resistance to Americanization that Mesa Verde in New Mexico makes possible for Jamie and that Mesa Verde on Mars confirms—but also for the fact that their refusal to be absorbed by other cultures is understood not simply as an affirmation of their own culture but as a suspicion of culture as such. Or perhaps, more precisely, as a suspicion of the idea that it is only humans or persons who have cultures. Hence, in Robinson's Mars, it is not exactly "Martian culture" that must be preserved; it is Mars itself, Martian rock, which is to say, Martian nature.[44]

We have already noted that Bova's *Mars* was published in 1992, the year of the Columbus quinquecentennial; Robinson's *Red Mars* was published in 1993, proclaimed by the United Nations The International Year of the World's Indigenous People.[45] The timing of the proclamation was, of course, as the then secretary general of the United Nations, Boutros Boutros-Ghali, put it, "no coincidence"; it was on Human Rights Day in 1992 that he issued his proclamation, making clear its status as a response to the violations of human rights set in motion by Columbus.[46] But the indigenous people who listened to the secretary general and who participated in the conference that he convened made it clear in response that they themselves understood the defense of their specifically human rights as only part of a larger project, a "struggle," as the Native American Council of New York City put it, for the "survival" of "the planet itself." Most human beings have "separated themselves from the land and nature," but "Indigenous people are one with the land," said William Means (the president of the International Indian Treaty Council), and "it is through their voice that nature can speak to us."[47] So the answer to the question posed by Hopi elder Thomas Banyacya—"Who in this world can speak for nature?"—was the "native peoples of the world." And, in Robinson, the answer to the question of who on Mars can speak for nature is the native peoples of that world: Mars is "part of our bodies," say the Martian natives. "Our bodies are made of atoms that until recently were part of the Martian regolith" (*Green Mars*, 589) so "we can speak for the land" (*Blue Mars*, 272).

If, then, we return to the question we began with—What is Mars's name for itself?—it looks after all like, whatever that name is, it must be the name used by the people who, because they have become indigenous to Mars, can "speak for" it. At the same time, however, we must recognize that Robinson himself, as committed as he is to imagining a people who are literally indigenous—whose bodies, insofar as they consist of Martian water and Martian regolith, are literally a part of the land—cannot quite accept the idea that such people could meet the demand for the land's name for itself. For the Martian natives are not Martian rocks but are only, as it were, part rock, which is to say that insofar as they are human and the land they speak for is not, their claim to speak for it testifies to what Robinson and a number of other writers associated with the deep ecology movement understand as a certain anthropocentric presumption. Our responsibility, according to ecotheorists like David Abram, "is to renounce the claim that 'language' is an exclusively human property" and to begin to listen to what "a world that *speaks*" has to say.[48] If, then, the science fiction concern for what languages are spoken on Mars articulates a commitment to respecting the rights of other peoples (and we will return to the question of why the question of their rights will be so deeply connected to the question of their language), it articulates also a commitment to respecting the rights of others who are not people.[49] "One had to let things speak for themselves," Robinson writes. "This was perhaps true of all phenomena. Nothing could be spoken for. One could only walk over the land and let it speak for itself" (*Blue Mars*, 96).

But how can the land speak for itself, how can things speak for themselves? If Mars is nothing but rock, what can it mean to think not just that it has a name but that it has a name for itself? The contrast with the rock on Bova's Mars is instructive here. For Bova, for Jamie, the fundamental question about the "rock formation" he discovers is whether it is "natural" ("Just a formation of rocks that look roughly like walls and towers made by intelligent creatures") or "artificial" (which is to say, "buildings," the "forerunners of Mesa Verde").[50] Because Jamie's ambition is to discover life on Mars, his hope is that the rock formation is artificial, which is to say, that the arrangement of the rocks testifies to the presence (if not now, once) of the humans, or at least persons, who did the arranging. But Robinson's Mars is "only rock." And his interest in knowing what it says, what it calls itself, is precisely a function of the fact that it does *not* testify to the presence of any persons. Indeed, it's only when the persons who see the rocks are themselves in some way impaired (both Robinson's central characters develop aphasia) that they begin to understand the rocks. On the one hand, "Things lost their names," which is to say, we can't remember the names we gave them. On the other hand—precisely because we can't remember the names we gave them—we can begin to see their own names: we can "see them and think about them in terms of shapes." "They are shapes without the names but the shapes alone [are] like names. Spatializing language" (*Green Mars*, 406).

Bova's Jamie thinks that the "shapes" of his rocks mean that there used to be Indians on Mars; no one on Robinson's Mars thinks that. But the important difference between these texts has nothing to do with the question of whether there ever was intelligent life on Mars, nothing to do with their differing narratives of how the rocks in which they're interested came to have their shapes. It has to do instead with their different accounts of the status of shape as such. The question raised by these two texts, in other words, is the question of the relation between what something is shaped like and what something is. They differ in their answers to that question: on Bova's Mars, the shapes of the rocks are regarded as clues, which is to say, the fact that they look like cliff dwellings is regarded as evidence that they might be cliff dwellings. On Robinson's Mars, the shapes aren't evidence of what the rocks are; rather, it is the shapes of the rocks that make them what they are. This is what it means for Robinson to imagine that there can be language on Mars without there being any persons (Martian, Navajo, whatever) to have spoken that language. And if this claim, put in these terms, seems slightly implausible—how, after all, can there be texts without persons to produce those texts?—it's not very difficult to imagine a way of enhancing its plausibility. Suppose that you're walking through the "stone and sand" of Mars, and you come across some curious squiggles in the sand, or a curious formation of the rock. You step back and you notice that they seem to spell out the following words:

> A slumber did my spirit seal;
>   I had no human fears.
> She seemed a thing that could not feel
>   The touch of earthly years.

On Earth, or on Ben Bova's Mars,[51] you might immediately think that someone had been there before you, writing. In the essay, "Against Theory," that Steven Knapp and I wrote in 1982, we suggested that it was only when, seeing these shapes on a beach, you then saw a wave wash up and recede, leaving behind this pattern—

> No motion has she now, no force:
>   She neither hears nor sees;
> Rolled round in earth's diurnal course,
>   With rocks and stones and trees.

—that you realized no person had made these marks. On Robinson's Mars, however, which is "only rock" and where there are no other persons, you know right away that the marks have not been made by anyone and that if what you're looking at is a poem (a poem apparently about Earth), it is the planet itself that has produced it.

The question raised in "Against Theory" was whether these marks *were* a poem or, more generally, whether they were language. If, Knapp and I argued, the marks were signs produced by some agent who meant something by them (in the way, say, that Bova's Jamie thinks of his rocks as artifacts produced by Martian Anasazi), then they were language; if, like Robinson's rocks, they were produced by what "Against Theory" called "natural accident," then they weren't.[52] "Against Theory" argued, in other words, that what these marks meant—indeed, what these marks *were*—was entirely determined by the intention of their author. Those who disagreed with it asserted in various forms the irrelevance of the author's intention, but even those, like John Searle, who were most sympathetic to the idea that a text could only mean what its author intended denied that the marks could only be words if they were intended to be. As Searle eventually put it, "In linguistics, philosophy and logic words . . . are standardly defined purely formally"; hence, "it is simply not true that in order for a physical token to be a word . . . it must have been produced by an intentional human action."[53] The appeal to the "purely formal" here is an appeal to the physical, to the shape of the signifier. Clearly the marks are shaped like language—they look just like English words. But is being shaped like language enough to be language? Is what makes a word a word the fact that it's being used as a word or the fact that it's shaped like a word?

On Robinson's Mars, as I've already indicated, the correct answer is shape. But, of course, Robinson doesn't exactly think there are English words on Mars, waiting to be discovered by colonists. Like other deep ecologists, he thinks that nature has a language, but he doesn't think that language is English. When Abram describes the "tribal hunters" who "once read the tracks of deer, moose, and bear printed in the soil of the forest floor" (95), he doesn't think that the moose were leaving messages for the hunters in the hunters' tribal language.[54] Rather, the moose left traces of their presence, and these traces are indeed entirely physical, formal. Which is just to say that their shape is the only thing about them that matters—the difference between the marks that mean deer and the marks that mean moose has nothing to do with the intentions of the creatures who made the marks. But, of course, most theorists of meaning would not consider these traces to be linguistic. Moose tracks mean moose only in the sense that they count as physical evidence that a moose has been there, and when theorists like Searle claim that the shape makes the word, they do not base their claim on the idea that the shape of the word is the shape of (some part of) the creature that made the word—their whole point is that it does not matter which, if any, creature made the word, that no narrative of how the marks were made is relevant to the question of whether the marks constitute a word. They think that the shape of the marks, however they were made, determines whether those marks are words and what words they are. But can this be true?

Suppose, walking along the Martian regolith, the marks you come across look a little like this: *"a slumber did my spirit seal."* They're in cursive, and you can't make out whether the third letter in the last word is an *a* or an *r* or whether the very last bit is the letter *e* or just the end of the *l*. Would the answer to the question which letter it is be which letter it resembles most? If you thought the letter had been produced by a person writing in English, shape would clearly not be definitive—it would function, in other words, as a clue rather than a criterion. This is why it can make sense to say of someone that her *a*s look like *r*s or vice versa. For an *a* to look like an *r* and not thereby become an *r*, the fact of its shape cannot be decisive. For if shape *were* decisive (and on Mars, shape is decisive), then something that looked like an *r* would necessarily be an *r*.[55]

But what are the criteria for looking like an *r*? There aren't any, not because we don't have some idea of what an *r* looks like but because, even if something looks to us like an *a*, we don't have any argument against someone who says that the same thing looks to him like an *r*. How could we? If to be an *r* involved more than just looking like an *r*, we might have arguments against it actually being an *r*. But the fact that some shape looks to somebody like an *r* is a fact about that person's experience, and it's hard to see how we could argue that the shape *didn't* really look to him like an *r*. And if being an *r* is a matter of looking like an *r*, then it is an *r*—at least to him. We may, in other words, disagree with someone about whether an *r* really is an *r*, but we don't disagree with him about whether it looks like an *r* to him. Or, to put the point in the opposite direction, we can't really disagree with someone about whether an *r* is an *r* unless we already think that being an *r* involves something more than looking like an *r*; without the appeal to something beyond shape, the difference between us is just a difference in our experience, not a difference of opinion.

And we may, of course, just as easily encounter this kind of difference—difference without disagreement, which is to say, without there being anything to disagree about—without reference to anyone *else's* experience. Suppose the areological formations we're calling letters are several hundred feet long and dozens of feet wide, so when you're walking around the Martian surface they just seem to you like irregular indentations but, seen from a couple of thousand feet above (when you're landing or taking off), they look like a line from a Wordsworth poem. From the ground there are no shapes that look like letters, but from the air there are. Are there letters on Mars? It depends on your perspective. But which perspective is the right one? You might be able to answer the question which perspective is the most beautiful or which perspective is the most interesting, but you obviously can't answer the question which is right. All you can say is there are areological formations that from one angle (or from a certain distance or at a certain time of day or in certain kinds of light) have the shape of letters and that from another angle don't. The question of whether those formations really are letters regardless of your perspective makes no sense, since, as long as the relevant criterion is formal (is shape), the question of whether the formations really are letters is a question that is crucially about your perspective. Hence the commitment to the primacy of the materiality of the signifier (to shape) is also a commitment to the primacy of experience (to the subject position). Because what something looks like must be what it looks like to someone, the appeal to the shape of the signifier is at the same time an appeal to the position and hence to the identity of its interpreter.

From the standpoint of the recent history of literary theory, the simultaneity of these appeals helps explain how the commitment to the materiality of the signifier that was so central to theory in the 1970s and early 1980s could so easily become (what without realizing it, it already was) the commitment to those categories of personhood (race, gender, above all, culture) that were so central to theory in the late 1980s and the 1990s.[56] Which is just to say that the redescription of difference of opinion (the difference between what you think that letter is and what I think that letter is) as difference in subject position (the difference between you and me) makes the literary critical critique of intentionalism into the posthistoricist valorization of identity. More generally—beyond the question of intention—it is difference itself that emerges as intrinsically valuable. Because there is no contradiction between the fact that from a certain distance, at a certain angle, in a certain light those formations on Mars do have the shapes of letters and the fact that from another distance, at a different angle and in a different light, they don't, there is no necessary or intrinsic conflict between these positions, no question of right or wrong, true or false.

That's why it's the name Mars calls itself (rather than, say, its true name) that matters to Robinson and why the "United Nations Draft Declaration of Indigenous Peoples Rights"—which begins by affirming a general "right of all peoples to be different" (159)—goes on to specify the right of indigenous peoples "to designate and retain their own names for communities, places and persons."[57] If we value "Mars's own name for itself," it cannot be because we think that name is correct; how could a name for something in one language (say, Martian) be more correct than the name for the same thing in another language (say, English)? If we value the Martian name, we must value it because we respect the rights of Martians to use their own language. And, by the same token, if we don't value Mars's name for itself, it cannot be because we think that name is mistaken. Insofar, then, as the exemplary conflicts become conflicts over what names things should be called, conflict itself requires a new explanation. The conviction that others are mistaken must be redescribed as dislike of the fact that they are different, and the desire to convince them of the truth must be redescribed as the desire to get them to be the same. And since this desire, even if it is regarded as in some sense inevitable, is nevertheless in principle indefensible (Why should our perspective be everyone's? Why should everyone use the names we use? Why should everybody be like us?), the recommended response to difference becomes appreciative—to protect the things that make us who we are, to respect the things that make others who they are. Hence the draft declaration's celebration of the "diversity and richness of civilizations and cultures" and hence its distinctive hostility not simply to genocide (of which, after all, no one approves) but to "assimilation" or "cultural genocide." It is the right to cultural difference and to cultural survival that those who wish to call things by their own names assert.

What's crucial here is not only (as we saw in the previous section) that the model of linguistic difference disconnects the commitment to the survival of cultures from the commitment to their value but also that the formalism of the signifier makes every instance of reading and writing into the emergence of linguistic difference and thus transforms people who believe different things into people who speak different languages. In literary theory, this transformation takes place in what Derrida has called the "substitution of mark for sign,"[58] the substitution that I have described as the emergence of the shape of the signifier as constitutive of the identity of the text, and that is foundational not only to deconstruction but to every account of literary texts that imagines they can have more than one meaning or, more particularly, that imagines they can mean something other than what their authors intended. For it is perfectly and, indeed, uncontroversially true that the same marks can have different meanings, and if we think of texts as composed of marks, then it must be equally true that the same text can have different mean-

ings—what it means to you may well be different from what it means to
me, just as what looks to you like an *r* may well look to me like an *a*.
For some, of course, the problem with this view is that it seems to make
impossible the resolution of our disagreements, but the real problem, if
there is one, is that it makes disagreement impossible, not resolution.
Hence political theories which take their inspiration from deconstructive
theories of language—like Judith Butler's effort in *Excitable Speech* to
"outline" a "theory of the performativity of political discourse"[59]—will,
like Huntington and Fukuyama, produce differences without differences
of opinion, conflicts without disagreements.

Butler calls these differences "conflicts of interpretation" (87), and she
identifies them as products of what she describes as "a permanent diversity within the semantic field," which, once acknowledged, enables us to
recognize that no "utterance" has "the same meaning everywhere" and
hence that the context in which meaning is assigned to an utterance "has
become a scene of conflict" (91). One of the points of *Excitable Speech* is
thus to argue against hate speech laws, which, by trying to "fix" the
meaning of terms like "queer" and "nigger," make both the theoretical
mistake of imagining that utterances can have a single meaning and the
political mistake of foreclosing the opportunity to "appropriate those
terms from the dominant discourse and rework or resignify" them and
thus "to rally a political movement" (158). The conflict, then, is a conflict
over the meaning of an utterance like "queer." But what exactly is this
conflict a conflict about? It clearly isn't a conflict about the interpretation
of an utterance; if one person uses the word "queer" as a term of abuse
and another person uses it as expression of resistance to that abuse, the
two speakers can hardly be said to have conflicting interpretations of an
utterance. They don't, in other words, disagree about what they mean;
they just mean different things. Perhaps, then, the conflict should be
understood not as a conflict over what they mean but as a conflict over
what "queer" means. But a conflict over what meaning to assign to
"queer" isn't exactly a conflict of interpretation either; we don't think,
for example, that speakers of Spanish who assign the meaning "royal" to
the marks "real" have a conflict of interpretation with speakers of English
who assign the meaning "not imagined" to the same marks. In fact, two
speakers who mean different things by the same marks ("queer") are in

the same situation as two speakers who mean the same thing by different marks ("Mars," "Ka"); they aren't disagreeing, they're just speaking different languages.

It is Butler's commitment to "resignification," her transformation of conflict over which interpretation of an utterance is correct into conflict over which language to use—a transformation made not only possible but inevitable by the reduction of the sign to the mark, the utterance to its shape—that produces her complete allegiance to the primacy of the subject position. And it is her conviction that this transformation makes possible a "more general theory of the performativity of political discourse" that marks the complete subsumption of her notion of the political by the posthistoricist identitarianism of Huntington and Fukuyama.[60] For if, from one standpoint (the standpoint of people whose commitment, say, to equal rights for gay people is not defined by their commitment to changing the meaning of the word "queer"), the "political promise" of Butler's project of "resignification" may look a little inadequate (even if we use "queer" insultingly, the people we call queer may flourish; even if we use it with pride, those of us who so use it may be discriminated against), from the standpoint of posthistoricism, the replacement of conflicting interpretations by competing efforts of resignification is an obvious gain. Because there can be no right answer about what "queer" (or any other set of marks) really means,[61] any conflict between you and me about what "queer" means is just that, a conflict between you and me: I use it to mean one thing, you use it to mean another. And this conflict has nothing to do with ideology; it is nothing but a conflict of subject positions. Insofar, then, as political conflicts can be understood as conflicts between meanings (it is our ability to "contest for meanings" that Donna Haraway claims the insights of postmodern theory will enhance)[62] they must be understood as above all conflicts of identity.

Another way to put this is just to say that because the difference between interpretations is here redescribed as a difference between languages, the effort to convince people of the truth of your interpretation must be redescribed as the effort to make them speak your language. Or perhaps it would be more accurate to say that the effort to convince people of the truth is confused with and thus replaced by the effort to make them speak the same language. Thus Haraway equates the "dream of a common language" with the dream of "a perfectly true language" (173) and, repudiating the commitment to truth, insists on the value of linguistic difference. And thus, even more strikingly, Boutros Boutros-Ghali, lamenting the disappearance of many of the world's languages ("on the eve of the year 2000, the number of languages and dialects spoken throughout the five continents was only half what it had been in 1900"), warns us that "if we are not careful," the world will be "reduced to a single culture, a single language," and, "although we will speak with one voice, we will have nothing to say."[63] The commitment to difference without disagreement appears here in its purest possible form, since the only conditions under which it is possible for us to disagree—our speaking the same language—are understood by Haraway and Boutros-Ghali as conditions under which we have nothing to disagree about. Haraway and Boutros-Ghali think, in other words, that to speak the same language is to say the same thing, or, turned around, that to say different things is to speak different languages. So the unhappy future they fear is a world in which we all speak the same language but have nothing to say to each other, and the happy ending they hope for is a world in which we all speak different languages and can't understand each other.

For Haraway and Boutros-Ghali, then, as for Butler, there can be no conflicts of interpretation, not because there can be no conflict but because there can be no interpretation. All conflict has been turned into conflict between those who speak one language and those who speak another or between those who wish to eliminate difference and those who wish to preserve it, and the act of interpreting what someone says has been reconfigured either as the act of saying the same thing or as the act of saying something else. It is for this reason—this calling into question the very notion of the interpretation of an utterance—that Derrida, as noted earlier, attempts to avoid both the term "utterance" and the concept of interpretation, substituting "the phrase 'functioning of the mark' " for " 'understanding' the 'written utterance.' "[64] If the very idea of understanding involves the idea of a common language, the very idea of an utterance—or, for that matter, of a sign—involves the idea of a single meaning to be understood. The same sign cannot, in other words, have different meanings because for the sign to be the same it must have not only the same signifier but the same signified, and if it has the same signified, then it doesn't have a different meaning. By the same token, what Butler calls an utterance that "does not have the same meaning everywhere" cannot be the same utterance.[65] If different people mean different things when they say "queer," it is not because they have produced the same utterance with a different meaning but because they have produced different utterances. They, have, however, used the same marks. The advantage of mark over utterance and over sign is thus that people can without disagreement give the same mark different meanings.

Hence Derrida, transforming different interpretations of the same text into different uses of the same mark, makes disagreement impossible from the start. And hence deconstruction emerges as a technology of identity, resolving differences of opinion (about what a text means) by turning them into differences of subject position (about what to make a mark mean). Its critique of the subject—its insistence that no one can control the meaning of an utterance—amounts from this perspective to nothing more than the reminder that there are, after all, other subjects. Because "one always risks meaning something other than what one thinks one utters," Butler says, "one cannot know in advance the meaning that the other will assign to one's utterance, what conflict of interpretation may well arise and how best to adjudicate that difference" (87). Insofar as the risk Butler describes is the risk of misinterpretation, then it must be true that everyone always takes it—there can be no way to guarantee that you will be understood, and the only alternative to being understood is being misunderstood. Which is just to say that there often are conflicting beliefs about the meaning of an utterance and, when there are, at least one of them must be mistaken. But the risk that the other will misunderstand your utterance is not the same as the risk that the other will make your utterance mean something different. And the risk that the other will make your utterance mean something different is a risk that no one ever runs. The other can't possibly make your utterance mean something different because when your utterance is made to mean something different, it isn't your utterance any more—it just looks and sounds a lot like yours. So the transformation of interpretation into resignification is only made possible by the transformation of the sign into the signifier, the utterance into the mark.

It's only when the sign becomes the signifier that the otherness of the other matters; it's only when the question of what you believe becomes irrelevant that the question of who you are becomes essential. That's how Butler's performative becomes as effective as Huntington's culture in replacing ideology with identity. The deconstructive commitment to the materiality of the signifier is linked in principle to a valorization of the subject position that makes the question of identity (both the reader's and the writer's) primary. And the "force of the performative," precisely because it goes "beyond all question of truth or meaning," will be to replace the understanding appropriate to the sign with the effect appropriate to the mark, to imagine a world in which what the text means will be entirely subsumed by what it does.

The End of Theory

In Bret Easton Ellis's *American Psycho* (1991), the best way to get through to a woman is by carving "words" "into her with an ice pick."[66] When you tell the girl who works in the video store that you "like the part in *Body Double* where the woman . . . gets drilled by the power driller . . . the best," she doesn't respond; she hands you the tapes "without even looking at" you; it's not even clear that she hears you—all she says is "Sign here." But when you start shooting a girl with a nail gun and you urge her to "scream," she does "start screaming" (245), and when you cut out her tongue with some scissors and she can't scream any more, the "blood" that "gushes out of her mouth" (246) is just as good as, even better than, the screaming. Because this is how women talk to men: "Everytime I talk to one of you," Abhor says in Kathy Acker's *Empire of the Senseless* (1988), "I feel like I'm taking layers of my own epidermis, which are layers of still freshly bloody scar tissue, . . . and tearing each one of them off so more and more of my blood shoots into your face. This is what writing is to me a woman."[67] In Ellis, making a woman bleed is a way of talking to her; in Acker, bleeding is the way she talks back.

Both these texts are, of course, notorious for their representations of violence and, although Ellis's sexual politics might look in some respects very different from Acker's (the publication of *American Psycho* was de-

layed by feminist objections, and when the book did appear, it was generally regarded as misogynistic; Acker, however, has sometimes been read
as a feminist and never read as a misogynist), the gendered speech acts in
both texts have the same nonreciprocal—only women bleed—structure.
Indeed, their violence is itself structural, which is just to say that if writing is bleeding, then it is the mere fact of the writing (not the violence
the writing represents) that is violent. In the appropriation of the end of
Huckleberry Finn that concludes *Empire of the Senseless*, the boys debate
whether to smuggle a pen or a penknife to Abhor for her to use in her
escape. Mark wants Abhor to use the penknife to cut off her leg, thus,
in the best *Huck Finn* tradition, making escape more difficult. But, in the
same tradition, Thivai wants her to use the pen to "write down, with
her own blood as ink, how we rescued her, how brave our hearts were,
how strong our arms" (200–201). "The pen is mightier than the sword,"
Acker says, and Thivai's Huck-like "morality" wins out—they give Abhor
the pen instead of the penknife. But if you need blood for ink, the superiority of the pen to the sword may look a little less decisive; if you need
blood for ink, the pen depends on the penknife, and the real point seems
to be that the penknife makes the difference between the pen and the
sword disappear. The one requires what the other produces; if you need
blood for ink, the representation of violence is subsumed by the violence
of representation.

But even though this familiar critical chiasmus clearly has its place in
both *American Psycho* and *Empire of the Senseless*, it would be a mistake to
understand Patrick Bateman's ambition to carve words into his girls or
Abhor's ambition to bleed in the face of her boys as ways of insisting on
the violence of representation—not because they don't really involve
violence (although, I will argue, there's a way in which they don't) but
because they don't really involve representation. It would be one thing
to read the words carved into your body; it's another to imagine that
you might understand them without being required (or even able) to
read them. Bateman doesn't exactly imagine that the girl on whose body
he writes with *his* penknife (the ice pick) will understand what he's writing in the way, say, that children understand you by trying to figure out
which letters you're tracing on their backs.[68] It's the pain the letters make
her feel that carries the meaning. And if, in Acker, it's one thing to write

by making your letters with blood, it's another to write by bleeding. Ellis's misogynistic writing *on* the body is here matched by Acker's feminist writing *with* the body; the affect is different, but the scene of writing is the same—it is the meeting of two bodies, the intermingling of bodily fluids. The happy end of this fantasy is Abhor and Thivai turned into Huck and Jim on the raft: we "talked to each other about nothing, the way people talk to each other when they don't have to listen to the other person cause they've partly melded into the other person" (191). Bateman's efforts of communication—the carving, the rapes—are the unhappy end. But—happy or unhappy—it's the melding, the redescription of communication as penetration, the idea of what Neal Stephenson calls "words" that can "sink right into your brainstem,"[69] that emerges as central in these texts.

In Stephenson's *Snow Crash*, such words are understood on the model of the "virus" and are, for the purposes of the plot, instantiated in a particularly powerful "metavirus," "the atomic bomb of informational warfare" (200). One way this virus spreads is through a drug called Snow Crash, made up of the "blood serum" of people who are already infected; language here is imagined as a biological entity. But in the cyberpunk tradition, and in science fiction more generally, viruses are also digital entities. So Snow Crash is also a "digital metavirus, in binary code," one that "can infect computers, or hackers, via the optic nerve" (350). If, in Acker, listening to Abhor means having her blood "shoot into" your face, in Stephenson, reading code means having "your optic nerve" "exposed" to "a hundred thousand bytes of information" (74). It's this exposure that makes your computer crash; more remarkably, it's this exposure that makes the hacker sick. "Why would anyone show me information in binary code?" asks one victim. "I'm not a computer. I can't read a bit-map" (74). And yet, in *Snow Crash*, the bodies of humans are affected by "information" they can't read; the virus, like the ice pick, gets the words inside you even if you haven't read them.

In fact, a good deal of *Snow Crash*'s plot depends upon eliding the distinction between hackers and their computers, as if—indeed, in the novel, just because—looking at code will do to the hacker what receiving it will do to the computer. And if this is rendered implausible on one level by the fact that humans can't interpret bitmaps (which are just

rectangular meshes of pixels), it is made plausible on another level by
the idea that computers can (by the idea, in other words, that what the
computer does with a bitmap is interpret it); "code is just a form of
speech—the form that computers understand" (211). So when a computer crashes, what crashes it is a text written in code, a virus. And while
it's implausible to think that a text written in binary code—the language
computers speak—could crash a person, it's not so implausible to think
that a text written in a different kind of code, say, the genetic code, could
have the same impact on persons that binary code has on computers.
The point, in other words, of the analogy between (or the identification
of) the biological virus and (or with) the computer virus is the promotion of the model of the code, which is to say, of the idea that languages
are codes. And because the virus that infects you does so not because of
what it means but because of what it is—you don't catch a virus by
understanding it—it's the model of the virus or code that produces the
critique of representation described earlier. On the one hand, as Richard
Powers puts it, "the world" is "awash in messages";[70] indeed, *The Gold
Bug Variations* (1991) is mainly about the attempt to break the code, the
genetic code, in which the most fundamental of these messages are written. So the self-understanding of these texts involves a world entirely
composed of messages that need to be decoded, of representations in
need of interpretation. On the other hand, however, there is no sense in
which the information strings that run through *Snow Crash* or the strings
of nucleotides that make up the "miracle sentences" of Powers's "molecular linguistics" are ever interpreted at all.[71] The body that is infected by
a virus does not become infected because it understands the virus any
more than the body that does not become infected misunderstands the
virus.[72] So the world in which everything—from bitmaps to blood—can
be understood as a "form of speech" is also a world in which nothing
actually is *understood*, a world in which what a speech act does is disconnected from what it means.

The analogy between the digital virus and the biological virus, between computer code and genetic code, thus performs a double function.
Its first function is to produce a world in which everything is a text—the
great theoretical advance of "modern biologies," Donna Haraway says,
is "the translation of the world into a problem of coding," and the idea

that, as Jacques Derrida has put it, "the text is not the book, it is not confined in a volume itself confined to the library" but that textuality is instead intrinsic to "history, to the world, to reality, to being" (*Limited Inc.*, 139) is surely one of the most influential claims of postmodernity. But if the first function of the translation of the world into codes is to make everything a text, its second function, I will be arguing, is to deny that there are such things as texts. Indeed, I will be arguing that the fantasy of a world without texts and without the interpretation of texts (a world, we might say, of information instead of texts) is an essential element of full-blown postmodernism, or posthistoricism. And the commitment to—or, at least, the desire for—such a world is expressed not only in the ontological fantasy of the text that is what it's made of (e.g., the transformation of letters written in blood to just blood) but also in the ethical form of that fantasy, the text that, because of the way it's made, can never tell a lie.

Sex in *American Psycho* features Bateman's commitment to making the "girls" come—as if coming audibly were not a performance but an emanation of the body (like bleeding)—but in order to guarantee their sincerity, he is required not just to make them come but to eviscerate them. After all, their pleasure can be faked in a way that their pain can't—with any plausibility. You can be confident that the girl screaming when you shoot her with a nail gun is not performing (in the sense of faking) her pain in the way that she might be performing (which is to say, faking) her pleasure.[73] Octavia Butler's *Xenogenesis* trilogy produces a more palatable (if even more moralistic)[74] version of this scenario. She imagines aliens who have never developed the "habit of lying" because they communicate with each other in what she calls "a sensory language," a language in which "relating . . . experience by direct neural stimulation, they could give each other whole experiences" (*Dawn*, 237). Humans, in Butler, lie "easily and often," so they can't "trust one another"; that's why Bateman has to use a nail gun to find out what people are really thinking. The Oankali just extend their "sensory arms" and, like Abhor and Thivai and Huck and Jim, meld into each other.

But if the fact that humans lie is a mark of their moral inferiority, it's hard to see how the fact that the aliens don't can count as a mark of their superiority. Insofar as their "sensory language" truly is sensory—

insofar as it enables them to "give each other whole experiences"—it makes lying impossible rather than immoral. If, in other words, to speak to someone of your experience is to produce your experience (if the way you tell someone what you experienced is by giving her the experience), then you can't possibly lie. The most you can do by way of concealing is, as Butler's heroine notes, "withholding information, refusing contact" (238). So it makes more sense to think of the Oankali as unable to lie than it does to think of them as unwilling to lie, and it doesn't make much sense to give them moral credit for honesty—why should you get credit for not doing something that you couldn't do even if you wanted to?

The point, however, is not really that the Oankali shouldn't get credit for telling the truth; the point is rather that they *aren't* telling the truth, that if they can't lie, they can't really tell the truth either. Insofar as the relevant alternatives are contact or no contact, giving the experience or not giving the experience, telling the truth is as impossible as lying. The Oankali never misrepresent the truth only because they never represent it in the first place. Their "sensory language" relates experience by embodying it rather than representing it, which is to say that, inasmuch as it really is "sensory," it isn't exactly a "language," or, if it is a language, it's a language without propositions, without statements that can be considered true or false. The virus you catch is neither true nor false; the DNA that constructs you is neither true nor false; the blood you shed is neither true nor false—it's a performative, not a performance. The ethical fantasy of speech acts that must be true thus finds its expression in a theoretical fantasy of speech acts that can be neither true nor false, that are instead, in Austin's terminology, felicitous or infelicitous, and the ideal of truth is thus replaced by the ideal of success. The successful performative doesn't tell you the truth, it gets you—in Austin's famous example—married; the biological virus gets you sick, the digital virus destroys your operating system.

The question of success or failure, in other words, is a question of effect, and the question of the effect of a speech act, thus construed, can be answered without recourse to the question of its meaning. Indeed, once the crucial thing about the text is its effect, the question of right or wrong interpretations of the text is as irrelevant as the question of its truth or falsehood. Just as the virus can be neither true nor false, no interpretation of the virus can be either accurate or inaccurate—that's what it means to say that the body doesn't interpret the virus, it just responds to it; it catches it or it doesn't. When Bateman imagines the "things I could do to this girl's body with a hammer, the words I could carve into her with an ice pick" (112), he is imagining for his reader the production of an experience that will not require her interpretation. Which is just to say, what Wimsatt and Beardsley said some time ago, that it doesn't make sense to think of your experience of a text—the effect the text has on you—as your interpretation of it.[75]

For them, of course, the question of interpretation was usually mixed in with and often subordinated to the question of evaluation, and their commitment to "objectivity" involved them in discounting the relevance of the reader's response to a wide range of phenomena—from Montgomery's strategy at El Alamein to the waterfall in Coleridge's *Biographia*. Thus the tourist who says the waterfall is pretty provokes Coleridge's disgust, since Coleridge thinks it's sublime. But their point here is not that Coleridge is right and the tourist wrong; their point is, rather, that one or the other of them must be right, that if the tourist says it's pretty and Coleridge thinks it's sublime, it's not "as if the tourist had said, 'I feel sick,' and Coleridge had thought, 'No, I feel quite well.'"[76] The difference between sublime and pretty is a difference in the object, not in the response to it, and the point of the commitment to objectivity is not to find some method for determining whether the waterfall really is sublime or pretty, it's just to note the question of whether something is sublime or pretty is a different kind of question from the question of how it makes you feel. If you say it's sublime and I say it's pretty, we disagree; if you say it makes you sick and I say it doesn't make me sick, we aren't disagreeing, we are just recording the difference between us.

So the main idea of "The Affective Fallacy" was that the question of a text's meaning (like the question of the waterfall's sublimity) is a question about it, whereas the question of its effect is a question about us—how are we feeling? The answer to this question may of course crucially depend on the text, and it may produce a certain kind of objectivity. Wimsatt and Beardsley at least feigned interest in the very crude psychological tests that could be employed to determine people's affective responses to certain words, and, of course, the model of the virus provides access to very sophisticated tests about what the effects of a given strain on a given population are likely to be. But when some people catch the virus and some people don't, we don't think of the sick people as disagreeing with the healthy ones. Indeed, this is precisely what it means to begin to conceive the text on the model of the virus; it means to understand differing responses to the text as different effects produced on different bodies by the same cause. The relevant question here will not be whether any individual response is right or wrong but whether it is normal or abnormal.[77] The normal (what people usually do) replaces the normative (what people ought to do), which means that the attempt to convince people that one interpretation of a text is true and another false is in principle inconceivable (since there can't in principle be any such things as reasons) and must be redescribed as the attempt to impose one's interpretation of a text on others (since if you can't convince people to change their beliefs you are required to coerce them to alter their actions).

This is what it means to think of conflicts of interpretation as, in Derrida's terms, "conflicts of force" and thus to think that they can only be resolved (albeit only provisionally and, in the end, inevitably indefensibly) by the "imposition of meaning" (145). The deconstructive mistake has always been, in Wimsatt and Beardsley's terms, to see the text as the cause of interpretation rather than its object, just as the reader response mistake was simply to reverse the causality and to understand the interpretation as producing the text rather than being produced by it. That's what Stanley Fish meant by insisting that readers write texts rather than read them, and that's why conflicts between communities of interpretation were also, since reasons were irrelevant, conflicts of force. Indeed, in their much more influential essay, "The Intentional Fallacy," even Wimsatt and Beardsley found themselves maintaining that because the author's intention could not be used as what they called a "standard" of judgment, it was relevant only as the "*cause* of a poem" (4). And, in another context, it would be possible to show that if you don't think of texts as meaning what their authors intended, you will end up required to think of them as meaning what they mean to you, which is to say, to think of them as not really meaning at all but just as producing some

effect on their readers. In other words, to stick with Wimsatt and Beardsley, if you don't commit the intentional fallacy, you will be required to
commit the affective fallacy.

But writers like Ellis and Acker and, especially, Stephenson are not, of
course, troubled by the redescription of questions about what the text
means as questions about how it makes you feel. In fact, the whole plot
of *Snow Crash* revolves around the attempt to destroy the virus without
reading it or, what amounts to the same thing, even looking at it, since
to look at it is to be infected by it. And the popular response to *American
Psycho*, which tended to treat the book as if it were a nail gun, has found
a more moderate and more theoretically sophisticated equivalent in
Richard Rorty's response to *Snow Crash*. Novels like *Snow Crash*, Rorty
says in *Achieving Our Country*, express the loss of what he calls "national
hope," and he contrasts their authors with people like Lincoln, Whitman,
and Dewey, who "tell inspiring stories about episodes and figures in the
nation's past" (3). Rorty's point here is not that Stephenson is wrong
about America and that his "heroes" are right. In fact, he says, "there is
no point in asking whether Lincoln or Whitman or Dewey got America
right," since "stories" about "a nation," he thinks, "are not attempts at
accurate representation, but rather attempts to forge a moral identity"
(13). So the problem with *Snow Crash* is not that it isn't true—after all,
it's a story—but that it isn't inspirational.

At the same time, however, as the tribute to "The Inspirational Value
of Great Works of Literature" that ends *Achieving Our Country* makes
clear, the problem with *Snow Crash* and books like it is not only that they
fail to inspire the "young intellectuals" who read them with "pride in
American citizenship" but also that they contribute to a more fundamental failure to appreciate the value of inspiration—and hence of literature—itself. These books produce in their readers the "state of soul" that
Rorty calls "knowingness," which he glosses as a "preference for knowledge over hope" (37), and which term—for reasons that will be obvious—
he prefers to Harold Bloom's word "resentment." Rorty agrees with
Bloom that English professors are turning the study of literature into
"one more dismal social science," but his objections are not so much to
the "dismal" and the "social" as they are to the "science." It's not resentment his intellectuals prefer to hope; it's "knowledge." So even though

Rorty complains that young intellectuals who read Stephenson "often become convinced that they live in a violent, inhuman, corrupt country" (7), his complaint isn't really about what they're becoming convinced of, it's about the fact that they're becoming convinced. Which is just to say that his objection isn't really to what the young intellectuals think they know, it's to their claim to know anything at all—to their "knowingness." Rorty's "knowingness" thus adds a properly philosophical dimension to Bloom's resentment; resentful young intellectuals merely have the wrong affect, knowing young intellectuals also have the wrong theory.

In this respect, then—in its comparative indifference to the question of what one knows about a text and its commitment to the question of what the text makes one feel ("pride" or "disgust")—*Achieving Our Country* is, interestingly enough, a lot like *Snow Crash* and, indeed, a lot like all the novels I have been discussing: we're not looking for "accurate representations" in or of the virus or the nail gun—we're only interested in how they make us feel. At the same time, however, the analogy between how the virus in *Snow Crash* makes its readers feel (bad) and how *Snow Crash* itself, understood as a virus, makes *its* readers feel (uninspired) may look like nothing but an analogy. Rorty's worry about the effects of texts like *Snow Crash*, that is, may thematize *Snow Crash*'s own conception of text as virus, but that doesn't mean that readers like Rorty understand texts to function in the way that a virus does. After all, the point of the virus, I have argued, is that it does not need to be interpreted, indeed, that the effect it produces on the reader has nothing to do with its meaning and that, as a virus, it can't really be said to have any meaning, whereas the texts that either do or don't inspire Rortyan readers presumably produce their effect primarily by way of their meaning. When Whitman writes, "The United States themselves are essentially the greatest poem," the pride we (we Americans, at least) are supposed to feel is presumably made available to us only through our interpretation of the text. The important thing may be the "shudders of awe" (126) that Rorty says great works of literature produce in us, but the shudders don't replace our interpretation, they follow from it.

In fact, however, for the pragmatist, the shudders—or at least a response that has their status—come first. The Romantic conception of literature that Rorty understands himself to be championing in *Achieving*

Our Country is anticipated in his work by a defense of Romanticism that speaks more precisely to the formal questions I have been addressing. The contribution of Romanticism, he says in *Contingency, irony, and solidarity*, was its promotion of "speaking differently" over "arguing well" in the hierarchy of human talents. To argue for a position is to give the reasons why you think it's right; the legacy of the Romantics was the ability (acquired, Rorty says, "somehow") "to juggle several descriptions of the same event without asking which one was right" (39), and nothing is more crucial to all of Rorty's writing than his hostility to "the whole terminology of 'getting right' and 'representing accurately' " (37). So the pointlessness of asking whether Whitman "got America right" is matched by the pointlessness of asking whether we're getting Whitman right. Questions about whether your interpretation of something is right, questions about whether your account is "true" or "false," are the characteristic questions of the school of "knowingness."

But if we are interested in asking whether the text made us shudder and not in asking whether our description of its meaning is right or wrong, in what sense are we interested in its meaning at all? The minute we see no point in asking whether we got a text right or wrong—more precisely, since I'm not trying to make a psychological point here—the minute we imagine that our interpretation of a text *is* neither right nor wrong, we cease to understand ourselves as interpreting the text at all and begin to understand ourselves as instead registering its effect on us. What *would* be our accounts of the text's meaning—the sort of thing about which we might disagree—become instead our accounts of what it makes us think of. If you say that *American Psycho* makes you think of your grandfather, and I say that it makes me think of my grandfather, we are not disagreeing about our interpretations of *American Psycho*, first because we aren't disagreeing (we're just thinking about different things) and, second, because we aren't interpreting *American Psycho* (we're just saying what it makes us think of). And the same thing is true even if what *American Psycho* makes you think of is how American corporate capitalism is structured by homophobic misogyny. The fact that it seems a lot more plausible to think of *American Psycho* as being about American corporate capitalism than to think of it as being about your grandfather doesn't bridge the gap between what a text makes us

think of and what we think it means; on the contrary, it dramatizes just
how unbridgeable that gap is because it makes it clear that even if the
text made us think of exactly what it was about, what it made us think
of would still be a fact about us, while what it was about would still be
a fact about it.[78]

So readers who prefer "hope" to "knowledge" will also prefer response
(inspired or not) to interpretation (true or false). And when there are
conflicts between such readers—not when they have different interpretations but when they are differently inspired—pragmatism's strategies of
conflict management must inevitably be those that are relevant to what
Derrida calls "conflicts of force." I have already noted the "fundamental
premise" of *Contingency, irony, and solidarity*, which is that "a belief can
still regulate action, can still be thought worth dying for, among people
who are quite aware that this belief is caused by nothing deeper than
contingent historical circumstance" (189). In one sense, of course, all this
means is that beliefs may still be *true* even if caused by nothing deeper
than contingent historical circumstance, which is to say that beliefs may
turn out to be true whatever their cause, which is to say that the cause
of a belief is irrelevant to the question of whether it's true, and that true
beliefs may be worth dying for. But also, of course, the question of
whether a belief is true is the kind of question that preoccupies the students in the school of "knowingness." The inspired don't care whether
their beliefs are true, and we have already noted the appropriateness,
indeed the inevitability, of the eagerness for martyrdom once the question of truth has been deemed irrelevant. The way to defend those beliefs that seem to you true is to give your reasons for believing them—
that's why the knowing are committed to "arguing well." But just as
the point of redescribing your beliefs as your language was to make
arguing for them unnecessary, the point of redescribing your beliefs as
your feelings (your interpretations as your responses) is to make arguing for them both irrelevant and impossible. It's impossible because you
can't give any reasons that justify your feelings (the most you can do is
explain why you have them); it's irrelevant because you don't need any
reasons to justify your feelings. You're entitled to them without having
to justify them. So the pragmatist is prepared to die for his beliefs not
despite the fact that they don't seem true to him but *because* they don't

seem true to him. It's because he can't give any reasons that he's so eager to give his life.

Hence the complete continuity between the pragmatism of *Contingency, irony, and solidarity* and the patriotism of *Achieving Our Country*. Pragmatism has always been committed to treating your beliefs as if they were your country, perfecting "my country, right or wrong" (a slogan that acknowledges considerations of right and wrong but subordinates them to a higher loyalty) with "my beliefs, neither right nor wrong" (which eliminates the need for any higher loyalty and which makes fighting for your beliefs—rather than arguing for them—the appropriate course of action). And it is, of course, the irrelevance of argument—which requires, as I've been trying to show, the transformation of texts into information (letters into blood) and so of meaning into force (intentions into infections, or inspiration)—that makes Rorty, like Stephenson, a posthistoricist writer.[79] History ended (in 1989) because the Soviet Union, as a distinctive ideological entity, collapsed, and, insofar as the Cold War was imagined by Fukuyama and Huntington as a war between beliefs—between liberalism and socialism—its end made ideological disagreement and political argument obsolete. But just as pragmatism perfects patriotism, posthistoricism in general improves upon the merely historical claims of the political scientists by turning what they thought of as an empirical event (the end of political disagreement) into a theoretical condition (the impossibility of any disagreement). And in a world of differences without disagreements, it is, of course, identities that matter; the relevant thing about you is not what you believe but who you are, who you were and who you want to be. In this respect, *Achieving Our Country*, concerned with "our nation's self-identity" (4), takes its place alongside books like Toni Morrison's *Beloved* and Art Spiegelman's *Maus* and even, although Rorty criticizes it along with *Snow Crash*, Silko's *Almanac of the Dead*. The relevant identity in *Achieving Our Country* is American, rather than African-American, Native American, or Jewish, but all these books are about those "contingent historical circumstances" that have produced their authors (when causes replace reasons, historicism will naturally loom large), and they all understand themselves as technologies for the production of that paradigmatically identitarian emotion, "pride."[80]

There is obviously a theoretical link between this historicism and the repudiation of representation that I have been discussing, if only because one's responses have histories rather than justifications—which is to say, their histories are taken to be their justifications. That's why Art's father in *Maus* is said to "bleed" history (Abhor bleeds literature), and that's why Silko's Indians execute the Cuban Marxist for "crimes against history": he wants to tell them what to do, they want to tell him who they are. And that's also why, as readers of another of his novels, *Cryptonomicon*, know, Stephenson dislikes the same intellectuals Bloom and Rorty do. He, too, is proud of being an American, and he, too, expresses that pride by telling what Rorty calls "inspiring stories about episodes and figures in the nation's past" (3). In fact, *Cryptonomicon* was one of several contributions—including Steven Spielberg's *Saving Private Ryan* and Tom Brokaw's *Greatest Generation*—to the late twentieth-century effort to give World War II the inspirational status for generically white Americans that, say, the revolt of Hateuy in 1510 has for Silko's Indians. But Brokaw and especially Spielberg emphasized the battlefield exploits of their heroes—indeed, *Saving Private Ryan*'s representation of the D-Day assault on Normandy's beaches was widely praised for a realism that went beyond representation and that, in making its viewers feel as if they were actually participating in the Normandy invasion, might be described in the present context as taking at least a step toward justifying their pride in actions that they had not, of course, actually performed; the intensity of identification at least makes the pride plausible. Stephenson, however, describes *Cryptonomicon* as mainly about the contribution of what he calls "technically inclined people" to the war effort.[81] Thus, although one of his war heroes is a marine, the other is a "hacker," and the novel's project is not only to link the hackers of today (working on the Internet) with the "great wartime hackers" (breaking Nazi codes) (which it does in the usual way, making the former the descendants of the latter) but also, what's more of a challenge, to make the hackers (of yesterday and today) as heroic as the marines.

That's where the Bloomian hostility to cultural studies comes in. One of the villains of *Cryptonomicon* is the about-to-be ex-girlfriend of the heroic computer programmer; she's an assistant professor of something humanities-like, and when the novel begins, she's participating in a conference called "War as Text," devoted to sweeping war and the soldiers who fight it into "the ash-bin of posthistorical discourse" (52). The complaint here looks like the familiar one: when you treat things as texts, you deny their reality. But, as we've already seen, the bad transformation of world into text can be made good by the redescription of text as code. The penknife replaces the pen; if you turn "War as Text" into "War as Code," you make it possible to think of the marines and the cryptographers not only as collaborating but as actually doing the same thing—interacting with information. So the posthistoricism in the ash bin is recycled—the proliferation of texts comes back as the disappearance of textuality.

It is the commitment to this recycling that I have described as characterizing the novel at the end of history. More generally, it is the description of the text as mark or virus and its consequent transformation into an object of experience rather than interpretation that provide the ontology for the political and epistemological positions of posthistoricism (for the valorization of difference and identity). The political position is that ideological differences have been replaced by differences that should be understood on the model of cultural or linguistic differences. (Capitalism may have triumphed over socialism, but the battles between cultures have just begun.) The epistemological position is that such differences, properly understood, make disagreement—with its unavoidable commitment to the idea that some beliefs are true and others false, some interpretations right and others wrong—impossible. (No language is right or wrong; conflicts on the model of conflicts between languages have to do with force, not truth.) The ontological position—the transformation of the object of interpretation, the sign, into the object of experience, the mark—turns disagreement about the meaning of texts into the registration of their different effects. Readers at the end of history bleed, or not; they differ, but they don't disagree. And they don't disagree because they have nothing to disagree about.

The point of "Against Theory's" call for the end of theory, on the other hand, was to give them something to disagree about. If the project of the end of history is to imagine a world of differences without disagreements, the "Against Theory" project was to explain disagreement—what the author intended mattered because what the author intended was what interpreters disagreed about. This was what was meant by denying that intentionalism had any methodological value—it didn't help you get at the truth about what a text meant, it just explained why you could think that there *was* some truth about what a text meant. Of course, there have been literary theories committed to denying the possibility of true (or false) interpretations of texts—indeed, I have been arguing that *every* theory must be committed to making true and false interpretations impossible and thus to eliminating interpretation itself, and that the end of history is just another name for the end of interpretation. But even if it is true that no one any longer thinks that capitalism is wrong, it is not true that no one thinks that anything is wrong, and it is certainly not true that anyone—except, perhaps, in theory—thinks that there are no more misinterpretations. Which is just to say that, if history has ended, it has only ended in theory. Theory is already over in history.

TWO

Prehistoricism

rocks

O n Kim Stanley Robinson's Mars, "the landscape itself speaks" in "a kind of glossolalia," a meaningless jumble" (*Red Mars*, 546); the geologist who nevertheless understands it speaks its "ideolect of shapes" (*Green Mars*, 409). This conjunction of the meaningless and the linguistic—sometimes by way of the appeal to glossolalia, sometimes by way of an appeal to the model of a computer virus, sometimes (as in Stephenson's *Snow Crash*) by both—is almost a staple of science fiction in the 1990s, but its interest was noted as early as 1967 by the artist Robert Smithson, who prefaces one of his own essays with an epigraph from J. G. Ballard and who associates what he calls Ballard's "environmental coding" with the "coded channels" of computers: "All the content is removed from the 'memory' of an automaton and transformed into a 'shape' or 'object' " (342). In Ballard, what this produces are "landscape[s]" "covered by strange ciphers," "tall palms" that look like "the symbols of some cryptic alphabet," lakes and limestone hills that speak in "inaudible voices."[1] Smithson says that in Ballard, "The abyss of language erases the supposed meanings of general history and leaves an awesome 'babel.' " (341). In *Snow Crash*, the "language of Nature" (206) is biological rather than geological, but it too is a kind of "babbling," and it too is depicted as erasing meaning. Indeed, this is the whole point of the double appeal to glossolalia and to the virus—they function as languages while bypassing meaning.

In Stephenson, what glossolalia and viruses have in common is the way they produce their effects. Because "glossolalia comes from structures buried deep within the brain, common to all people" (206), someone speaking in tongues, "bypassing all the higher, acquired languages," produces "words" that, as I have already noted, "sink right into your brainstem" (395). The model of communication here is a disease (Stephenson compares it to smallpox) penetrating the human "immune system," and, although no computer virus "passes through the cell's walls and goes to the nucleus and messes with the cell's DNA," it is, of course, as we have also seen, precisely the overlap between genetic code and computer code—the idea that both the body and the computer exchange information with other bodies and computers through codes—that makes Stephenson's vision of the "neurolinguistic" both powerful and widespread. In *Children of the Mind*, for example, Orson Scott Card imagines a species that conveys information through a molecular code: "The code comes in and they somehow interpret it . . . by—what, smelling it? Swallowing it? The point is, if genetic molecules are their language, then they must somehow take them into their body as appropriately as the way we get the images of our writing from the paper into our eyes" (266). In Card, as in Stephenson, the language of nature is a code; this is science fiction's way of celebrating, with Haraway, "the translation of the world into a problem of coding" that constitutes the great theoretical advance of "modern biological science."

This subsumption of the linguistic under the model of the virus or code, computer or biological, produces two effects. On the one hand, it expands the field of language; on the other, it alters our sense of what it means to use a language—indeed, it alters our sense of what meaning is. The virus in Stephenson is a code "that can infect computers, or hackers, via the optic nerve" (405). Hackers are susceptible to the virus not, in other words, because they understand the virus (in the way, say, that French speakers understand French) but because their optic nerves are vulnerable to infection, a vulnerability that is a function of what Stephenson calls their "immune systems" rather than of their interpretive abilities. Because infection is not interpretation, you don't need to understand a virus in order to catch a code. Instead, what Smithson praised in the work of the Minimalist sculptor Donald Judd, his transformation of "printed matter" into something that "he looks at rather than reads" (18), turns the question of what a thing means into the question of what it looks like or smells like or tastes like.

Smithson's enthusiasm for Ballard and for the computer—for the replacement of "supposed meanings" by "shapes and objects"—is thus a version of his enthusiasm for Judd; Judd is doing what Ballard imagined, removing the "content" and replacing it with the "shape" or "object." And, indeed, it was precisely the status of shape—what Michael Fried called the difference between "shape as a fundamental property of objects and shape as a medium of painting"[2]—that emerged as central not only to Smithson's work but to the debate over Minimalism (or, as Fried called it, "Literalism"). What was literal about literalism was its refusal precisely of content, a refusal impossible for painting, Smithson thought, because painting as such—even abstract painting (so called)—was intrinsically representational: "There is nothing abstract about any kind of painting—it all represents space" (390). In contrast, Judd's "specific objects" (or the new work by Morris, Serra, and Smithson himself) inhabited rather than represented space; they existed in what Judd called "real space" or "actual space."[3] But, of course, this point could be put in just the opposite way: paintings, even abstract paintings, also existed in real or actual space; the conditions toward which specific objects aspired was a condition which every object—as an object—could not help but achieve. Indeed, it is precisely because all objects have shapes that the point of Modernist painting, as Fried described it in "Art and Objecthood," was to make the painting have a shape that was not simply the shape of the object that the painting is—"otherwise they are experienced as nothing more than objects."

Smithson's distinction between the content that paintings have and the shape that objects have appears in Fried as the distinction between "depicted" and "literal" shape, the distinction between the irregular polygon that is the shape of Frank Stella's *Moultonboro II*—the shape of the support—and the triangle that is painted on the support. And the Mini-malist critique of painting (Smithson's attack on "content") was a critique precisely of the very idea of the support, of the distinction between the painting and its support required by the idea of painting—the idea of putting something (paint) *on* something else. So if the goal of Fried's Modernism is to insist on the irreducibility of art's content (the irreduc-ibility of what, in the work of art, exceeds the object it is), the goal of Minimalism is to produce the work of art precisely as the object it is: "It aspires not to defeat or suspend its own objecthood, but on the contrary to discover and project objecthood as such." This is what Smithson is getting at when he cites approvingly Judd's description of a work by Lee Bontecou: "The black hole does not allude to a black hole . . . it is one" (80).[4] What Smithson values here is the substitution of exemplification for allusion and, more generally, the substitution of what he will call the "material" (209) for the "representational and illusionistic" (361). It is this substitution that Fried rejects as literal and that, in a very early piece—written before Minimalism/literalism came into existence and about a painter, Larry Poons, whom he admired and subsequently champi-oned—he criticized not simply because it produces inferior art but be-cause it "runs counter to art" (310).

The paintings Fried describes involved "the placement of colored dots in . . . patterns on a colored field," and Fried criticizes them for being "literally irresistible," comparing them to "those tests for color blindness in which colored dots form one number under normal vision and an-other number if the subject's vision is defective" (310). In *Snow Crash*, the virus that destroys hackers' brains is, as we have seen, communicated to them through a bitmap, "a series of white and black pixels" mounted on a scroll. The only way to avoid the effect is not to look at the bitmap and, although the effect of the Poonsian eye test is less dire, Fried's resis-tance to these paintings is expressed in terms of the similar "coercion" they exercise over the spectator, which he characterizes as their refusal to acknowledge "even the barest notion of individual sensibility." Insofar as the paintings are like eye charts, everyone who sees them will inevita-bly respond to them in the way that every eye patient responds to the chart (in the way that every hacker responds to the bitmap). But to put the point in this way is to realize that Fried isn't really concerned about

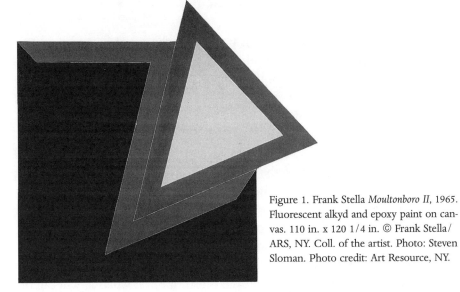

Figure 1. Frank Stella *Moultonboro II*, 1965. Fluorescent alkyd and epoxy paint on canvas. 110 in. x 120 1/4 in. © Frank Stella/ ARS, NY. Coll. of the artist. Photo: Steven Sloman. Photo credit: Art Resource, NY.

Figure 2. Robert Smithson, *Nonsite (Mica from Portland, Ct.)*, 1968. Mica, 5 x 9 x 64 3/4. Estate of Robert Smithson. Courtesy James Cohan Gallery, New York. © Copyright Estate of Robert Smithson/Licensed by VAGA, New York, NY.

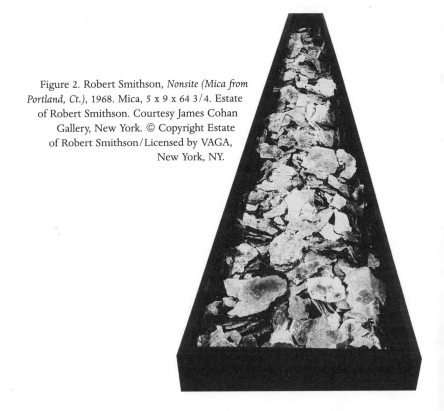

the failure of these paintings to acknowledge the spectator's individual-ity; after all, people who aren't color-blind respond differently to eye tests than people who are, and there are many other kinds of diagnostic tests that reveal subtle differences between every spectator, thus calibrating rather than ignoring their individuality. The real problem is not that the tests render the differences between spectators irrelevant; the real prob-lem is that, in functioning like tests, the paintings make the spectator as such irrelevant: their "mode of address," he says, is "to us as subjects, not spectators."

Several years later (in "Shape as Form"), Fried makes this distinction more perspicuous by quoting Judd—"A work of art needs only to be interesting"—and by claiming in response that "some work" is "more than just interesting. It is, I want to say, *good*" (98). And in "Art and Objecthood" (1967), he will return to Judd's claim that the work need only be interesting and oppose that claim not only to the Modernist demand that the work be good but to the demand that it be *convincing*, that paintings, as he puts it in "Morris Louis," "compel conviction as paintings" (128). So the address to the subject becomes the appeal to the subject's interest, while the address to the spectator appeals to his or her sense of what is good, of what compels conviction. And if one more or less inevitable way to understand this distinction is as a disguise for the distinction between paintings he likes and paintings he doesn't, Fried's insistence that good paintings compel conviction seems designed pre-cisely to counter this objection, to counter the criticism that the differ-ence between interesting and convincing objects is just the difference in our attitude toward those objects. For what makes conviction superior to interest is the fact that interest is essentially an attribute of the sub-ject—the question of whether we find an object interesting is (like the question about how the waterfall makes us feel) a question about *us*—whereas objects that compel conviction do not leave the question of our being convinced up to us.[5] Compelling conviction is something the work does, and it is precisely this commitment to the work—*it* is good regard-less of whether we are interested—that Fried wants to insist on.

To put the point this way, however, is obviously to render problematic the critique of the early Poons paintings as "literally irresistible" and as hence running "counter to art." Why isn't the great work of art, the one that compels conviction, coercive in exactly the way that the Poons paintings are or the eye test is? And if great works of art are the ones that compel conviction, why are so few (as the famous ending of "Art and Objecthood" cheerfully points out) convinced? Should we understand people who can feel the force of great art as the aesthetic equivalents of people who aren't color-blind or as the fortunate version of people whose immune systems are susceptible to viruses that the rest of us easily reject? And, if that's true, aren't we all "subjects" rather than "spectators" after all?

From this standpoint, it seems obvious that the difference between being interested and being convinced cannot do the work (the work of distinguishing between art and objects, between spectators and subjects) that Fried wants it to. But, as these essays also make obvious, it doesn't really need to. The reason that interest and conviction collapse into each other is that (compulsory or not) both are irreducibly attributes of the subject; they are elements of or, more precisely, descriptions (I am interested, I am convinced) of what Fried will call the subject's "experience." The reason it doesn't matter is that Fried's fundamental commitment in these essays is not to distinguishing between kinds of experience (between, say, interest and conviction) but to distinguishing between those objects to which our experience is relevant and those to which it isn't. The test for color blindness is what it is, for example, only in virtue of what it reveals about the people who look at it, namely, whether or not they are color-blind. Insofar as the test exercises coercion over the beholder, it does so only in the sense that it produces a response in us that is automatic. And it is not the automatic as such to which Fried objects; it is the automatic precisely as a mark of the relevance of our response. Modernist paintings, he wants to argue, are the sorts of objects to which we might *not* respond. This is why he insists not only that Modernist paintings compel conviction but that they "compel conviction as paintings." In other words, it is no more his freedom than it was his individuality that distinguishes the subject from the spectator. Everyone responds in some way to eye tests; we cannot help but respond to—be more or less interested by—objects in the world. Fried's description of the effort of Modernist paintings to defeat their objecthood ("as though a work of art—more accurately, a work of modernist painting or sculpture—were in some essential respect *not an object*" [152]) is a description rather of the effort to imagine objects to which we do not respond. All objects coerce (in the sense of produce) some response; it is this coercion, the coercion built into the concept of experience, that "runs counter to art" and that demands a subject who is as little a subject as the object is an object.

Hence, theatricality, which Fried understands as the production of objects designed exclusively to produce a response (or some range of responses) in the beholder and which he presents as "the negation of art,"[6] involves only incidentally the insistence on the object. What's crucial is that the transformation of the art object into an object like any other requires the transformation of the beholder's experience of it into a version of experience tout court: "Whereas in previous art 'what is to be had from the work is located strictly within [it],' the experience of literalist art is of an object in a situation—one that, virtually by definition, includes the beholder." The "virtually" here is a little misleading because, as Fried goes on to say, although the "object, not the beholder, must remain the center or focus of the situation," "the situation itself *belongs* to the beholder—it is *his* situation" (154). The presence of the beholder is structural rather than empirical, since without him there is no situation and therefore no literalist art. The point here is not a kind of general idealism, not the idea that the object comes into existence only when the beholder encounters it and therefore that there is some sense in which he creates it. Although this position will quickly emerge as central to certain forms of literary theory, in Fried's account of Minimalism, the object exists on its own all right; what depends on the beholder is only the experience. But, of course, the experience is everything—it is the *experience* instead of the *object* that Minimalism values.

This is why the often retold story of the artist Tony Smith's night drive on the unfinished New Jersey Turnpike—"It was a dark night and there were no lights or shoulder markers, lines, railings, or anything at all except the dark pavement moving through the landscape of the flats, rimmed by hills in the distance, but punctuated by stacks, towers, fumes, and colored lights"—is so central to Fried and Smithson both: "I thought to myself," Smith says, "it ought to be clear that's the end of art. Most painting looks pretty pictorial after that. There is no way you can frame it, you just have to experience it." The opposition between what can be framed and what can only be experienced is foundational. The removal of the frame means that in Minimalism there is nothing within the beholder's field of vision that "declares its irrelevance to the situation, and therefore to the experience, in question. . . . Everything counts—not as part of the object but as part of the situation" (Fried, 155). Smithson calls this "making contact with matter" and identifies it with "limitlessness" and with "Freud's notion of the 'oceanic' " (103), but the replacement of what can be framed with what is experienced doesn't exactly remove all limits; there are always limits to what you can see. The point, in other words, is not that your experience is unbounded—it is, of course, bounded by the physical limits that go with it being your experience. The point is, rather, that there are no boundaries *within* your experience, no boundaries other than the physical limits. Everything that is contributing to the experience (the wall on which the painting is hung as well as the painting) is as much a part of it as everything else. Some things, no doubt, will be more prominent features of it than others, but everything will continue to count, since if *anything* were changed, the whole experience would be different. This is how the gallery—or, more generally, the site—will become part of the work, not simply the place where the work can be seen but a component of it. You don't go to Holland to see Smithson's *Broken Circle* in the way that you might go to New York to see Stella's *Alpha Pi* because the *Alpha Pi* you see in New York you might also see in Chicago (New York is just where it happens to be), whereas *Broken Circle* can be seen only in Holland. And this is not because *Broken Circle* is too big or too fragile to move; it's because to see it anywhere else, in a different place at a different latitude or longitude, would be to have a different experience and hence to be seeing something else.[7]

By contrast, the Modernist work refuses to be absorbed into its site. It is "exclusive" rather than "inclusive," and what it excludes is precisely the beholder; the context in which you encounter the work—where you see it, when you see it, who you are—is not a part of what it is. This is why Fried will invoke "the concept of meaning" (161) as against experience on its behalf. The idea here is that our experience of any work will vary with place, time, and so forth—the experience of reading some text on an airplane will be different from the experience of reading the same text in one's study—but the meaning of the text will not. Of course, this claim can be disputed; not only will the experience of reading, say, *The Scarlet Letter* be different in the twenty-first century from what it was in the nineteenth or twentieth, but the meaning of the novel, according to a set of literary theoretical arguments developed in the late 1960s and early 1970s, will be different too.[8] What these arguments will require is an equation of the text's meaning with the reader's experience, like that proclaimed in Stanley Fish's reader response criticism, or a reduction of the reader's interpretation of the text to his experience of it, like that performed in the work of Paul de Man and Jacques Derrida (it is this reduction—to anticipate the arguments of the next two sections—that will make the meaningless signifier "Marion" central to de Man and that will in Derrida turn the understanding of the sign into the functioning of the mark). In Smithson, however, the question of the frame will have less to do with the difference between the meaningful and the meaningless than with the difference between the limited (framed) and the unlimited (unframed because unframeable). And, although in "A Sedimentation of the Mind," written more or less explicitly as an attack on "Art and Objecthood," Smithson identifies his own aesthetic as a version of Tony Smith's (and although the opposition between Smithson and Fried is more or less canonical in contemporary art history), his actual account of the construction of his *Non-Sites* will reproduce Fried's insistence on the frame.

Both the identification with Smith and the attack on Fried involve the commitment to "non-containment" (Smithson, 102), to "an empty limit, or no limit at all" (102), to the "oceanic" and the "infinite." The need for limits is attributed to the "critic" who "cannot risk the rhythm of dedifferentiation" (103), and Fried's description in "Morris Louis" of the "dazzling blankness of the untouched canvas" in Louis's unfurleds, his comparison of that blankness to an "infinite abyss" that only the "innumerable conventions" of "art and life" can contain, is cited as evidence of both the power of the limitless and the critic's fear of it. But if this moment is deeply problematic in Fried, what makes it problematic is not primarily its affective quality. The problem is, rather, the temporary transformation of the framed work of art (framed blankness) into the unframed experience (the transformation of Morris Louis into Tony

Smith) that is produced precisely by Fried's allusion to the "consequences" (which is to say, to the effects rather than to the meaning) of
the artistic "act" and by his consequent appeal to the "conventions of art
and of life" to shore up the limits that seem to have been breached. The
conventions are required to draw us back from the abyss of the infinite,
to "restrict the consequences of our act within narrow bounds" (103)
because it must of course be true that the consequences of our acts *are*
infinite—in the sense that any act of ours plays a role in innumerable
causal chains over which we have no control and about which we have
no knowledge. It is precisely this unbounded quality that is an aspect of
every part of everyone's life, and it is this abyssal unboundedness that
Smithson values and associates with nature, which is to say, with "raw
matter" ("the physical abyss of raw matter" [104]). But on Fried's own
account of the ontology of works of art, their *consequences* (the effects
they have on us) are part of what they are only as objects and are in no
sense part of what they are as works of art. Which is just to say that if
someone looking at a Louis unfurled found himself so deeply interested
in the painting that he neglected to watch where he was going and
bumped into a sculpture by Caro, severely injuring himself, the injury
would in an important sense be one of the consequences of the act that
produced the painting, but it would not thereby count as part of the
meaning of the painting. And if the injured person won a judgment
against the museum and put it out of business, that would also be a
consequence of Louis's making the painting, but it would not be part of
what the painting meant. Ad infinitum. Indeed, insofar as the abyss opens
with respect to the consequences of our acts, no set of conventions can
very neatly draw us back from it, which is why Fried's appeal to convention seems to Smithson like a panic response (and which is why in Derrida the attempt to limit such effects will be understood as belonging to
"the order of ethical-political"—rather than, say, hermeneutic, "responsibility" [116]—as the decision, for example, to hold the museum liable for
your injuries surely does).

But the whole point of Fried's insistence on the irrelevance of the
subject's experience is to make it unnecessary to worry about the consequences from which conventions are supposed to save us. In Fried, the

real problem with the abyss is not that it's terrifying in its infiniteness but that its infiniteness has nothing to do with its status as a work of art; it belongs to the art object as object and not as art. To insist on the abyssal is to imagine the work of art as a thing and to convert the interpretation of the work of art into the experience of the thing. And actually, despite his attack on Fried and despite his commitment to "making contact with matter" (103) (the black hole that *is* rather than *alludes* to a black hole), Smithson is himself entirely committed to the production of limits and to the idea that it is the limit that marks the difference between the object and the work of art. Visiting slate quarries in Pennsylvania (quarries in general are privileged sites for Smithson), he insists that they literalize the "oceanic," which is to say that "all boundaries and distinctions lost their meaning in this ocean of slate" (110). The quarry is here an exemplary instance of experience as such, which has no boundaries except the limits of one's own perceptions. For a boundary to count as a boundary, in other words, it must be a boundary within the perceptual field, not the boundary of the perceptual field, not the boundary that *is* the perceptual field. So what Smithson does is collect "a canvas bag full of slate chips for a small *Non-Site*." The *Non-Site*, materials from the quarry enclosed by a frame, contains the slate in a way that the quarry does not—which is what he means when he says that "if art is art it must have limits." The point here is not that art cannot succeed in being as oceanic as the quarry; the point is rather that it's the act of containment that produces the concept of art. It is the "container" (the frame) that makes the art because it is the frame that renders much of the experience of the beholder (his experience of everything outside the frame) and thus his experience as such irrelevant. It is when it is contained (and only when it is contained) that the world becomes art, that, as Smithson says, "The ground becomes a map" (111).

The ground that becomes a map is the opposite of the black hole that is rather than alludes to the black hole, since what makes the black hole distinctive is that it *is* what it is, while what makes the ground as map distinctive is that it *represents* what it is. It is because they are irreducibly representational (whether or not they are mimetic) that maps are crucial to Smithson. Even if, in other words, they cannot be understood as looking like the thing they represent, they also cannot be understood except as representations. Hence the position of the beholder is utterly irrelevant to their meaning; the scale of a map has an essential relation to the world outside of the map (e.g., one inch equals one hundred miles), which is part of what it means to think of the map as representing the world, but it has no relation to the position of the beholder in that world. It doesn't matter whether the distance between two points looks longer because you are looking at it head-on or shorter because you're looking at an angle. The relations between the elements in a map, in other words, have nothing to do with where the map is or where you see it from; they are entirely internal.

One way to express this internality is just to say that maps are flat. Greenberg had, of course, identified the flatness of Modernist painting with its attempt to repudiate pictorial illusion, but Judd insisted that painting was irreducibly tied to illusionism and had linked his commitment to "specific objects" to the repudiation of what he regarded as the inevitability of even the flattest painting's need to represent three dimensions in two. Specific objects, as objects, were already in three dimensions and hence were free from this necessity; thus, "Actual space is intrinsically more powerful and specific than paint on a flat surface." Actual space, however (what Smithson calls "the ground"), is transformed when it "becomes a map." The "last monument" mentioned by Smithson in "A Tour of the Monuments of Passaic, New Jersey" (1967), is a "sand box," which he immediately describes as a "model desert": "Under the dead light of the Passaic afternoon the desert became a map of infinite disintegration and forgetfulness" (74). The transformation of the object into a model and then of the model into what he would call "a three-dimensional map" repudiates illusion not by locating the object in "actual space" but by removing it—despite its three-dimensionsionality—from actual space. Like the frame that turns an "uncontained site" into a *Non-Site* (turns a place into a work of art), what Smithson will call the "glance" of the artist (the glance that turns a sandbox into a map) turns rocks into representations ("of infinite disintegration and forgetfulness") without even having to flatten them. It's as if you could achieve the two-dimensionality of painting without flatness, without the delusion that you were producing the ineluctable essence of painting. The relevance of flatness, in other words, is only as a mark of representation, and the point here is—against but actually in the spirit of Greenberg— you don't need flatness for representation.[9] For although it may look like the whole point of abstraction on the Greenbergian model is to repudiate representation, the point actually is to insist on the primacy of representation—the (impossibly) flat object is the representing object.

It's in this sense—the sense in which the container and the ground can become maps—that "a great artist can make art simply by casting a glance" (112). The glance leaves the shape of the ground—its topography—untouched but utterly alters its ontology; it is the difference between the infinite and a map of the infinite, between a thing and a thing that represents. And it's this difference—a difference in ontology that can be made just by casting a glance—that is brought to the fore by what Smithson calls the impossibility of abstraction in painting and by the emergence in response of a post-Minimalist photographic practice that will insist, by contrast, on the inevitability of abstraction in photography. If Smithson's characterization of painting as always being *of* something seems counterintuitive, it is bound to seem even more counterintuitive to say of any photograph, as James Welling does, that it is *not* of something. Indeed, it is precisely because all photographs do seem to be photographs of something—because Welling's own photographs are of buildings or trains or pieces of tin foil and because even the ones he calls abstractions record the presence of the strips of paper that were used to make them—that it seems to make sense to insist that photography is essentially representational and that photographs have an irreducible relation to the objects they are photographs of.[10] But, of course, it is precisely the relation they have to objects—the fact that they record their presence—that makes it unclear whether we want to call any photograph a representation. When you look at yourself in a mirror and see your presence recorded, you don't see a representation of yourself, you see yourself; when you look at *Movable Bridge, New York, NY, 1990*, you don't see a representation of that bridge, you see the bridge. Understood in these terms, photographs are different from paintings not because all photographs represent the world while only some paintings do but because no photograph represents the world. When we look at photographs, as Kendall Walton puts it, we are not seeing representations of the world, we are seeing the world itself.[11]

The reason for this is that the object a photograph is of—the bridge
or the train—plays an essential causal role in the production of the photograph that the object a painting is of does not. You can make a painting
of a movable bridge even if the movable bridge you're painting never
existed, or if you've never seen a movable bridge, or if there are no
such things as movable bridges. But you cannot make a photograph of
a movable bridge without a movable bridge. That's why if, say, I accuse
you of stealing a movable bridge and produce a photograph I took of
you stealing it, the photograph will count as evidence (though not, of
course, necessarily conclusive evidence) in a way that a painting I made
of you stealing the bridge would not. We might say that the photograph
has value as evidence of the truth of the accusation, whereas the painting
is just another way of making the accusation. And we might put the
point more generally by saying that the causal history of the painting
runs through the painter in a way that it doesn't run through the thing
he or she is painting, whereas the causal history of the photograph runs
through the thing being photographed in a way that it doesn't run
through the photographer.

Indeed, this difference has been invoked almost from the beginning
of its history as a reason why straight photography cannot count as an
art. As early as 1907, in an essay called "On the Straight Print," the
pictorialist Robert Demachy put the point sharply by claiming that a
"straight print may be beautiful . . . but it cannot be a work of art."[12]
The reason for this, according to Demachy, was that a straight print can
only be a copy of what he calls "nature" and that "there is not a particle
of art in the most beautiful scene of nature." Sunsets, to take a standard
example, are beautiful, but they are not works of art, so the photograph
of a sunset may be beautiful but, insofar as its beauty is derived from the
beauty of the sunset, the photograph is not art, it's just a technology for
helping those of us who weren't there see the beautiful sunset. So when
Sadakichi Hartmann urged the photographer as artist to rely "on your
eye, on your good taste and your knowledge of composition" and to
"patiently wait until the scene or object of your pictured vision reveals
itself in its supremest moment of beauty,"[13] Demachy's response was that
the photographer could demonstrate all the taste in the world and could
position himself wherever he liked, but the beauty he recorded was nev-

ertheless not that of the picture he made but that of the object he had seen. And both Demachy's sense of the primacy of the object in photography and his sense of photography's consequent inappropriateness as a medium for art not only have survived but more recently—above all in the emergence of a distinctively postmodern theory and practice of photography—have flourished.

Thus, in an important essay called "Photography after Art Photography," Abigail Solomon-Godeau could argue that photography had come to "figure as a crucial term in postmodernism" precisely insofar as it had repudiated the ambition to make photographs into works of art and had taken instead "an instrumental approach to the medium."[14] What this involved was "using photography" to make art rather than making photographs that were themselves art, a distinction she derives from Peter Bunnell's remark that he finds Cindy Sherman "interesting as an artist, but uninteresting as a photographer" (113) and that Arthur Danto's subsequent analysis of Sherman—"photography is not her medium. It is rather a means to her artistic ends. Her medium is herself"[15]—makes perspicuous. In all these analyses, it is what the photograph is of that makes it art. Even a more or less explicitly deconstructive manifesto like Craig Owens's essay "The Allegorical Impulse: Toward a Theory of Postmodernism" praises "untitled photos for film stills" in terms of Sherman's cleverness as a *model*: the "perfection of her impersonations," Owens says, turns "disguise" into "parody" and thus into criticism of the "alienating identifications" of the mass media.[16] Photography is, of course, necessary for this project—without it there would be no record of Sherman's virtuosity and, in fact, there would have been no occasion for the virtuosity: the pose that is recorded by the photograph is also produced for the photograph. But this double function of the camera in relation to the pose—it both causes and records it—in no way detracts from the primacy of the pose. Instead, insofar as the pose thematizes photography, transforming the photograph into an element in the history of the pose (subsuming the photograph in the narrative of its own existence), the photograph is even more rigorously subordinated to the pose than it would otherwise be, for the pose becomes, in effect, a critique of the photograph. What the photograph shows is an object that has been called into the world by the existence of cameras; the pose, as pose, calls attention to this fact and criticizes the world the camera has made; the camera, then, records this critique. The parodic element in Sherman consists in her insistence that the object the camera records is an object the camera has made, but the status of the photograph as record is asserted rather than challenged by the parody.

That's why Danto can say that "untitled film stills" "are art and not a transcription through photography of the real world" (121). What he really means is that the photographs are art because they're transcriptions of artifice rather than of the "real world"; insofar as actresses pose for photographs only because there are photographs for them to pose for, the "untitled film stills" series insists on the centrality of the camera. At the same time, however, this centrality is understood as extrinsic to the actual photograph, which treats the object as if it were autonomous, as if it were there to be seen in the world in the same way that sunsets are. Thus the narrative dependence of the object photographed on the photograph is overridden by its formal independence, that is, by its position in relation to the camera as an object that can be seen through the camera. In this respect, Sherman's photographs, although they are not, of course, photographs of nature (in postmodernism, as Owens says, "nature is treated as wholly domesticated by culture" [94]), nevertheless participate in the natural aesthetic criticized by Demachy—they place the photographed object (Sherman herself) in the position occupied by nature in that aesthetic. Demachy's point was that there was no art in nature and therefore that there was no art in "straight prints" of nature, that is, in pictures that could be understood above all as records of nature. Sherman's poses are vividly unnatural—which is to say, conventional— but insofar as the function of the camera is to record them, their position in relation to the camera might as well be that of a sunset. In the end, then, the form of these pictures reasserts the priority of Hartmann's "pictured object"—what the photographs show is what is there to be seen even if (unlike the sunset) what is there to be seen could never have come to be there without the existence of photography.

So the problem of photography as art is finally not solved by the practice of photographers like Sherman or by the theorizations of photography in such writers as Owens, Douglas Crimp, and Abigail Solomon-Godeau. One way of putting the problem—the way Demachy and his contemporaries tended to put it—is as a problem about agency. Where the painter "sits down in front of his subject . . . and makes a careful study of it with his unaided hands," the photographer just "presses a button." By contrast to the painter, in other words, the photographer doesn't *do* anything. And while the attempt to replace the work done by the painter's hand with the work done by the photographer's eye may solve one problem, it does so only by creating another. The problem it solves is the problem of what the photographer does—he or she *sees*. But the problem it creates is why the record of things one has seen—however insightful one's vision or however clever one has been at arranging or inventing interesting objects of that vision—should count as art. In fact, what Sherman's practice shows is that even when the objects seen through the camera are themselves works of art (like Sherman's *tableaux vivants*), the picture produced by photographing them is not. These photographs have no way of detaching their interest from the interest of the objects they are photographs of; they have no way of detaching what they show from what the photographer who made them has seen. So the problem with what the photographer does is at the same time a problem with what the photograph is—a view of an object rather than a representation of an object.

That's the point of saying that the object a photograph is of plays a causal role in its production that the object a painting is of doesn't; the photograph requires the object, the painting doesn't. But we can also complicate this point by thinking for a minute about the things that do play a similarly crucial role in painting. The making of Welling's photograph *Movable Bridge* required the bridge; the making of a painted movable bridge would not—all you would need is the paint. So saying that the object a photograph is of is causally crucial to the photograph is like saying that the paint in a painting is causally crucial to the painting: you need paint to make paintings; you need objects to make photographs. And from this standpoint, the insistence that a photograph is always a photograph of something is less an insistence on the uniqueness of the photograph's referential relation to the world than a reminder of the material conditions of the photograph's production. Of course, the difference is that the photograph looks like—is an image of—the conditions of its production. (The painting is made with but does not look like paint.) But it is precisely because looking like something does not in itself amount to representing something (the reflection looks like but does not represent the thing reflected; the word represents but does not look like the thing represented) that the photograph's effort to represent things will require it to overcome its ability to look like things. If, in other words, it is true that the photograph is in an important sense transparent—it cannot help but show us the world—it will also be true that this transparency can be employed to make photographs that are of objects but are not views of those objects.

Such photographs cannot help but be ways of seeing the world, but they will also be ways of *not* seeing it, or at least of not showing what an eye—the photographer's eye—has seen. No one, for example, has seen what Welling's aluminum foil images or drapery images show. By this, of course, I don't mean that no one has ever seen foil or even that no one has ever seen the piece of cloth used to make the drapes. I mean instead that these objects in the world—the foil and the cloth—pushed forward in the photograph so that they fill the picture and lose their outlines, are not allowed by the photograph to emerge as objects of vision. So the objects we see in the photographs are not objects we see in the world. One way to put this would be to say that, unlike objects we can see, they have no shape; another way would be to say that the shape they have is the shape of the photograph.

The point of this description—and of the claim that Welling deploys the shape of the photograph against the shape of the objects photographed in order to defeat the camera's ability to let us see objects in the world and to employ those objects instead in the making of photographs (to use them like paint)—is made clearer in the *Diary/Landscape* series. Here the pages of Elisabeth Dixon's diary fill the picture just as the foil and the cloth do, but that fact is not enough to separate them from the world, not enough to deprive them of the shape they have as objects in the world. And since that shape (the shape of a page of writing) is so similar to the shape of a photograph, these pictures run the risk of subordinating their shape (the shape of the photograph) to the shape of the object (the written page). That is, instead of the shape of the photograph being seen to *determine* the shape of the photographed object, the shape of the photograph would be seen as corresponding to (as determined by) the shape of the pages. So in the photographs, the pages tend to be angled; more important, the objects photographed are not really pages but are instead parts of pages because parts, in themselves, in the world, have no shape. In Welling, its shapelessness is the meaning of the part object. Thus the shapes of the photographed objects are determined not by the shapes of the diary pages but by the shape of the photograph. In the *Diary/Landscape* series, then, the shapes of the objects being photographed (the diary pages) are acknowledged but are overcome by the shapes of the photographed objects (parts of diary pages). The object seen in the world is *replaced* by the photograph rather than made visible through it.

We have, of course, already seen a version of this insistence on the shape of the representing object from the other direction—in Fried's account of Stella's effort to overcome it. And we can see it also in Smithson's cut and/or folded maps, like the *Negative Map Showing Region of the Monuments along the Passaic River* (on the jacket of this book). The map is already, like the writing on the page, a representation; the cut map, replacing the shape of Passaic with the shape of the *Negative Map*, is a different representation. But it's in photographs (understood as ways of seeing the world rather than as representations of it) and especially in photographs of objects which are not themselves representations (photographs of trains and buildings rather than pages of writing) that the effort to negate what the artist sees, to eliminate the photographer's eye, is most vividly and problematically on display. *Pennsylvania Railroad, 1990*, for example, repeats a fundamental gesture of the earlier photographs in eliminating every object but one from the picture and in showing only a part of the object that remains. The parlor car is both pushed forward and cut off, but because of the resistance of the object—it can't be crumpled or angled or curved in the way foil, cloth, and paper can—the effort to render it partial emerges with a special clarity, which is just to say that the discontinuity between what we see in the photograph and what we would see if we were looking at the train is made particularly vivid. And not only does the object defined by the frame of the photograph not exist in the world, it is not to be understood as a detail of some object that does exist in the world. Photographs of details are ways of looking more closely at some object, and the aesthetic of the detail necessarily insists on the primacy of the object—it is the object the detail is a detail of. The detail, in other words, is like the part objects in Welling's photographs precisely because it is a part. But in my account, Welling's interest in parts of objects is not an interest in the objects themselves. It is not so much a way of seeing them better as it is a way of not seeing them at all, of asserting the primacy of the photograph over the object, of detaching the object of the photograph from the object in the world. The detail alludes to the object outside the frame by presenting itself as part of a larger whole. But the part we see of the parlor car in *Pennsylvania Railroad* is made by the camera into a new whole. The unity of the photograph is thus not derived from but is asserted against the unity of the object it's a photograph of.

And as its shape removes the photograph from the world of objects, it also removes the viewer from the world of subjects. In those photographs (like the aluminum foil and the drapery images) that most blatantly repudiate the view, this removal is obvious—there can be no viewer without a view. But in a photograph like *Movable Bridge, New York, NY, 1990*— once actually printed in a set called *Railroad Views*—the elimination of the subject is both more problematic and more definitive. It's problematic because it invites the viewer to look through or across the bridge as if he or she were standing somewhere along it. It's definitive because that invitation is accompanied by the photograph's insistence on the discrepancy between what the viewer of the photograph sees and where that viewer would have to be in order to see what the photograph shows. Representing simultaneously an object that is so close to the camera as to be virtually parallel to it and (through a kind of continuous recession of framing) an object that is so far from the camera and seems so reduced in size as to be virtually a parody of perspective, what the picture does is exploit an evenness of emphasis that no eye could experience. In this respect, the camera functions here as a displacement rather than an extension of the human eye.

Again, the point may be illustrated by an appeal to the *Diarys*. I argued earlier that the likeness between a page of writing and a photograph (a likeness emblematized by the photocopy—there are no photocopies of bridges) requires these photographs to assert their priority over the pages they're photographs of by turning the objects photographed into part

Figure 4. James Welling, *August 16B, 1980*.
From *Untitled, 1980–81*. Courtesy the artist.

Figure 3. James Welling, *Diary/Landscape 9*,
1977. From *Diary of Elizabeth and James Dixon
(1840–41)/Connecticut Landscapes, 1977–86*.
Courtesy the artist.

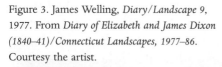

Figure 5. James Welling, *Pennsylvania Railroad*,
1990. From *Railroad Photographs, 1987–94*.
Courtesy the artist.

Figure 6. James Welling, *Movable Bridge, New
York, NY, 1990*. From *Railroad Photographs,
1987–94*. Courtesy the artist.

objects: the shape of the photograph supplants the shape of the page. But—as the allusion to photocopying suggests—the problem posed by the page goes beyond its shape. Insofar as the photograph of a page makes that page readable, the photograph is reduced to a technology of reproduction. (A photograph of a word will have the same status as a photograph of Cindy Sherman posing.) Hence the requirement in the *Diary/Landscape* series that the words be made, if not always unreadable, at least difficult to read—because of the way the pages are angled or the way the ink on the other side is made to show through. Welling treats the diary, in other words, the way Howe treats the text of Shephard's *Autobiography,* insisting on its materiality and, like de Man, identifying that materiality with a certain illegibility. The difference, of course, is that the de Manian critique of signification is here transformed into its technology; the diary as a signifying object is denied only in order that the photograph as a signifying object may be affirmed. In these photographs, the relation that a reader might have to the diary is turned into a view of the diary in order that the relation the viewer of the photograph has to the photograph can be, in effect, as a reader of it.

This is the difference, in Smithson's terms, between the view of a quarry and the ("great artist's") "glance" that turns the quarry into a map. Where the view is entirely dependent on where the viewer is—the view is a relation between the viewer and what he or she sees; the view is how things look to a certain person from a certain position—the text or map is its opposite. Two people in two different positions will see two different views; two readers in two different positions will read the same text. That's why Fried, in his discussion of the Morris Louis unfurleds, insists on what he calls the "illusory closeness" of the rivulets of paint while simultaneously describing the "blankness" of the canvas into (parts of) which the rivulets are stained as the "blankness . . . of an enormous *page*" (119). The closeness of the rivulets consists in the fact that they make the beholder feel as if he or she is standing too close to see them properly; the closeness is illusory because stepping back makes no difference. It has nothing to do with where you stand: it belongs "not to one's actual situation viewing them but to the paintings themselves."

It's this irrelevance of the viewer that turns "the blankness of the canvas" into that of the "page." Like the transformation of the ground into a "three-dimensional map" (111), the transformation of canvas into page makes the beholder into a reader instead of a viewer. The point here is not that painting is a kind of writing or even, more generally, that painting is like language. (Indeed, it might more plausibly be argued that this view casts some doubt on the utility of the very idea of a language—what language are the eighty-six "blank pages" of Shepard's *Autobiography* written in?) The point, rather, is that once the object becomes a representation, the beholder's relation to it is that of a reader rather than a viewer: the closeness of the unfurleds is no more affected by the distance between your eyes and the paint than the meaning of a page of writing is affected by the distance between your eyes and the words. What *is* affected, of course, is your experience of the object. So the claim that it doesn't matter how far your eyes are from the words is the claim that your experience as such doesn't matter. Or, conversely, that the object as such doesn't matter; if the blankness of the blank page is crucial, its size or texture or weight won't be. But its size and weight and texture are nonetheless a part of what it, as a material object, is, and of our experience of it. So to say that the size of Shepard's blank pages doesn't matter, or, for that matter, that the size ("enormous") of Louis's does, is to say that for certain kinds of objects—texts and paintings and rocks made into points on a map—the question of what they are cannot be answered by a description either of them or of our experience of them.

and stones

Fried thought of such objects as striving to defeat their objecthood; it is as though, he wrote in "Art and Objecthood," "a work of art . . . were in some essential respect *not an object*" (152). And Smithson (although he and Fried understood themselves as violently opposed to one another) agreed: the difference between the rocks he saw in the quarry and the (same) rocks he "collected" for *Non-Sites* was the difference between "raw matter" and "art." Two years after Fried and a year after Smithson, Paul de Man sought to express his version of this distinction (without the appeal to art but with the same conceptual apparatus) by characterizing it as the difference between two kinds of objects, "natural" and "intentional." The problem with American formalism, he wrote in "Form and Intent in the American New Criticism," is that it fails to observe this distinction, or at least fails to apply it correctly with respect to poetry. There are "certain entities" the "full meaning" of which, de Man says, "can be said to be equal to the totality of their sensory appearances"; thus, for "an ideal perception . . . the 'meaning' of 'stone' could only refer to a totality of sensory appearances."[17] Stones are natural objects. There are other kinds of objects, for example, chairs, which cannot be fully described by an inventory of their sensory appearances. "The most rigorous description of the perceptions of the object 'chair,' " he writes, "would remain meaningless if one does not organize them in function of the potential act that defines the object; namely, that it is destined to be sat on" (24). The difference between the natural object and the intentional object is thus that the intentional object "requires a reference to a specific act as constitutive of its mode of being." The mistake of the New Critics, a mistake made doctrinal in Wimsatt and Beardsley's "The Intentional Fallacy," is to treat what is in fact an intentional object as if it were a natural object, to treat, in effect, poems as if they were stones.

Wimsatt and Beardsley, of course, would hardly have recognized this description of their procedures. Far from naturalizing the poem, they insisted on the importance of the "designing intellect" in its production and, indeed, announced as their first theoretical "proposition" or "axiom" the claim that "a poem does not come into existence by accident" (4). The alternative to by accident is on purpose, and what the axiom is supposed to recognize is that poems do indeed require something like a reference to an intention as constitutive of their "mode of being." As they go on to say, "The words of a poem . . . come out of a head, not out of a hat." Why, then, is the intentional fallacy a fallacy? Because the axiomatic insistence on the "designing intellect" is meant to provide an account of how poems come into existence, not of what they mean. The importance of the intention, in other words, is as a "cause." The intentions of the poet are causally relevant to the production of the poem in the way that the carpenter's intentions are relevant to the production of the chair and in a way that no one's intentions are relevant to the production of the stone. Once the poem has been created, however, "it is detached from the author . . . and goes about the world beyond his power to intend about it or control it" (5). So when it comes to understanding the poem, we want to know not "what the author in-tended" but "the meaning of his words" (11) independent of what he intended. We want, in other words, to know the "public" meaning of what the poet has written as determined by the syntactic and semantic rules of the "language"—the meaning of the poem as a "linguistic fact" (10)—rather than the "private" history of the poem's (why, say, he wrote it) origin.

The New Critical reader's rejection of intention thus commits him not to thinking of the poem as a natural object like a rock but to thinking of it as a "linguistic" object whose meaning is determined by a particular set of syntactic and semantic rules—by a language. And what the reader needs is to know not what the poet meant by the words he used but what the words mean in the language in which he wrote. So, to take a famous example, to understand the meaning of the word "vegetable" in the couplet "My vegetable love should grow / Vaster than empires and more slow' " from Marvell's "To His Coy Mistress," the reader needs to know not what Marvell meant by "vegetable" but what "vegetable" means in English. But, of course, the reason the example is famous is because the answer to this question depends on whether the English in question is seventeenth-century English (in which case "vegetable" means growing) or twenty-first-century English (in which case it's more likely to be a kind of plant). And although some theorists have argued that both meanings should be considered correct,[18] the point of Wimsatt and Beardsley's insistence on the causal relevance of authorial intention would seem to be that seventeenth-century English is the right answer. If, in other words, a text should be read according to the rules of the language the text is in, and if the text was written by someone who spoke seventeenth-century English, seventeenth-century English is the language it's in, and the seventeenth-century rules are the ones to use.

At the same time, however, if the author's intention is only relevant as a cause of the text and does not determine its meaning, it's hard to see why that intention should be relevant to figuring out what that mean-ing is. Even if we say that "To His Coy Mistress" is in seventeenth-century English because it was written by Marvell, who wrote it in seventeenth-century English, it is open to a defender of twenty-first-century English to ask why—if we are truly formalists, if we truly think that the meaning of the text is determined by the rules of the language and not by the intention of the author—we should count the fact that the text's author used a particular set of rules as a reason for us to use the same set of rules. For it makes sense to care about what rules the author meant to use if we care about what the author meant to say, and if he was using the seventeenth-century rules but we are using the twenty-first-century rules, we obviously won't be able to figure out what he meant. But if we don't care about what he meant, if we think it's fallacious to think that the poem means what he meant, why should we care which rules he was using? Why should we use his rules rather than some other set of rules? So while it's certainly possible to interpret the text according to the rules Marvell used, and it's even possible to say the text was produced according to Marvell's rules, it's not possible—without recourse to the author's intended meaning—to say that the text is really *in* seventeenth-century English and that it therefore means what it means in seventeenth-century English. And if we are nonetheless inclined to think of seventeenth-century English as the language the text *is* really in, we must recognize that this inclination is derived from our sense that the set of rules the author used is the relevant set, and that what makes it relevant is our interest in what he meant—for if we don't care what he meant, the rules he used are just one among many possible sets of rules, and our preference for them will be utterly arbitrary. But if we are interested in the rules he used because they will make it possible for us to understand what he meant, then, of course, we aren't formalists at all—we're intentionalists.

The point might be put more generally by saying that if (like Wimsatt and Beardsley) we assign the author's intention a merely causal role in the production of texts, the question of what language a text is in and the question of what language it was written in are not the same question. And once we put the point this way, we can feel the force of de Man's claim that the New Critics treat the poem as a "natural object." For as long as we assign the author's intention a merely causal relation to the poem, it's hard to see how the claim that the "poem does not come into existence by accident," that "words come out of a head, not out of a hat," can count as a theoretical axiom. No doubt it's true that most (perhaps all) poems do not come into existence by accident, but if the author's intention is relevant to the poem *only* as its cause and has nothing to do with its meaning, then a poem that did somehow come into existence by accident (e.g., a poem washed up on a beach on Mars) would be just as much a poem as any other—it would mean whatever its words meant regardless of where the words came from. So Wimsatt and Beardsley's assertion that a poem does not come into existence by accident is more an empirical observation than it is a theoretical axiom. Indeed, the possibility of a poem coming into existence by accident is essential to the claim that the cause of the poem (the fact that the "words come out of a head, not out of a hat") is irrelevant to its meaning. And de Man is thus correct in characterizing New Critical theory by its "rejection of the principle of intentionality."

De Man, however, also insists that this New Critical blindness to the difference between "literary language" and "natural object" produces what he characterizes as its accompanying insight. Texts are not like stones because stones are the objects of what he calls "perception"—to perceive a stone is to perceive "a totality of sensory appearances"—while texts are the object of what he calls "interpretation," which involves "an *understanding* of the intent" (29). But treating poems like stones nonetheless turns out to have its advantages, since the New Critical attention to the text's "sheer surface" (the surface it would have if it *were* a stone) leads to the discovery of complexities that those who treat the text simply as the product of some author's intention have overlooked. It is, in other words, just because they turn "the literary act into a literary object" that the New Critics are committed to the practice of close reading and are thus able to discover not the "single meaning" that might be thought to have been produced by some author's "act" but a "plurality of significations" (28): "Because such patient and delicate attention was paid to the reading of forms, the critics pragmatically entered into the hermeneutic circle of interpretation, mistaking it for the organic circularity of natural processes" (29).

On de Man's own account of the difference between natural objects and intentional objects, however, it's hard to see how this is possible. For on his account, the difference between such objects, the difference between a stone and a text, cannot be the difference between an object that is understood to have a "single meaning" and one that is understood to have a "plurality of significations." We don't, according to de Man, *understand* stones at all—we *perceive* them, which is only to say that the difference between stones and poems is not, on this account, that stones have only one meaning while poems have many; it is, instead, that, however many meanings a poem may have, a stone has none. But when the meaningless stone becomes the route through which the polysemous poem is discovered, it begins to look like the real work of this essay is not so much to insist on the distinction between object and text as to call it into question, to redescribe the difference between texts and objects as a difference between two forms of textuality and, in keeping with a certain, well-established reading of poststructuralism (and postmodernism more generally), to leave nothing—not even the natural forms of geology—outside the text. Thus, on the one hand, the deconstructive apothegm, "Il n'y a pas de hors texte," could be read as an attempt to treat the world as if it contained no "natural objects," as if everything were, in de Man's early formulation, an object of "understanding" rather than "perception." Or, on the other hand, it could be read as an attempt to treat texts as if they themselves should be understood as objects of perception rather than interpretation. "My sense of language is that it is matter and not ideas," Smithson said in a 1972 note to his 1967 piece "Language to Be Looked At and/or Things to Be Read." If natural objects are to be looked at ("perception") and intentional objects are to be read ("understanding"), the double gesture performed by Smithson and de Man will be to imagine things to be read (texts) as natural objects and things to be looked at (rocks) as intentional objects.

But there is a sense also in which the doubleness of this double gesture is, for both writers, unsustainable. After all, Smithson's 1972 note makes language into a thing to be looked at *rather than* read ("matter and not ideas"), and by the time of "The Purloined Ribbon" (published in 1977 but written at least as early as 1975), de Man had begun to think of its materiality as not only the necessary condition of but the deep truth about language. For if "The Purloined Ribbon" begins by reprising the distinction between the natural object (the object of perception) and the intentional object (the object of interpretation), it will end by treating the very idea that language can be interpreted (the idea, as Smithson would say, of language as idea rather than matter) as an "illusion."[19] De

Man will offer a series of interpretations of what the young Rousseau meant when, accused of stealing a ribbon, he blurts out in response to the accusation the name of his fellow servant, "Marion"—he meant to blame her, he meant not to blame her but to confess his desire for her, he meant not to confess his desire for her but to produce what he really desired, a shameful scene of exposure—but he will reject these interpretations in favor of the claim that "Marion" is actually "meaningless" (289). If, then, "The Purloined Ribbon" begins with a distinction between what is perceived and what is interpreted that is familiar to us from "Form and Intent"—there it was called the distinction between the natural and the intentional, here it's between the "referential" and the "verbal," but in both places it consists in the fact that "the latter process [the verbal] necessarily includes a moment of understanding that cannot be equated with a perception" (281)—it ends by going in a very different direction. In "Form and Intent," as we have seen, the description of the natural as an object that has *no* meaning slides into its redescription as an object with only *one* meaning, and the description of the intentional as an object with one meaning slides into its redescription as an object with many meanings. The tropism in the essay pulls the perceptual toward the textual, and so the opposition between the meaningless and the meaningful is turned into an opposition between two kinds of meaning: single and multiple. In "The Purloined Ribbon," however, the tropism works the other way; it is the "moment of understanding," not the "perception," that begins to disappear, and it disappears because the "meaning" that would be the object of "understanding" (290) is shown to be an "illusion" (298). When Rousseau says "Marion," he doesn't mean just one thing (Marion did it), and he doesn't mean many things (Marion did it, and I want her); he doesn't mean anything. " 'Marion' is meaningless" (289), de Man says; Rousseau "was saying nothing at all," he was just "making whatever noise happened to come into his head" (292). "Properly interpreted" (292), "Marion" would not be interpreted at all—it would be perceived instead of understood.

If, then, according to the argument of "Form and Intent," the mistake made by the New Critics is to treat intentional objects as if they were natural objects, according to the argument of "The Purloined Ribbon," the mistake made not only by readers of Rousseau but by all users of language (since de Man understands himself to be describing not merely a fact about one text but a fact about textuality as such ["There can be no use of language" (294), he says, that does not work the way "Marion" does] is to treat intentional objects as if they were *not* natural objects. Rousseau's readers misinterpret his utterance not because they give it the wrong meaning but because they give it any meaning at all: "properly interpreted," the text "stands free of any signification" (292)—it is just a "noise" or a "sound" (288). Replacing "significance" with "sound," de Man radicalizes Smithson's commitment to "the physical properties of language" (55) by insisting that those physical properties are determinative, by insisting that the sign, stripped of the "illusion of meaning," reveals itself not only to include the physical but to be the physical that it includes. It is this insistence on the "linguistic" as opposed to the "hermeneutic" that makes the word—as sound, as noise—into an object of perception rather than understanding. And if, in the context of deconstruction, the primacy of sound seems somewhat anomalous (it was, after all, as a critique of the spoken word and a revaluation of the written word that Derridean deconstruction announced itself), it is materiality as such rather than the particular form of the materiality that is crucial here. Once we are interested in what "Form and Intent" calls the "sensory appearance" of the text, then the way it sounds is as important as the way it looks; indeed, as Derrida suggests in *Limited Inc*, the "surface of the paper" it is written on and the ink it is written with may be regarded as crucial. "Are we now going to integrate such fringes into the text and take account of such frames?" (45). Derrida imagines a skeptical reader protesting; to which skepticism he responds, "Why not?" Once, in other words, we are concerned with the sensuous appearance of the text, any effort to render part of that appearance irrelevant will look—will, in fact, *be*—arbitrary. This is why Smithson takes Fried's appeal to the "innumerable conventions both of art and of practical life," which rescue us from the "infinite abyss" that would otherwise be opened by the "dazzling blankness of the untouched canvas" of Louis's unfurleds, as a confession of defeat. Conventions *are* arbitrary; if it is only conventions that keep us from taking the surface of the paper (or the shape of the paper, or the amount of white space on the paper, or the room the paper is in, or the color of the paper) into what Derrida calls "our calculations," then every frame we place around the text, every limit we impose on it, will seem just that, an imposition—something that may be necessary but that cannot be justified.

The transformation (in de Man) of the sign into the sound or (in Derrida) of the sign into the mark thus counts as a version of Minimalism's effort to remove the frame from the work of art, to insist on the inadequacy of our interpretation of the text—which inevitably imposes limits on it, makes some part of it (the paper, the ink, whatever) irrelevant—to our experience of the text (since we nonetheless can see the ink and the paper), and to insist also on the inadequacy of our experience of the text to the text itself, since what others can or will see (the same paper but in different places at different times) will be different from what we have seen. Once, in other words, the text is turned into an object of perception, it is made literally uninterpretable but also literally inexhaustible, since how it is perceived—not only what it looks like but what it makes you feel like, what it makes you think of—must be a function not only of what it is but of who you are.

To put the point this way is thus to say, with respect to the materiality of the signifier in deconstruction, what Fried said with respect to the materiality of the object in Minimalism. Because the "materials" of Minimalism "do not represent, signify, or allude to anything" (because of what de Man would call the signifier's "essential non-signification" [292]), the beholder's relation to them is not like his relation to what Fried called "previous art" but is instead like his relation to the world. "There is no way you can frame it," Tony Smith writes of his drive down the unfinished New Jersey Turnpike, "you just have to experience it." The frame turns the object into a representation and, making the beholder's experience of everything outside the frame irrelevant, makes his experience *as such* (which is to say, his experience of everything but the representation) irrelevant. The removal of the frame turns the representation back to object (the sign back to signifier—sound, shape, or mark) and makes the beholder's experience of the object *identical* to his experience as such. Insofar, in other words, as the work is transformed into an object, the beholder's experience of it is constitutive rather than incidental. Indeed, the primacy of the object is simultaneously and without contradiction the primacy of the subject.

Like the question of whether there are letters on Mars, what the claims for Minimalism and the critique of it reveal is thus a complete continuity between the theoretical interest in materiality (which characterized the "high theory" of the 1970s) and the theoretical interest in identity (which has characterized "low theory" ever since).[20] Indeed, it is only the deconstructive answer to the question what is the text (the mark) that makes the identitarian question—who is the reader—relevant. As long as the text is understood to consist not only of its marks but of its marks and their meanings, the identity of the reader is in principle irrelevant—who the reader is makes no difference to what the text means. When, however, the meaning of the text is subsumed by the experience of it—when, for example (to cite perhaps the most characteristic claim of poststructuralist theory), the meaning of the text is said to be altered by the context in which it is read—then the position of the reader, not only who he or she is, but where, when, and why he or she reads, *must* matter. For if the meaning of the text exists independent of the reader, it makes no sense to think that it can change from reader to reader, but it is obviously true that the experience of a text can and, indeed, must: different readers will inevitably have different experiences. When, in other words, you're interpreting a speech act, the questions of what shape it is, how loud it is, where and when you saw or heard it, are relevant only insofar as they bear on the question of what it means. But when you're hearing a noise or seeing a mark, those questions—and everything else about both it and you—are always relevant. What you hear and see—which is to say, what you experience—is in principle a function of who you are.

The text as mark or sound thus solicits the participation of the reader; it is the reader's response to the mark or sound that gives it meaning. In denying the relevance of the author's intention, Wimsatt and Beardsley had also denied the relevance of the reader's response; they thought of the intentional fallacy and what they called the affective fallacy as two aspects of the same problem, "two forms of irresponsibility" (5). Because the poem is "embodied in language, the peculiar possession of the public," they argued, it "belongs to the public"; "it is not the critic's own and not the author's." We have already begun to see, however, how little help the appeal to language provides in getting us out of the choice between writer and reader. The only way to decide which language "vegetable" is in (which public it belongs to) is by deciding between writer and reader. So even though Wimsatt and Beardsley offer up the public rules of language as an alternative to that choice, the rules the reader invokes must necessarily be a consequence of the choice.

More fundamentally, absent the appeal to some author, there's not only no way to decide what language a text is in, there's no reason to think of it as actually being in any particular language. The fact that we can interpret "vegetable" according to the rules of seventeenth-century English doesn't mean that it's in seventeenth-century English—we can also interpret it according to the rules of twenty-first century English, and we could make up a language (call it Schmenglish) and interpret it according to the rules of Schmenglish. So the appeal to the rules of language is actually a way of committing rather than avoiding the affective fallacy. For as long as the reader must decide which rules to use in interpreting the text, the meaning of that text—even if the reader chooses Marvell's English—will be determined by the reader's choice. But if we insist that the reader has no say in deciding which language the text is in, if we insist that the text is in the language its author wrote it in, then the rules of the language become relevant only insofar as they give us information about what the author might have meant. And once we are interested in what the author meant, we have already subordinated the question of what the words mean in the language the author used to the question of what the author meant by them. For if the language in which the words the author wrote *are* words is determined by his or her intention, why aren't the meanings of the words he or she wrote also determined by his or her intention? In fact, we treat interpretive controversies precisely as controversies over what somebody meant by a word rather than as controversies over what the word means. No one ever thought that the old debate over whether Wordsworth's "A Slumber Did My Spirit Seal" was a pantheist poem could be resolved by looking up its words in a nineteenth-century dictionary—which is just to say that no one ever thought that the dictionary definitions of "rocks" and "stones" would tell us whether they were inhabited by some kind of living spirit. The question of whether Lucy—"rolled round in earth's

diurnal course / with rocks and stones and trees"—is utterly dead or
more alive than ever is a question about what Wordsworth meant by
"rocks" not about what "rocks" means in English.

That's why the very possibility of interpretive controversy implies—
or, rather, depends upon—the belief that texts mean what their authors
intend. The point is not only that questions about what a word means
in a language are generally irrelevant to such disputes (or are relevant
only as clues to what some author might have intended). The point is
also that when differences in interpretation are both explained and defended by reference to the differences between readers, the very idea of
an interpretive dispute disappears. Which is just to say that two different
people with two different experiences don't disagree, they just differ—
" 'I feel sick,' " " 'No, I feel quite well.' " There's nothing for them to
disagree about. This emerges most vividly as a literary theoretical issue
in Stanley Fish's account of what he calls the construction of texts by
their readers ("Interpretation is not the art of construing but the art of
constructing. Interpreters do not decode poems; they make them" [327]).
Because, according to Fish, the texts we read are the products of our
"intrepretive strategies," two readers with radically different interpretations of, to repeat Fish's example, *Lycidas*, may well feel they cannot be
"reading the same poem" (168), and they will, in fact, be "right": the two
different readers are reading the two different poems they have "made."
But once, of course, they understand themselves to be reading different
poems, the conflict between them disappears: your view that one poem
means one thing and my view that another poem means something else
are entirely compatible. On Fish's theory, or on any theory that claims
a participatory role in the creation of meaning for the reader, disagreement can only be an illusion.

If, then, there are such things as interpretive disagreements, no text
can mean either what the rules of the language make it mean or what
its readers make it mean. It can't mean what the rules of the language
make it mean because our disagreements are not about the rules. It can't
mean what the readers make it mean because different readers giving
texts different meanings do not disagree. Perhaps, then, we want to say
that the meanings of texts really aren't the sorts of things it makes sense
to disagree about. Indeed, this is the claim built into the idea that the

meaning of a text—or of any work of art—is the experience we have of
it, since it really is true that our different experiences don't count as
disagreements.[21] But the problem with this claim is not only that it requires us to give up the idea that our beliefs about what texts mean ever
conflict with other people's beliefs; the problem is also that it requires
us to give up the idea that we have any beliefs about what texts mean;
in fact, it requires us to give up the idea of meaning. For our beliefs are
necessarily either true or false, which is just to say that having a belief
about something involves disagreeing with anyone who has a different
belief about the same thing. So when we stop thinking of ourselves as
disagreeing, we also stop thinking of ourselves as believing, which is just
to say that we cannot think of our different responses to poems (what
they make us think of) as different interpretations of those poems. To
put the point more strongly, once we turn the meaning of the poem into
our experience of it, we begin to treat the poem as if it had no meaning.
Either we commit the intentional fallacy, and treat the text as if it meant
what its author intended, or we commit the affective fallacy—and don't
interpret it at all.

We are accustomed to thinking that there are at least three competing
accounts of the interpretation of textual meaning—those that appeal to
the author (intentionalist), those that appeal to the rules of the language
(formalist), and those that appeal to the reader (affective)—and that the
literary theorist must either choose among them or cobble together
some combination of them. But the point of the preceding argument has
been to discredit this scenario. The appeal to the reader, as we have just
seen, is more a refusal of interpretation than an account of it. And the
appeal to the rules of the language—to the extent that it really is an
account of interpretation—is only a disguised form of intentionalism: if
we need to know what language the author wrote in, we need to know
what the author intended, and once we care about what the author intended, the rules of the language are relevant only because they help us
figure out that intention. If, on the other hand, our appeal to the rules
of the language is *not* a disguised intentionalism, if we are, like John
Searle, more purely formalist—that is, indifferent to the question (by
whom or by what?) of how the marks or noises we interpret were produced—then we treat them perforce as accidents and, once again, do not

interpret them at all. This is the point of de Man's "radical" formalism: he sees that the only alternative to thinking of "Marion" as meaning whatever (more or less complicated thing) Rousseau meant by it is to think of it as meaning nothing—as a rock instead of a speech act.

and trees

"We thought that we would never see / A suit to compensate a tree," begins the decision of the Oakland, Michigan County Appeals Court in the case of *Fisher v. Lowe* (No. 60732 [Mich. CA], 69 A.B.A.J., 436 [1983]). The decision, which went against the tree, is cited in the introduction to a 1996 collection of essays by Christopher D. Stone (!) which reprints (and is named after) Stone's famous essay "Should Trees Have Standing? Toward Legal Rights for Natural Objects" (1972). Like the original essay, the collection as a whole argues that natural objects—not only trees and forests but also rivers and rocks—should, when damaged or threatened, be entitled to seek legal redress and protection, as Stone puts it, "in their own behalf" (12). It has always, of course, been possible for the owners of natural objects to seek legal redress for damage done to those objects; Stone's point is that we should now recognize the rights of the objects themselves to be represented in court and to have lawyers who will "speak for them" rather than speaking for their owners. The idea is that natural objects have rights—or, more generally, have value—independent of the value ascribed to them by humans, and therefore that trees and rivers should be protected not because some humans value them (this would be the position of an "anthropocentric" environmentalism) but because they are intrinsically valuable (this is the position of what is called deep ecology).

Stone makes this argument—the argument that natural entities should now be understood to have rights—through an analogy with other entities once denied rights. Children, for example, and women and slaves have at different times and in different places been regarded as having no rights. But if we understand our history to have consisted in what Stone calls "a widening of the circle" (140) of those deserving moral consideration, why shouldn't other entities—"animals, plants, . . . the entire planet"—come to be included in the circle? And if the analogy between women and children on the one hand and trees and rocks on the other seems significantly flawed—after all, once their rights were acknowledged, women and blacks could speak for themselves (indeed, their ability to speak for themselves is part of what made it plausible to think of them as having the relevant rights in the first place); trees, rivers, and rocks can't—Stone points out that "corporations cannot speak, nor can states, estates, infants [or] incompetents," and recommends that "the legal problems of natural objects" be treated like "the problems of legal incompetents—human beings who have become vegetable" (12). The tree or rock, which "cannot speak," should thus be appointed a lawyer— "to speak for it" (13).

The general position here—that nature has value independent of its value to humans—is controversial, but, of course, the acknowledgment that nature, even if valuable, is not articulate is not. Although, as we have already seen, some writers (like Kim Stanley Robinson) treat even the project of speaking for nature as inappropriately anthropocentric and imagine the possibility of a nature that speaks for itself ("One had to let things speak for themselves," as Saxe says. "Nothing could be spoken for" [Blue Mars, 96]), not even very many deep ecologists believe that nature really can speak for itself. Indeed, given the idea's implausibility, what's just as striking as the fact that the occasional writer affirms it is the necessity some other writers have felt to deny it. It's one thing, in other words, for a science fiction novelist to imagine that the planet he calls Ka instead of Mars "suggests the sound" that is its true name; it's another for the philosopher Richard Rorty to insist that "the world does not speak. Only we do" (Contingency, 6). Who except for the deepest of ecologists thinks the world does speak? Why does Rorty feel compelled to remind us that it doesn't?

For Rorty, the idea that the world speaks is identified with the idea that if we could just learn the language it's speaking in we could also learn the truth about what it really is. This is the dream of what he calls foundationalism—the dream, precisely, of knowing what Mars calls itself, of knowing, as Rorty says, "Nature's *own* conventions of representation" (italics mine).[22] And the point of Rorty's antifoundationalism—the point, more generally, of all those who insist that nature is, as Donna Haraway puts it, a "construction"—is that because nature has no conventions by which it represents itself (because none of the vocabularies in which different languages describe the world is the world's *own* vocabulary), there can be no true or false descriptions of the world. Haraway makes this point by asserting that "language is not about description, but about commitment" (214), and that "science" should no longer be understood as a "univocal language" but as a collection of competing "cultural dialects"; Rorty makes it by saying that "cultural change" should no longer be understood as a consequence of "arguing well" but rather as a consequence of "speaking differently" (*Contingency*, 7).

In Rorty and Haraway both, the replacement of "arguing well" by "speaking differently" links the possibility of different vocabularies to the impossibility of any correct vocabulary. To *argue* about Mars's real name is to imply that there is some fact of the matter about which the arguers disagree. To *speak differently* is to deny the relevance of argument, since, if the Arabs call Mars Qahira and the Japanese call it Kasei, they are not disagreeing. It can only make sense to say that people who give Mars different names are disagreeing if they think that the name they are giving it is not merely its name in their language but its right name—its name for itself. And even if—to imagine an instance of "cultural change"—the people who call Mars Qahira should begin calling it Kasei, it wouldn't be because they had been *argued* out of the old name. It would be rather because they had accepted what Rorty would call a "redescription" of Mars, what Haraway would call its "resignification." Indeed, the prominence of the term "resignification" in recent theoretical discourse can be entirely understood as an attempt to describe (diachronically) the phenomenon of difference and (insofar as it is diachronic) of change without disagreement. This is why Rorty understands people who begin to "speak differently" from the way they used to speak as having been "tempt[ed]" rather than, say, convinced, by their new vocabulary. Resignification understands giving things new names as giving them the names you want them to have, rather than as giving them what seem to you the right names.

But, of course, the concept of the right name—both the assertion and the denial that you can know it—seems a little beside the point here. To know the right name of something may be to know what it calls itself, but to know what something calls itself is not exactly to know the truth about it. I may understand your language and hence know what you're saying, but you may, of course, be lying, or you yourself might be mistaken. Which is just to say, as I've already had occasion to note, that languages are not in themselves either true or false, and hence the claim that nature doesn't have a language is just as irrelevant as the claim that it does to the question of whether we can know the truth about it. Which is why the idea that Martian rock might have a name for itself—the idea more generally that the natural world has its own language—is in recent writing just as deeply identified with the critique of scientism as is the idea that it doesn't. When, as if in reply to Rorty's claim that "the world does not speak," the ecophilosopher David Abram describes a world saturated with "language," "a world that *speaks*" (81), he means not to praise scientific objectivity but to repudiate it. Abram is as critical as Haraway of the "positivism" that turns the world into an "object"; his point in insisting that the world speaks is to turn the antifoundationalist denial that the world is an object into the deep-ecological claim that the world is a subject.

From this standpoint, we should understand the question about Mars's name for itself as a question not about our ability to know reality but about our ability to acknowledge "otherness" (Abram, 10). Indeed, the very idea that rocks have an "intrinsic worth," a "mineral reality" with its own "rock ethic," might lead us to think of them not as the object of our scientific knowledge but as a term in Haraway's series "women, people of color, animals, the non-human environment" or in Stone's series—children, women, blacks, Indians—of those whose personhood the law has learned to recognize. Here the Mars trilogy's "little red people"—mythical and yet functional, functional because mythical—usefully blur the distinction between what Mars calls itself and what Martians call it. After all, rocks and aliens both belong to the "non-human environment," and the point of thinking of the nonhuman environment as the final term in a series that begins with "women" and "people of color" will be precisely to turn the foundationalist encounter with the real into an antifoundationalist encounter with the other. When red rocks are figured as red men, geologists must also be anthropologists, and the effort to rescue endangered environments becomes indistinguishable from the effort to rescue endangered cultures. On Mars, it is the "little red people" who represent this transformation of nature into culture; on Earth—and, in particular, on what they call "Mother Earth" (19)—it is "indigenous peoples" who identify the threat to their own survival as a threat to the survival of "the planet itself." Tied, by definition, to "the land," indigenous peoples map the social commitment to cultural diversity onto the ecological commitment to biological and indeed geological diversity. The interest in what Mars calls itself can now be understood not as a way of discovering Martian truth but as a way of preserving the Martian environment and respecting Martian difference.

What's problematic about this, of course, is that it's difficult to conceive of the personification of rocks, rivers, and trees as anything other than a form of pathetic fallacy, which is to say not only that we will have a hard time understanding "brooks" that "babble in the courts / seeking damages for torts" (that's why they need lawyers to speak for them) but also that we will have a hard time assessing what will count for them as damages. Because persons have interests (whether or not they can express them), they can be compensated for damage done to them—the law, as Stone says, can protect their "welfare." But rivers and rocks have no interests; you can't compensate a river for its diminished flow (due, say, to damming) by paying it off. So if the law is to protect a river, it can only do so, Stone thinks, by appealing to what he calls its "right" to "intactness" (54) and thus protecting not its personhood but its "riverhood" (62). And it is this respect not for the river's interests or feelings (since the whole problem is that it doesn't have any) but for its identity— its right to be the river it is—that links the deep-ecological conception of nature to the multicultural concept of culture. For the sense that identity is intrinsically valuable, a sense expressed in our feelings of loss when, say, one culture is assimilated by another, relies as little on the attributes of personhood as Stone's right to intactness. Persons can be *compensated* for the loss of their culture. In fact, assimilation can be described as nothing but a structure of compensation—you only stop speaking your old language if you find there is some advantage to be gained by speaking your new one. So when we nonetheless deplore the loss of the old culture, the old language, we are deploring not the harm that has been done to a person or persons (there is no harm) but the harm that has been done to an identity. It is, in other words, because cultures are as uncompensable as rivers that protecting them can only take the form of preserving them, and if we believe that cultures are intrinsically valuable, we will also be ready to believe that rivers and rocks are.

The deep-ecological defense of nature as a subject is thus more a defense of nature as an identity—of nature as a culture—than it is a defense of nature as a person. By the same token, the deep-ecological claim that nature can speak doesn't really require the fantasy of what Robinson calls "mineral consciousness" or even of Abram's defense of the "animistic proclivity" to "perceive the angular shape of a boulder" as "a kind of meaningful gesture" (130). It needn't, that is, take the form of imagining a nature that (contra Rorty) produces its own representations because it takes the form instead of imagining a language that isn't itself a representation. We've already seen the science fiction version of this fantasy in the "sensory language" of Butler's Oankali, through which, "relating . . . experience by direct neural stimulation, they could give each other whole experiences" (*Dawn*, 237). The point there was that just as the Oankali couldn't tell a lie (they could only give you the experience or withhold it), they couldn't tell the truth either—they weren't, in other words, *telling* you anything at all; they were letting you feel what they felt, see what they had seen. What giving each other the experience meant was *not* giving each other representations of the experience. And we saw also that this fantasy of meaning without representation—the text written in blood, the computer virus, the genetic code (we might call it the fantasy of information)—is foundational for posthistoricism.

Information as such, of course, is not itself a fantasy. The moan of pain from the woman the pyscho shoots with a nail gun really does give him information about how she's feeling. The fantasy comes in only when you think of that moan as a kind of text, when you think of the noise that reveals her pain as a speech act that announces her pain. Or, conversely, when you think of the virus you've caught as a text you've interpreted. And the fantasy only takes its specifically posthistoricist form when you think of the moan or the virus—the noise or the mark—as exemplary not only in the way it means but also (in fact, especially) in the way it doesn't mean. It's one thing, in other words, to think with Abram of the "terms we spontaneously use to describe the surging waters of the nearby river," "words like 'rush,' 'splash,' 'gush,' " as determined by the sound that "the water itself chants as it flows between the banks" (82); this onomatopoetic ideal of the sound that means what it *is* has always been crucial to the idea of nature's language. But it's another thing to insist simultaneously that because no sounds really are intrinsically meaningful, not only must the language of nature fail but all meaning must be a kind of "illusion." [23]

The specifically posthistoricist fantasy, in other words, is of a certain reversibility between the speech act which, because it isn't a representation, cannot be a misrepresentation and can be understood by all and the speech act which, because it isn't a representation, isn't a speech act and cannot "properly" be understood by anyone. That's the reason that, in writers like Robinson and Stephenson, "the language of nature" (*Snow Crash*, 205–26)—the language that does not depend on some particular set of conventions of representation—is more or less simultaneously imagined as universal and as meaningless. It is, on the one hand, a kind of "glossolalia," imagined in the form of a "neurological phenomenon" that (once "mystical explanations are ruled out") can be referred to "structures buried deep within the brain, common to all people." But it is at the same time "a meaningless jumble" (*Red Mars*, 546), since shapes and sounds—signifiers without signifieds—are experienced (seen and heard) rather than understood. Like "semen," as Stephenson puts it, it's a "carrier of information" (258), but, also like semen, or like a virus or the genetic code, it's not a carrier of meaning. Which is just to say that the response people have to shapes (getting sick or not, getting pregnant or not) is not in itself an interpretation of those shapes and that the spatialized language of nature—insofar as it really is spatial—isn't really a language.

The point here is not just that when David Abram describes "the angular shape of a boulder" as "a kind of meaningful gesture" (130) he is mistaken; no doubt even the deepest of deep ecologists doesn't literally believe in the language of rocks. It is instead that the critique of the sign that we have already outlined in de Man and that—when, for example, Derrida urges us to replace the concept of "the sign" by "the trace or mark"—we can find elsewhere in recent literary theory depends ultimately on the same transformation of speech act into "sensory language" and text into shape at work not only in Abram but also in the more general redescription of meaning as information. For if the sign—the combination of signifier and signified—consists of something more than or other than its shape (two different signs, e.g. "bank" [First National] and "bank" [of the Mississippi], may have the same shape), the mark is and must be nothing other than its shape. Which is just to say that a mark with a different shape is a different mark, and a mark with the same shape is the same mark. So just as the same sign must have the same meaning (if the meaning—the signified—isn't the same, it isn't the same sign), the same mark (or the same sound) can be used to mean many different things (the same signifier can be linked to many different signifieds). And it is this fact—the fact that the same mark or the same sound can be used to mean many things—that requires Derrida to insist that no one can control the meaning of a text and that produces the characteristic deconstructive pathos of the author who strives but necessarily fails to achieve such control. If (and only if) we think of signs as marks and therefore of texts as made up of marks, we must necessarily think of writers as producing texts that mean more or less than the writers themselves mean by them. Writing, in deconstruction, becomes "abandon[ing]" the text to "its essential drift" (9) because writing in deconstruction is essentially the production of marks (which in different contexts will come to mean different things) rather than signs (which will always mean whatever they were made to mean).

Once the point is put this way, it is obvious that what Derrida calls the "scriptor-author" has at most a contingent relation to the text; authors may be useful for the production of marks, but they are by no means essential.[24] If, in other words, it is the shape or the sound that makes any word the word it is, why should it matter whether the shape was produced by or (for that matter) is used by humans? Why can't it be produced by the flow of a river or the pressure of an earthquake or the lapping of the waves against the shore? Once we are willing to count the marks that appear on the beach as the text of "A Slumber Did My Spirit Seal," we have already accepted the idea of a world that speaks. In deconstruction and deep ecology both, it is the commitment to the materiality of the signifier (to the primacy of the mark) that makes the world into a text—"there is nothing outside the text," as Derrida famously put it, or, as Abram less elegantly says, "Language is as much a property of the . . . landscape as of the humans who dwell" (139) in it.[25]

And not only in deep ecology and deconstruction. In fact, the commitment to the mark that culminates in the commitment to nature's languages is mobilized by every literary critic who thinks that the same text can have different meanings. What else could make texts with different meanings the same text? Obviously not the fact that they have the same meanings, which is just to say—in the language of shape—not the fact that their signifiers have the same signifieds; they don't. Rather, their signifieds have the same signifiers; they have different meanings but the same shapes, the same marks, the same sounds. And if shapes make texts, then the world, which not only contains many shapes but in fact consists of nothing but shapes, will have a lot to say. Many of the shapes in the world will look like signifiers in some language we know, and every shape in the world may look like a signifier in the many languages we don't know, in languages that have disappeared or haven't yet been invented. If, then, a world in which one text can have many meanings is a world in which shapes make texts, a world in which shapes make texts is a world that can speak, that can, like Robinson's Ka, say its name. From this perspective, the great interest of Robinson's Mars trilogy is not that it takes us to an inventively imagined Mars but rather that it shows us we're already there.

No doubt, however, the literary critics and theorists committed to the idea that the same text can have more than one meaning are not primarily interested in the idea that the same mark in different languages will have different meanings. When Derrida describes writing as the "abandoning" of the mark to its "essential drift" (9), what he means is that the same mark in different contexts will be understood to have different meanings and that the author's attempt to control the meaning of his or her utterance is in principle doomed to failure, since for the utterance ever to function as an utterance (for the mark to mean), it must be able to function in contexts other than the one in which it was produced—it must be able to mean something else. That's why Derrida wishes to replace the idea of "understanding" the sign or "utterance" with the idea of the "functioning of the mark." To think that you have understood an utterance is to think that you have figured out and fixed its meaning;

indeed (as we have already seen), the meaning of the sign is, as it were, fixed by definition, since a sign with a different meaning is a different sign. But when we recognize that texts consist not of signs but of marks, we see both that our responses to them cannot exactly be thought of as understandings of them and that our responses to them will necessarily vary—not only from person to person but from context to context. Which is just to say that if there were such things as signs, they would have the same meanings in different contexts, whereas the marks that replace the signs can be seen to function differently in different contexts. So the "substitution of mark for sign" is necessarily accompanied by the substitution of "intentional effect for intention" (66) and by a concern more generally for "effects of speech" and the "effect of ordinary language," which is to say, for effects as such. Indeed, it is the commitment to effect that makes sense of what I described earlier as the pathos characteristic of deconstruction, since the effect is what the author cannot control and what the reader registers rather than understands. That's why Derrida, acknowledging that there is in practice a "relative specificity" of effects, at the same time correctly insists that they are in principle "illimitable." As a producer of effects, the text is like the unfinished New Jersey Turnpike and like everything else in the world: you can't put a frame around it.[26]

But, of course, while it's easy to see that texts do have effects, it's hard to see why we should think of those effects as replacing their meaning, as requiring the "substitution" (66) of mark for sign, of intentional effect for intention. We don't in general identify the meaning of an act with the effects it has; we don't think that the act performed by the assassin of Archduke Ferdinand at Sarajevo was the act of starting World War I, even though we may believe that World War I was indeed a consequence of this act. And we certainly don't identify the meanings of texts and speech acts with their effects. We don't treat the fact that it bores or amuses you as part of the meaning of my utterance; we don't treat the fact that it makes you think of one thing instead of another thing as part of its meaning; we don't even think the fact that it makes you think what I want you to think (that it communicates what I mean) or that it doesn't is part of its meaning. The failure to communicate is not, after all, a failure to mean, as is obvious any time one person understands a speech act while another person doesn't. So although we might say that one reader's understanding of the text is an effect produced by it, and that another reader's different understanding is also an effect produced by it, the meaning of the text remains independent of (and may even be different from) both these effects.

Or, to put the point a slightly different way, if we treat the text like the unframed turnpike—if we imagine that it consists of marks that produce an effect rather than signs that have a meaning—it's hard to see why we should still think of it as a text. After all, the world is filled with things that produce effects, and if we think of texts as things that produce effects (e.g., as shapes that may make some of us think of words in English), then, on the one hand, anything may become a text (since anything may make us think of words) while, on the other hand, nothing is a text—since the effects of the mark—the things it makes us think of— are not its meaning. If the mistake made by those who think that texts can have many meanings is the mistake of confusing the truly illimitable effects of the mark with the single meaning of the sign, de Man's insistence that, "properly understood," the mark has no meaning, not many, is the correction. And the conviction that the world can speak—whether it takes the naive form of imagining brooks that babble or the more sophisticated form of imagining that there is nothing outside the text— is just another way of making the mistake. What's really asserted by the claim that there is nothing outside the text is that there is no such thing as a text.

THREE

Historicism

Remembering

I n Art Spiegelman's *Maus*, Jews are mice, Germans are cats, Poles are pigs, Americans are dogs, and African-Americans are black dogs. Several questions—several kinds of questions—are raised by this typology: What does it mean to represent different groups of humans as animals? Is it a successful parody of Hitler's dehumanization of the Jews, or does the parody end up repeating that dehumanization? What about the principles on which the typology is based? Do the different animals constitute different racial groups? Or different nationalities? Or perhaps different religions, since Art's French wife, once a frog, becomes, when she converts to Judaism, a mouse? Part of the interest of *Maus* is that in raising these questions without making it possible definitively to answer them (actually while making it impossible to answer them), Spiegelman registers—instantiates—the posthistoricist commitment to seeing the world as organized by identities. But I want to begin this discussion by asking a question not so much about the overall logic of the typology as about one of its categories: Why are African-Americans dogs? Or, to begin to give the question some point, why aren't Jewish Americans dogs?

In his "Epilogue" to *The Autobiography of Malcolm X*, Alex Haley records a remark Malcolm X made while watching "several cherubic little chil-

dren" playing and "exclaiming in another language" as they waited for
their baggage at the airport: "By tomorrow night, they'll know how to
say their first English word—*nigger*."[1] The point of the story is not just
that the United States is or was a racist country; it is, rather, that learning
how to say "nigger" marks a crucial stage in the Americanization of the
immigrant; it marks the fact that in laying claim to a new national identity, the immigrant is also gaining access to a new racial identity. In eastern Europe, Art's father, Vladek, belonged, as a Jew, to a racially op-
pressed group; under the Nazis, he would be defined by opposition to
Aryans. But America makes the Jew white, and it does so by distinguishing him from blacks. Indeed, Malcolm X's point was that America's racial
binary has functioned as a machine for making a wide range of people
white: not just the Jews but the Irish, Italians, Poles, and, more recently,
one might argue, Asians, all of whom, while being subjected to various
forms of prejudice and discrimination, have nonetheless found themselves transformed into the racial brothers of what used to be called
Anglo-Saxons.[2] (Indeed, insofar as economic success is a measure of success in American society, the most recent data rank Asian Americans at
the top of the charts and African-Americans at the bottom.)

From this standpoint, the fact that *Maus*'s American Jews remain mice
is remarkable both because all its other immigrants have melted into dogs
and because even those people whose racial distinctiveness has enabled
the melting—African-Americans—are depicted as dogs. *Maus*'s primary
concern is not, of course, racial difference in the United States; the animals
it deploys are meant to represent the racial categories of eastern Europe
before and during the Holocaust. At the same time, however, its extensive
frame story, extensive enough to introduce an African-American presence
and even to embarrass Art with his father's hostility to *"schvartsers,"*[3] does
a certain racial work of its own. It shows us the United States through the
lens of the Holocaust. And through that lens, the United States is divided
not into blacks and whites but into dogs and mice, Americans and Jews.

It is this use of the Holocaust, this insistence not simply on its enor-
mity but on its relevance to racial life in America (an insistence officially
sanctioned by the creation of the federally funded U.S. Holocaust Museum in Washington, D.C.), that has sometimes produced an angry response from African-Americans. Hence the famous dedication of Toni

Morrison's *Beloved* to the sixty million and more, a figure used also by Leslie Marmon Silko, although applied in *Almanac of the Dead* to Native Americans: "I have to laugh at all the talk about Hitler," says one of her Mexican Indians. "Hitler got all he knew from the Spanish and Portugese" (216). Although comparisons of the numbers of Jews killed by the Nazis with the number of blacks killed in the middle passage and in slavery or of the Native Americans killed by the European conquest of the Americas have been criticized as a kind of competitive victimization, this criticism misses the point of what Hilene Flanzbaum has called "the Americanization of the Holocaust,"[4] the way in which the deployment of the Holocaust in contemporary America functions to make the victimization of Jews a fact of American history. In its criticism of the recent proliferation of holocausts, it misses also the new appeal of the very idea of holocaust, an appeal that has nothing to do with a debate over numbers but everything to do with holocaust precisely as an idea.

Holocausts are not, after all, statistical events. A holocaust is not just a mass murder; the murder even of millions of people, if they were randomly selected, would not amount to a holocaust. It is the attempt to exterminate a people, not the number of people exterminated, that confers its specificity on holocaust. What turns mass murder into holocaust is that the target of holocaust is only incidentally some number of persons; it is more fundamentally that thing that makes those persons who they are— holocaust is a crime of identity. Hence the claim to have been the victim of a holocaust is not only the claim to be a victim; it is also the claim to an identity. It is because Hitler's goal was not to exterminate some large number of people but instead to exterminate a particular group of people—Jews—that *Maus*'s American Jews remain mice in America. Art's parents remain mice to mark the distinctiveness conferred upon them by the Holocaust; Art and his children remain mice to mark the fact that this distinctiveness, the distinctiveness of the European Jew, is retained by, indeed inherited by, the American Jew. All *Maus*'s other Americans are dogs because none of them has inherited the Holocaust. And the fact that today in America it is African-Americans rather than Jewish Americans who are marked as nonwhite and are more usually and more destructively the objects of racism is rendered irrelevant by the appeal to history (the history that Art's father is said to "bleed") as the guarantee of identity. It is this

appeal, turning blacks and whites into Americans (dogs) and distinguishing
only between Americans and Jews (mice), that makes sense of the otherwise inexplicable Jewish fear of black anti-Semitism that played such a
prominent role in the public discourse of the late 1980s and early 1990s.
And, of course, it is only another version of the appeal to history that
makes sense of the otherwise equally inexplicable interest of some African-
Americans in the fact that there were some Jewish slave traders.

Indeed, this appeal to history, to the idea that it is only the heritage
of a holocaust that can confer the desired distinctiveness, is accepted even
by writers like Morrison and Silko. That is why, despite the fact that
slavery ended more than a century before *Beloved* was written, Morrison's book is an antislavery novel. And that is why, in *Almanac of the
Dead*, we have already seen the Cuban Marxist who wants to organize
the people to fight against private property and doesn't want to listen to
their stories about "the Native American holocaust" be indicted by them
for "crimes against history" (516). The prosecutor at his trial reads a
chronicle of Native American resistance to and oppression by Europeans
(e.g., "1542—Mexico—Indian rebellion at Mixton is put down, and all
the rebels are branded and sold into slavery" [528]; a few years before
Silko, Simon Wiesenthal published a Jewish version of this almanac called
Every Day Remembrance Day: A Chronicle of Jewish Martyrdom).⁵ But Silko's
Marxist keeps on insisting on the primitiveness of "tribalism" and on the
primacy of the class struggle, and so, because he "has no use for indigenous history" and because he "denies the holocaust of indigenous Americans" (531), he is, as we have also already seen, executed. Crimes against
history—holocaust denial or revisionism—are the worst crimes of all.
They are worse than capitalist exploitation because the capitalist steals
the worker's labor, not his identity. And, in a way, they are even worse
than the holocausts themselves, because where the holocausts destroy
life, at least they acknowledge identity—indeed, they are a tribute to it.
But indifference to or denial of the holocausts refuses identity.

Hence the urgency in Silko's turn to history and hence, in the same
year that *Almanac of the Dead* appeared (1991), Arthur Schlesinger Jr.'s insistence on the importance of history to American life and, indeed, to the
very idea of what it means to be American. "History is to the nation,"
Schlesinger wrote in *The Disuniting of America*, "rather as memory is to the

individual. As an individual deprived of memory becomes disoriented and lost, . . . so a nation denied a conception of its past will be disabled in dealing with its present. . . . As the means of defining national identity, history becomes a means of shaping history" (20). Memory is here said to constitute the core of individual identity; national memory is understood to constitute the core of national identity. Insofar, then, as individuals have a national as well as an individual identity, they must have access not only to their own memories but to the national memory; they must be able to remember not only the things that happened to them as individuals but the things that happened to them as Americans. The way they can do this, Schlesinger says, is through history. Each of us has his or her own memories of the things that have happened to us personally; history can give us memories of the things that happened to us but not to us personally, the things that happened to us as Americans (or Native Americans, or Jews). And it is in giving us these memories that history gives us our "identity." Indeed, it is because our relation to things that happened to and were done by Americans long ago is the relation of memory that we know we are Americans. We learn about other people's history; we remember our own.

But how can we be said to remember not just things that happened to us but things that didn't happen to us? Taken literally, the effort to imagine this possibility may produce exotic results. Under hypnotic regression therapy, for example, a writer named Whitley Strieber began to remember a series of encounters with creatures who looked, he thought, like the ancient Babylonian goddess Ishtar. When he subsequently met several of these creatures in person, he realized that they were in fact alien "visitors," and he began to "wonder" whether what he had thought were memories of his childhood in Texas were really memories of Babylon and "of the shadowy temples where the grey goddess reigned." "Do my memories come from my own life," he wondered in his best-selling memoir *Communion* (1987), "or from other lives lived long ago?"[6] And, in an equally literal although more explicitly fictional (the subtitle of *Communion* is *A True Story*) mode, Greg Bear's science fiction novel *Blood Music* (1985) imagines the restructuring of blood cells so as to enable them to perform a kind of memory transfer, first from father to son— "The memory was there and he hadn't even been born, and he was seeing it, and then seeing their wedding night"[7] (111–12)—and then more

generally: "And his father went off to war . . . and his son watched what
he could not possibly have seen. And then he watched what his father
could not possibly have seen." "Where did they come from?" he asks
about these memories, and when he is told, *"Not all memory comes from
an individual's life,"* he realizes that what he is encountering is "the transfer of racial memory" and that now, in "his blood, his flesh, he carried
. . . part of his father and mother, parts of people he had never known,
people perhaps thousands of years dead" (217). *Blood Music* imagines
as science what *Communion*, identifying its "visitors" with the "Greek
pantheon" and speculating that they are the "gods" who created us,
imagines as religion.

   Both *Blood Music* and *Communion*, however, should no doubt be considered marginal texts, partly because of what I have already characterized
as their literality, but just as importantly because their account of what
Blood Music calls "racial memory" is, in a certain sense, significantly
anachronistic. By "racial," Greg Bear means "human"; it's the human
race, not the white or the black or the red race, that his transfusions of
blood unite. And while it is true that, in a remarkable moment, Whitley
Strieber speaks of "visitor culture" and imagines our encounter with it
along vaguely multicultural lines (it may be only "apparently superior";
we will come to understand "its truth" by understanding its "weak-
nesses" as well as its "strengths"), it is essential to remember that the
"visitors" he has in mind are not merely foreigners. Strieber does produce
the familiar nativist gesture of imagining himself a Native American,
the "flower" of his "culture" crushed by "Cortez"-like invaders, but the
vanishing race for which he is proleptically nostalgic is, like Greg Bear's,
human rather than American. It would only make sense to understand
Communion's aliens as relevant to the question of American identity if we
were to understand them as allegories of the aliens threatening American
identity. Insofar, however, as the apparatus of the allegory requires the
redescription of differences between humans as differences between humans and others, it has the effect of establishing the human as an inter-
nally undifferentiated category and thus of making the designation of
some humans as American irrelevant. In *Communion* and *Blood Music*, the
emergence of "racial memory," of a history made almost literally universal, unites us all.

So the technologies of memory imagined in *Blood Music* and *Communion* provide an image, but only a partial image, of what is required by Schlesinger's invocation of history as memory. If the obvious objection to thinking of history as a kind of memory is that things we are said to remember are things that we did or experienced, whereas things that are said to belong to our history tend to be things that were neither done nor experienced by us, *Blood Music* and *Communion* imagine ways in which history can be turned into memory. But they don't meet Schlesinger's and Silko's and Spiegelman's requirement that this history be national. Which is to say that they don't deploy the transformation of history into memory on behalf of the constitution of identity; in *Communion*, the remembered past is merely a testament to the visitors' persistence; in *Blood Music*, the moment in which the past can be remembered actually marks the disappearance of nationality. It is instead in a much more important and influential text of 1987, Toni Morrison's *Beloved*, that Schlesinger's identification of memory, history, and national identity is given a definitive articulation.

And this is true despite the fact that *Beloved*, according to Morrison, is a story about something no one wants to remember: "The characters don't want to remember, I don't want to remember, black people don't want to remember, white people don't want to remember."[8] What no one wants to remember, she thinks, is slavery, and whether or not this characterization is accurate, it succeeds in establishing remembering or forgetting as the relevant alternatives. It establishes, in other words, that although no white people or black people now living ever experienced it, slavery can be and must be either remembered or forgotten. Thus, although Sethe's daughter, Denver, thinks early on that "only those who lived in Sweet Home [where Sethe was a slave] could remember it," it quickly turns out that memories of "places" like Sweet Home can, in fact, be made available to people who never lived there.[9] A "house can burn down," Sethe tells Denver, "but the place—the picture of it—stays, and not just in my rememory, but out there, in the world" (36). Thus people always run the risk of bumping into "a rememory that belongs to somebody else," and thus, especially, Denver runs the risk of a return to slavery: "The picture is still there and what's more, if you go there— you who never was there—if you go there and stand in the place where it was, it will happen again; it will be there for you, waiting for you." Because Denver might bump into Sethe's rememory, Sethe's memory can become Denver's; because what once happened is still happening—because, as Denver says, "nothing ever dies"—slavery needn't be part of your memory in order to be remembered by you.

From Sethe's standpoint, this is, of course, a kind of threat; she and her contemporaries are, as one critic has put it, "haunted by memories of slavery that they seek to avoid."[10] But if *Beloved*'s characters want to forget something that happened to them, its readers—"black people," "white people," Morrison herself—are supposed to remember something that didn't happen to them. And in insisting on slavery as the thing they are supposed to remember, Morrison not only gives *Blood Music*'s "racial memory" what counts in posthistoricism as its proper meaning but also establishes what we might call, in contrast to the marginality of *Blood Music*, the centrality of *Beloved* or, at least, its discursive distance from the genres of science fiction and New Age space invasion. This distance involves, as I have already noted, the political difference between a certain universalism and a certain nationalism, but in fact it's much greater than that. For Morrison's race, like Schlesinger's nation, provides the mechanism for as well as the meaning of the conversion of history into memory. *Blood Music* requires weird science to explain how people can "remember stuff" they haven't "even lived through" (197); *The Disuniting of America* needs only the nation, *Beloved* needs only race. And while probably almost no Americans now believe that blood transfusions can make us remember things that did not happen to us, and probably only some Americans now believe that "visitors" can help us remember the lives we lived long ago, probably a great many Americans believe that nationality (understood by Schlesinger as citizenship in a state, transformed by Morrison and by multiculturalism more generally into membership in a race or culture) can do what blood transfusions and visitors cannot. It is racial identity that makes the experience of enslavement part of the history of African-Americans today.[11]

On the one hand, then, the supernatural presence that haunts 124 Bluestone Road outside of Cincinnati, Ohio, should not be understood as a version of the supernatural presence that haunts Whitley Strieber's cabin in upstate New York. On the other hand, however, it is a striking fact about *Beloved* that it presents itself as a ghost story, that its account of the past takes the form of an encounter with a ghost, a ghost who is, as Valerie Smith has said, "the story of the past embodied."[12] And if one way to regard this ghost is (along the lines I've just suggested) as a figure for the way in which race can make the past present, another way to regard the ghost is as the figure for a certain anxiety about the very idea of race that is being called upon to perform this function. For while races are, no doubt, more real than "visitors," it isn't quite clear how much more or in what ways they are more real. To what extent, for example, are the races we believe in biological entities? Nothing is more common in American intellectual life today than the denial that racial identity is a biological phenomenon and the denunciation of such a biologism as racial essentialism. The race that antiessentialists believe in is a historical entity, not a biological one. In racial antiessentialism, the effort to imagine an identity that will connect people through history is replaced by the effort to imagine a history that will give people an identity.

If, then, we must not see the ghost in *Beloved* as a real (albeit biologically exotic) entity (like a visitor), we should not see her either as a figure for a real (and also biologically exotic) entity (like a race). She is a figure instead for a process, for history itself; *Beloved* is, in this respect, not only a historical but a historicist novel. It is historical in that it's about the historical past; it's historicist in that—setting out to remember "the disremembered"—it redescribes something we have never known as something we have forgotten and thus makes the historical past a part of our own experience. It's no accident that the year in which *Communion* and *Beloved* were published (1987) was also the year in which the University of California Press series *The New Historicism* was inaugurated, or that the year in which *Beloved* won the Pulitzer Prize (1988) was the year in which *Shakespearean Negotiations*—written by the editor of *The New Historicism* and beginning with the author's announcement of his "desire to speak with the dead"—was also published.[13] The ghost story, the story in which the dead speak, either like Beloved in a voice that's "low and rough" or like Shakespeare through "textual traces," is the privileged form of the new historicism.

If, in other words, the minimal condition of the historian's activity is an interest in the past as an object of study, Stephen Greenblatt's accounts of the origins of his vocation ("I began with the desire to speak with the dead") and of the nature of that vocation ("literature professors are salaried, middle-class shamans") both insist on a relation to the past (he calls it a "link") that goes beyond that minimal condition, and beyond also (it's this going beyond that the model of the shaman is meant to indicate) various standard accounts of the continuity between past and present. Greenblatt is not, that is, interested in the kind of continuity offered by the claim that events in the past have *caused* conditions in the present or in the kind of continuity imagined in the idea that the past is enough like the present that we might learn from the past things that are useful in the present. Indeed, the interest proclaimed here has almost nothing to do with taking the past as an object of knowledge—what he wants is to *speak* with the dead, "to re-create a conversation with them," not to find out or explain what they did. And although he himself proclaims this ambition a failed one, from the standpoint of the heightened continuity that the New Historicism requires, the terms of failure are even more satisfying than success would be: "Even when I came to understand that in my most intense moments of straining to listen all I could hear was my own voice, even then I did not abandon my desire. It was true that I could hear only my own voice, but my own voice was the voice of the dead." (1). If what you want is a "link" with the dead that is better achieved by speaking with them than by studying them (which is achieved, that is to say, by understanding studying them as a way of speaking with them), then the discovery that what one hears when one hears the dead speak is actually the sound of one's "own voice" can't really count as a disappointment. "My own voice was the voice of the dead"; the link envisioned in conversation is only made stronger by the discovery that the conversation is with oneself. Continuity is turned into identity.

For both Morrison and Greenblatt, then, history involves the effort to make the past present, and the ghosts of *Beloved* and *Shakespearean Negotiations* are the figures for this effort, the transformation of history into something that can be remembered and, when it is not remembered, forgotten. Without the idea of a history that is remembered or forgotten (not merely learned or unlearned), the events of the past can have only a limited relevance to the present, providing us at best with causal accounts of how things have come to be the way they are, at worst with objects of antiquarian interest. It is only when it's reimagined as the fabric of our own experience that the past can be deployed in the constitution of identity and that any history can properly become ours. A history that is *learned* can be learned by anyone (and can belong to anyone who learns it); a history that is *remembered* can be remembered only by those who first experienced it and it must belong to them. So if history were learned, not remembered, then no history could be more truly ours than any other. Indeed, no history, except the things that had actually happened to us, would be truly ours at all.

This is why the ghosts of the New Historicism are not simply figures for history; they are figures for a remembered history. But this is also why there is a problem in thinking about these ghosts as *figures*, as well as in my earlier characterization of *Beloved* as less literal than *Blood Music* or *Communion*. For without the ghosts to function as partners in conversation rather than objects of study, without rememories that allow "you who never was there" (36) access to experiences otherwise available to "only those who" *were* there, history can no more be remembered than it can be forgotten. The ghosts cannot, in other words, be explained as metaphoric representations of the importance to us of our history because the history cannot count as ours and thus can have no particular importance to us without the ghosts. It is only when the events of the past can be imagined not only to have consequences for the present but to *live on* in the present that they can become part of our experience and can testify to who we are. So the ghosts are not merely the figures for history as memory; they are the technology for history as memory—to have the history, we have to have the ghosts. Remembered history is not merely described or represented by the ghosts who make the past ours; it is *made possible* by them. *Beloved's* ghosts are thus as essential to its historicism as *Communion's* visitors are to its New Age mysticism; indeed, *Beloved's* historicism is nothing but the racialized and, hence, authorized version of *Communion's* mysticism. Without the visitors, the remains of UFOs are just fragments of old weather balloons; without the ghosts, history is just a subject we study in school.[14] It is only accounts like Sethe's of how other people's memories can become our own that provide the apparatus through which our history can, as Arthur Schlesinger puts it, define our identity.

Reliving

Writing about "literary history in the shadow of poststructuralism," Cary Nelson argues that "poststructuralist" historiography is distinguished from the "conventional" kind by its recognition that it can "never actually contain or fully represent the history it engage[s]."[15] Where "conventional literary histories often aim for a confident sense that history is effectively relived within their narratives," Nelson's own history of early twentieth-century American poetry, as he describes it, acknowledges that it could not "find the lived time of history," that "the actual lived time of history would remain elsewhere," "unknowable" (47, 51). In one sense, of course, this view is simply mistaken. Insofar as Nelson's skepticism is founded on the recognition that our accounts of the past are "mediated" by our own interests and so are never "neutral," it cannot lead us to conclude that our beliefs about the past—interested though they must be—may not nonetheless be true. Only a geneticism that conflated true with disinterested would require such a conclusion. Nelson is, of course, on stronger ground when he says that "we need to admit that we will never know for certain what it was like to live in an earlier period" (50), but the ground is stronger only because the claim is so much weaker; who would deny it? What it was like to live in the past is one of the many—actually innumerable—things we will never know for certain. And since our inability to know things for certain is even less an obstacle to our knowing them than our inability to be "neutral" is, it's hard to see why we can't more or less cheerfully admit it.

More striking, however, than Nelson's conflation of not knowable for certain with not knowable is his conflation of knowable with relivable, his claim that the reason we can never "fully represent" history is because we can never relive it. "Conventional" historians might criticize this claim by reminding Nelson that representing history has nothing to do with reliving it—we can know that Caesar crossed the Rubicon without ourselves getting wet. But we have already begun to see how irrelevant to posthistoricist historicism this criticism is. Where the conventional historian may be happy to settle for knowledge, Morrison and Greenblatt are more interested in experiencing the past (if only by talking to it) than they are in having true beliefs about it. If, in other words, Nelson makes the mistake of thinking that knowing about the past involves experiencing it, Morrison and Greenblatt correct this mistake not simply by disconnecting knowledge from experience but by preferring experience to knowledge. In fact, from this perspective and with respect at least to certain events, knowing about the past instead of experiencing it may come to look not like an impossibility but like an easy way out, a way of trying to avoid the reality of slavery or the Holocaust, and we thus see the emergence of a certain hostility to the idea that the Holocaust is the sort of thing that can be known.

Claude Lanzmann, for example, has insisted that the purpose of his documentary *Shoah* is "not to transmit knowledge" and has instead characterized the film as "an *incarnation*, a *resurrection*,"[16] thus identifying his ambitions in terms that we may understand as characteristically New Historicist: the incarnated dead are the ones with whom Stephen Greenblatt wishes to speak. But where, in the New Historicism, understanding the past is at worst an irrelevance and at best an aid to the more crucial task of remembering it, understanding the Holocaust seems to Lanzmann an "absolute obscenity," and to try to "learn the Holocaust" is, in fact, to "forget" it.[17] The representations and explanations of historians, he thinks, are "a way of escaping," "a way not to face the horror";[18] what the Holocaust requires is a way of transmitting not the normalizing knowledge of the horror but the horror itself. And it is this "transmission"—what Shoshana Felman calls "testimony"—that the film *Shoah* strives for and that, according to Felman, is the project of many of the major literary and theoretical texts of the post–World War II period as well as of *Shoah*.

But how can texts *transmit* rather than merely represent "horror"? How, as Felman puts it, can "the act of *reading* literary texts" be "related to the act of *facing horror*?" (2). If it could, then, of course, reading would become a form of witnessing. But it is one thing, it seems, to experience horror and another thing to read about it; the person who reads about it is dealing not with the experience of horror but with a representation of that experience. And Felman has no wish to deny this difference; on the contrary, she wishes to insist upon it, and it is out of her insistence that she produces her contribution to the theory of testimony. For when testimony is "simply relayed, repeated or reported," she argues, it "loses its function as a testimony" (3). So in order for testimony to avoid losing its proper function, it must be "performative" (5); it must "accomplish a speech act" rather than simply "formulate a statement." Its subject matter must be "enacted" rather than reported or represented. The problem of testimony is thus fundamentally a problem about "the *relation between language and events*" (16). Language that represents or reports events will fail as testimony, will fail, that is, to be properly "performative" or "literary." Language that is itself an "act" and that therefore can be said to "enact" rather than report events will succeed. The reader of the "performative" text will be in the position not of someone who reads about the "horror" and understands it; he or she will be in the position of "facing horror."

But how can a text achieve the performative? How can a text cease merely to represent an act and instead become the act it no longer represents? The idea of the performative is, of course, drawn from Austin's speech act theory, where it is famously instantiated in the marriage ceremony: "When I say, before the registrar or altar, etc., 'I do,' I am not reporting on a marriage: I am indulging in it."[19] Austin's opposition between reporting and indulging anticipates (in a different key) Felman's opposition between reporting and enacting. But in *Testimony*, the first exemplar of the performative will not exactly be, as it is in Austin, the act of *"saying certain words"* (13); it will instead be what Felman calls the "breakdown" or "breakage of the words" (39). Citing these lines from Celan,

> Your question—your answer.
> Your song, what does it know?
>
> Deepinsnow,
>   Eepinow,
>   Ee-i-o.

she argues that it is "by disrupting" "conscious meaning" that these "sounds testify" (37). It is, in other words, at the moment when the words as words begin to "break down" that they become performative, that they begin to enact rather than report. And it is at this moment that the readers of those words are "ready to be solicited" not by the "meaning" those words convey (since, as they break down, it is precisely their meaning that is put in question) but by what Felman calls the "experience" of their author, Celan.

The genealogy of this version of the performative is, of course, as much de Manian as Austinian and is articulated most explicitly in the discussion of Rousseau's *Confessions* that I have already cited, where de Man analyzes Rousseau's effort to escape being blamed for stealing a ribbon from his employer by blaming the theft instead on the young servant girl, Marion. Recognizing, with Rousseau, that the crime of having named Marion as the thief is a good deal more serious than the theft itself, de Man works through a series of accounts of what Rousseau might have meant when he said "Marion," moving from his desire to blame Marion to his desire to possess Marion to his desire for a public scene in which both the previous desires are shamefully displayed but concluding that none of these interpretations is adequate. For, ultimately, de Man argues, Rousseau never meant to and did not in fact name Marion; he was "making whatever noise happened to come into his head," he was "saying nothing at all."[20] So, no attempt to understand what "Marion" means can succeed because, properly understood, " 'Marion' is meaningless." And de Man goes on to assert that the "essential non-signification" of this text is exemplary of textuality as such: "It seems to be impossible to isolate the moment in which the fiction stands free of any signification. . . . Yet without this moment, never allowed to exist as such, no such thing as a text is conceivable." On the one hand, it is the "arbitrariness" of the sign that makes meaning possible; on the other hand, it is the revelation of that same "arbitrariness"—"the complete disjunction between Rousseau's desires . . . and the selection of this particular name . . . any other name, any other word, any other sound or noise could have done just as well"—that "disrupts the meaning." For de Man, the speech act becomes performative only in the moment that it becomes illegible.

In the wake of the discovery of de Man's wartime journalism, some critics read "The Purloined Ribbon" and the theory it articulates as a kind of alibi for de Man's own disinclination to acknowledge whatever involvement he may have had in the apparatus that produced the Holocaust. According to Felman, however, the refusal to confess is a sign not of indifference to one's own morally scandalous behavior but of a heightened sensitivity to exactly what is scandalous about it. The "trouble" with confessions, she writes, "is that they are all too *readable*: partaking of the continuity of conscious meaning and of the illusion of the restoration of coherence, what de Man calls 'the readability of . . . apologetic discourse' (*AR*, 290) pretends to reduce historical scandals to mere sense and to eliminate the unassimilable shock of history, by leaving 'the [very] assumption of intelligibility . . . unquestioned' (*AR*, 300)." What is scandalous in "historical scandals" is what, in Felman's view, marks the Holocaust above all, its resistance to intelligibility. Insofar as confession produces a "referential narrative," it necessarily diminishes the crime it confesses to. Thus, following Lanzmann, who identifies the Holocaust as a "pure event" and who characterizes the effort to make sense of it as a "perverse form of revisionism" (*YFS*, 482), Felman insists on the "refusal of understanding" (*YFS*, 477) as, in Lanzmann's terms, "the only possible ethical . . . attitude" (*YFS*, 478). The attempt to explain it can only be an attempt to reduce it.

Felman thus regards what some have thought of as de Man's worst sin, his failure to confess, as his greatest virtue. For confession, diminishing the crime, would excuse the criminal. But, whatever we may think of de Man's personal morality, his real contribution here is not his (from Felman's standpoint admirable) refusal to confess; it is his discovery of the linguistic form that, unlike the "referential narrative," *is* adequate to the Holocaust, the "performative." The essence of the performative is, as we have seen, its irreducibility to "mere sense," and it is precisely this irreducibility that makes it appropriate as a technology for what Lanzmann calls the "transmission" (*YFS*, 486) rather than the representation of the Holocaust. Felman thus focuses intensely on the moment in *Shoah* when Lanzmann, listening to some Polish peasants describe the efforts of a Ukrainian guard to keep his Jewish prisoners quiet, hears sounds that he recognizes right away are "no longer simply Polish" (230). The Poles are saying, "So the Jews shut up and the guard moved off. Then the Jews started talking again in their language . . . : *ra-ra-ra* and so on" (230). The "*ra-ra-ra*" here is the aural equivalent of "eepinow, / ee-i-o," and both "ee-i-o" and "*ra-ra-ra*" are occurrences of the performativity theorized in "The Purloined Ribbon" and embodied in Rousseau's "Marion." "Rousseau was making whatever noise happened to come into his head" (39), de Man writes;

testimony from "inside" the "horror" can only be heard as "pure noise" (232), according to Felman. If to understand is, inevitably, to misunderstand, to bear false witness, it is only the "mere noise" one "does not understand" (231) that makes it possible to bear true witness.[21]

The point of the performative, then, is that, itself an event, it "transmits" rather than represents the events to which it testifies. This is what Felman means when she says that *Shoah* "makes the testimony *happen*" (267), and even that it happens "as a second Holocaust." So the Holocaust, like slavery, is never over—it is "an event that . . . *does not end*" (67). And just as the transformation of history into memory made it possible for people who did not live through slavery to remember it, so the transformation of texts that "make sense" of the Holocaust into events that "enact" it makes it possible for people who did not live through the Holocaust to survive it. "The listener to the narrative of extreme human pain, of massive psychic trauma," says Felman's collaborator, the analyst Dori Laub, "comes to be a participant and a co-owner of the traumatic event: through his very listening, he comes to partially experience trauma in himself" (57). "Is the act of *reading* literary texts itself inherently related to the act of *facing* horror?" (2) asks Felman. De Man's account of the performative, of the replacement of "meaning" by "event," makes the answer yes.

But what de Man characterized as the failure of reference—in order for a text "to come into being as text," he says, its "referential function" has to be "radically suspended" (44)—Felman cannily characterizes as the return of reference, "like a ghost" (267). Reference has returned because the text, insofar as it ceases to refer to things, has become a thing that can be referred to; it has returned "like a ghost" because the thing it is is a kind of absence, "the very object—and the very content—of historical erasure" (267). When he said "Marion," Rousseau "was making whatever noise happened to come into his head; he was saying nothing at all, least of all someone's name" (39). Both erased and embodied by performativity itself, Marion, like Beloved, walks. But this turn to the ghost makes clear not only an important point of resemblance between deconstruction and the New Historicism but also an important point of difference. For the ghosts of New Historicism are, as we have seen, essential to its functioning, but, as the simile—reference returns "like a ghost"—suggests, in deconstruction they are essentially supererogatory. In deconstruction the texts do what, in New Historicism, the ghosts must do. Indeed, if we take the ghosts of New Historicism as a figure for its ambition to turn history into memory, we can understand the "mere noise" of Felman's deployment of de Man as an effort to provide the thematics of historicism with its formal ground. Deconstruction requires no ghosts because the emergence of a meaningless and untranslatable signifier in the poem of Celan or in the film of Lanzmann can actually produce what Lanzmann calls the "resurrection" that a text like *Beloved* only narrates. Understood in these terms, deconstruction is the theory of (rather than the alternative to) the New Historicism; deconstruction explains how texts not only can thematize the transformation of the historical past into the remembered past but also, by way of the performative, can actually produce that transformation.

And it is, as we have already seen, this transformation that is required to make it possible for us to remember things that happened when we weren't there and thus make it possible for those things to count as testimony to who we are. For Jews, as Geoffrey Hartman has written, this necessity has recently come into sharp focus: "As the eyewitnesses pass from the scene and even the most faithful memories fade," Hartman says, "the question of what sustains Jewish identity is raised with a new urgency."[22] What the eyewitnesses witnessed, and what they have begun to forget, is, of course, the Holocaust, so if the idea here is that memories of the Holocaust have sustained Jewish identity and thus that the imminent disappearance of those memories (as even the survivors die) poses a threat to Jewish identity, the task becomes to keep those memories alive if only in order to keep Jewish identity alive. Like slavery, the Holocaust must never die. So if the passing of eyewitnesses and the fading of memories does indeed give the question of what sustains Jewish identity a new urgency, this new deployment of deconstruction helps make the Holocaust available as a continuing source of identitarian sustenance. But in seeking to ensure that the Holocaust is not forgotten, deconstruction contributes not only to the maintenance of but also to a change in Jewish identity. For insofar as Jewish identity is understood to depend on what Michael Krausz has called "identification" with the "narrative" of the Holocaust as "the most salient episode in contemporary Jewish history," it is significantly detached from the racial base that was definitive, for example, for the perpetrators of the Holocaust.[23] The primacy of the Holocaust as a guarantor of Jewish identity marks, in other words, the emergence of an explicitly antiessentialist Jewishness.

This antiessentialist Jewishness is disarticulated from the idea of a Jewish race and also, albeit less sharply, from the idea of a Jewish religion. Many of those who think of themselves as Jews do not think that they are Jews because they have Jewish blood and are, in fact, skeptical of the very idea of Jewish blood. For them, as for many members of other races (so called), cultural inheritance takes the place of biological inheritance. And many of those who think of themselves as Jews do not think that they are Jews because they believe in Judaism. But by redescribing certain practices that might be called religious (circumcision, for example) as cultural, Jewishness can sever their connection to Judaism, enabling Jews to give up their belief in Jewish blood and their belief in a Jewish God while still remaining Jewish. What they can't give up is Jewish culture. Hence the significance of the Holocaust and of the widespread insistence that Jews remember it, and hence the importance of the idea that "understanding" the Holocaust is a kind of "obscenity." For the prohibition against understanding the Holocaust is at the same time formulated as the requirement that it be *experienced* instead of understood, and this requirement—supposedly fulfillable through technologies like the deconstructive performative—makes it possible to define the Jew not as someone who has Jewish blood or who believes in Judaism but as someone who, having experienced the Holocaust, can—even if he or she was never there—acknowledge it as part of his or her history.[24]

And just as remembering the Holocaust is now understood as the key to preserving Jewish cultural identity, the Holocaust itself is now retrospectively reconfigured as an assault on Jewish cultural identity. "The commanding voice at Auschwitz," Lionel Rubinoff writes, "decrees that Jews may not respond to Hitler's attempt to destroy totally Judaism by themselves co-operating in that destruction. In ancient times, the unthinkable Jewish sin was idolatry. Today, it is to respond to Hitler by doing his work" ("Jewish Identity and the Challenge of Auschwitz," 150). Jews who might today be understood to be doing Hitler's work are not, of course, murdering other Jews, which is to say that Hitler's work, the destruction of Jewishness, is understood here as only incidentally the murder of Jews. Rather, the Jews who today do Hitler's work are those who "survive" as people but not "*as Jews*" (136); they stop thinking of themselves as Jews, they refuse the "stubborn persistence" in their "Jewishness" that is required by Rubinoff as the mark of resistance to Hitler. What this means is that the concept of "cultural genocide," introduced in analogy to the genocide of the Holocaust, now begins to replace that genocide and to become the Holocaust. "A culture is the most valuable thing we have" ("Custodians," 122), says the philosopher Eddy M. Zemach, and this commitment to the value of culture requires that the Holocaust be rewritten as an attack on culture. Thus the "Judaism" that Hitler wanted to destroy ceases to be a group of people who had what he thought of as "Jewish blood" and becomes instead a set of beliefs and practices, and the Hitler who in fact "opened almost every discussion on Jewish matters with the assertion that the Jews are not primarily a religious community but a race" is now reimagined as a Hitler who wished above all to destroy Jewish religion and culture.[25] From this standpoint Hitler becomes an opponent of cultural diversity and those Jews who have, as Zemach puts it, "lost the will to retain their culture" (129) become not only his victims but his collaborators. They do his work by assimilating, and insofar as, according to Zemach, American Jews in particular are abandoning their culture, what Jews now confront is the threat of a second Holocaust: if American Jews give up their Jewishness, Jews "will have lost the greatest and most advanced part of their people" . . . "for the second time this century" (129).

This revaluation of assimilation as Holocaust marks the complete triumph of the notion of culture, which now emerges not merely as the defining characteristic of persons ("the most important thing we have") but as itself a kind of person, whose death has a pathos entirely independent of the death of those persons whose culture it was. The Jew is here subsumed by his Jewishness[26]—the person is transformed into an identity, and the identity is treated as a person, albeit a person without a body or, for that matter, a mind. An identity has no body because it can die without any bodies dying; Holocaust by assimilation is like the Great Train Robbery—"no loss of train."[27] And it has no mind in the sense that it doesn't require any beliefs—that's what it means to be culturally instead of religiously Jewish. To be a Jew—or an African-American—is, we might say, to inhabit a subject position rather than to be a subject, and it is this transformation of subjectivity into subject position that is, as we have already seen, posthistoricism's defining parallel to the transformation of text into object.

Dismembering

Unlike identities, however, ordinary persons do have bodies so; despite appearances, there is no contradiction when, in *American Psycho*, Patrick Bateman professes disapproval of anti-Semitism ("Just cool it with the anti-Semitic remarks" [37], he tells his friend Preston) and of a joke about black women ("It's not funny. . . . It's *racist*" [38]) while at the same time butchering dozens of men and women, some of them Jews and African-Americans. Of course, the temptation to think of this behavior as something like hypocrisy is more or less inevitable. After all, the conversation in which the psycho objects to his friend Preston describing the guy who got the Fisher account as a "lucky Jew bastard" will be followed a few chapters later by his regaling Preston and some other friends with the serial killer Ed Gein's reflections on women: "When I see a pretty girl walking down the street," Gein says, "I think two things. One part of me wants to take her out and talk to her and be real nice and sweet." "What does the other part think?" someone asks Bateman. "What her head would look like on a stick." And the psycho's complaint that Preston's joke about JFK and Pearl Bailey is "not funny but *racist*" (38) will be followed by his vicious attack on a homeless black man, in which he himself will enthusiastically use the racial epithet ("you crazy fucking nigger") he disapproved of in the joke. Nevertheless, I want to suggest, it isn't anyone's identity that Bateman is interested in attacking. When, for example, he ends up beheading the man whom Preston called a "lucky Jew bastard," it's not exactly a hate crime—his motive, insofar as he has some recognizable motive, is his own desire for the Fisher account.[28] And, more generally, the categories of difference in which *American Psycho* is relentlessly invested—say, the difference between Armani and Armani Emporio or between a "hardbody" from Vassar and one from Queens—have nothing to do with either respect for or hostility to racial or cultural difference. The difference between Armani and Armani Emporio is not cultural but economic, and the difference between girls from Vassar and girls from Queens is also economic; it's a difference in class.

It's this interest in money and class rather than culture and race that establishes *American Psycho* as the novel of manners (rather than mores) it declares itself (beginning with the epigraph from Judith Martin) to be, with its notorious insistence on documenting the dinners, the toys, and above all the clothes of its "yuppie scum" and with its establishment of Bateman himself as the rightful heir of men like Edith Wharton's Larry Lefferts. Lefferts, Wharton says in *The Age of Innocence* (1920), was "the foremost authority on 'form' in New York": "As a young admirer had once said of him: 'If anybody can tell a fellow just when to wear a black tie with evening clothes and when not to, it's Larry Lefferts.' "[29] And Bateman is "total *GQ*," the man who can answer questions about "the correct way to wear a cummerbund" (316) or the "right way to wear a tie bar" (160) or about how a vest should fit—"trimly around the body. . . . It should peek just above the waist button of the suit jacket" because "if too much of the vest appears, it'll give the suit a tight, constricted look that you don't want" (87). As *American Psycho* understands them, what the people interested in these questions belong to is a class instead of a culture—what brings them together is their money. That's what it means for Bateman not to have "anything in common" with the bum on the street, and that's why, even when "things are getting bad" (385), he's "left with one comforting thought: I am rich—millions are not" (392).

Books like *Beloved*, *Maus*, and *Almanac of the Dead* imagine societies organized by identity. The injustices against which they protest fundamentally involve disrespect for difference; their murdered bodies (six million Jews, sixty million and more African-Americans, another sixty million Native Americans) died, as these novels understand it, for their cultures, the victims of genocide and Holocaust. But the butchered bodies of *American Psycho* don't have a culture—even the group that constitutes Bateman's preferred target, pretty "girls," doesn't constitute a people: women are not a culture. And, more generally, what the rich don't have "in common" with the poor is not a culture either. It's money. To call *American Psycho* a novel of manners, then, is just to say it is a novel in which the world is fundamentally organized by class rather than by culture and in which people's behavior represents their relation to their money—how much or how old.[30] The utopian ideal of the novel of identity—the novel of cultures—is a world in which since, as Gordon and Newfield insist, cultures must be understood as essentially equal, difference is respected. But class differences, as we have already had occasion to note, are constituted by inequality, and the novel of class (the novel of manners) is thus in principle no respecter of difference.

Nowhere is this more visible than in the contrast between the way that texts like *American Psycho* and texts like *Beloved* and *Maus* imagine the transmission of difference from one generation to the next. The mechanism in both cases, of course, is inheritance, but what the psycho gets from his parents is a brokerage house, while what Denver and Art get from Sethe and Vladek is their identity. In the novel of manners, what you inherit is property. Thus *American Psycho* has no need to imagine the relation between generations, whereas *Beloved* and *Maus* are fundamentally concerned with that relation and with the scenes of instruction—about slavery, about the Holocaust—through which the young learn who they are. And if the contrast with *American Psycho* is sharp, the contrast with a text like the African-American writer Samuel Delany's *The Game of Time and Pain* (published in 1987, the same year as *Beloved*) is even sharper, since *The Game of Time and Pain*, like *Beloved*, is a story about slavery and, like *Maus*, is told by an older man to a younger one. But where the characteristic scenes of identity in(and con)struction in *Maus* and *Beloved* involve the narrative transmission of a heritage from parent to child (virtually all of *Maus* consists of Vladek telling Art about the Holocaust, and much of *Beloved* involves Sethe telling Denver about slavery), the parallel scene in *The Game of Time and Pain* involves a middle-aged Gorgik ("the Liberator"—he's a former slave who led the rebellion that ended slavery) telling about slavery to a boy (Udrog) young enough to be his son but about, instead, to be his partner in what the boy hopefully describes as "real rough" sex.[31] *The Game of Time and Pain* has its "holocaust" (80), but it isn't an effort at genocide, it's just a lot of people killed in the mine where Gorgik used to be enslaved, and he mentions it just in passing. Indeed, although Gorgik does, like Morrison, complain that the slaves had been denied "our history," he isn't really interested in reclaiming it. Instead he asserts the importance of what he says the slaves had replaced it with—"a personal history," one that he imagines to be founded on "desire" rather than "memory." Hence, what brings Gorgik and Udrog together is not the filial piety required by the transmission of a history that is something more than "personal"—the transmission of a heritage—but their shared "desire": to "fuck real rough."

What's being passed on here—as if it were but precisely because it isn't a heritage—is the sexual practice of what Delany calls "sadomasochism." Slavery, of course, is crucial to this practice, but the history of slavery is not, and the racialized identity that Morrison anchors in that history isn't either. What this means in part is that being a masochist is obviously different from being an African-American or a Jew—masochists are not a "people."[32] If, in other words, slavery is important to them, its importance doesn't consist in its being part of their shared past. Udrog never was a slave; he wears "willingly" (it's the crucial element in their "rough sex") the "collar" that was "clapped and locked" around Gorgik's "most unwilling neck" (32) when his parents were killed and he himself sold into slavery. But just as Delany's text has no particular interest in the fate of Gorgik's parents (here again the contrast with *Maus* and *Beloved* could hardly be more striking), it has no particular interest in the slave narrative as a recruiting device. The point, in other words, is not that by listening to the history of slavery, Udrog will come to see himself as an heir to it. Just the opposite; Udrog spends most of his time wishing Gorgik would stop talking and start fucking. What Udrog is interested in is not the *history* of slavery but the *idea* of slavery, and what *The Game of Time and Pain* is interested in is the slave collar as both a political and an erotic device for representing and revising that idea.

Politically, of course, the collar is the mark of enslavement, and there's nothing very erotic about the short and brutal lives Delany imagines for Nevèrÿon's slaves. At the same time, however, there's nothing erotic in *The Game of Time and Pain* without the collar either, since it's the collar—the token of one man's submission to another—that makes masochism (the text's sexual dominant) possible. But if there is no masochism without slavery (without the idea that one man can be enslaved to another), there is no masochism in slavery either. For what excites Gorgik is not the fact of the collar being fastened on him by his captors but his first vision years later of a "lord" placing the collar around his own neck: "I had known that the masters of Nevèrÿon could unlock the collar from my neck or lock it on again. What I had not known was that they could place it on their own necks and remove it" (55). The first of these acts— a master locking the collar around Gorgik's neck—is "as empty of the sexual as it is possible for a human gesture to be" (54); the second— placing it around one's own neck—Gorgik describes as a "sexual gesture" so intense that it makes his "joints go weak." And when the lord who's wearing the collar looks back at Gorgik, when "the slave and master" exchange a look, Gorgik says, "I became myself" (76).

One way to understand this moment of self-realization is as the re-placement of a racial or cultural identity by a sexual identity. But, even setting aside the structural difference between culture and sex (the differ-ence marked by the irrelevance or merely antiquarian interest to the masochist of the history and traditions of masochism), Delany makes it clear that Gorgik's excitement involves not just the discovery of his sex-ual preferences but the deployment of those preferences as the eroticized form of a political position. The "tingling" of "lust" that Gorgik feels for the "Lord" is, he says, "the same tingling" he feels when he is liberating slaves by murdering their masters—it is the feeling of "freedom" (62). Hence the meaning of his masochism goes beyond its irrelevance to the idea of a people. It's not just that what you are is replaced by what you want; it's that what you want is articulated both as a desire and as a political principle—the commitment to freedom. And the fact that it's masochistic desire that Delany identifies with freedom gives that prin-ciple its full political meaning. If the slave is someone who is owned— whose freedom belongs to another—the masochist is someone who, owning himself, willingly relinquishes his freedom, who exercises his will and insists on his freedom precisely by relinquishing his freedom. "I knew," Gorgik says, "that the power to remove the collar was wholly involved with the freedom to place it there when I wished" (57). Insisting that if he is truly free, he must be free to give his freedom up, the masoch-ist understands his freedom as the right to convey it to another, as, in other words, the fundamental freedom of liberal capitalism—freedom of contract.

This is why masochism has from its inception (in the texts of Sacher-Masoch) been identified with contract, and why in Delany, too, putting the collar on and taking it off are understood as the elements of contract, of a "proposition"—"Let me put a proposition to you" (149), as one man says to another. "Wear the collar" (173), and "I will pay you whatever you ask" (174). Insofar, then, as masochism involves taking one's freedom to market, it enacts the commitment to freedom by turning the slave (whose body belongs to his master) into a prostitute (whose body is sold to a customer); before Udrog realizes that Gorgik wants him "to be my slave," he imagines that after they have sex Gorgik might give him "a coin" (18–19). But masochism also goes beyond prostitution as an exercise of freedom. The problem with prostitution is that while, on the one hand, it makes sex into a celebration of the free market, on the other hand, it counts as a continual critique of the market by way of its implicit reference to an unprostituted alternative, one that would involve sex without exchange, without contract. In prostitution, in other words, giving up one's freedom—which is to say, freedom itself—need not be eroticized; the prostitute need take no pleasure in prostitution. He may (and no doubt characteristically does) sell himself not for the pleasure of selling himself but for the money. But masochism is different. In masochism the contract is intrinsic to the pleasure, since what's desired is the transformation of submission into choice. The prostitute exercises his freedom in giving up his freedom; the masochist not only exercises his freedom but finds his pleasure.

Gayle Rubin begins to make this point (in "The Leather Menace: Comments on Politics and S/M") when she writes that "you can do S/M by agreement *and* it can still be a turn-on,"[33] but the surprise embodied in the italicized *"and"* makes it clear that she still thinks of the masochist's consent to the loss of her freedom as something essentially extrinsic to her pleasure. For Rubin and for many of the other writers in *Coming to Power*, a collection of essays and stories first published in 1981 (just after Delany began the Nevèrÿon series), "sadomasochism" (especially lesbian sadomasochism) was always defended against the accusation that it reproduced men's oppression of women by the insistence that masochism was a "consensual exchange of power" (30)—that the "distinction" between "men's violence against womyn" (remember?!) and "lesbian

S/M" was that lesbian S/M was "consensual" (37). "It is the presence of consent," as another writer put it, "which legitimates acts that in a different, nonconsensual context would be oppressive, degrading, or criminal" (87). The fact that it is chosen thus guarantees the legitimacy of the choice: the members of SAMOIS are to battered women what Gorgik the Liberator is to Gorgik the slave. And SAMOIS's critique of those who seek to deny masochists the right to exercise their freedom parallels the critique of the state's effort to deny prostitutes the right to sell themselves in the market and of the government's efforts more generally to limit people's ability to do what they want. "I want lesbians to understand that anything you want is alright as long as you don't coerce or abuse anyone to get it" (35), says Juicy Lucy in Coming to Power. If it's consensual, it's not criminal ("In sex law, consent is what distinguishes sex from rape" [224]). Juicy Lucy and her friends are outraged by the idea of the state interfering with a woman's desire to be spanked in the same way that Bateman and his friends are outraged by the government's attempt to put an unwilling homeless woman in a shelter: she actually "*wants* to be out on the streets . . . and we have a mayor who won't listen to her, a mayor who won't let the *bitch* have her way" (6). Letting the bitch have her way (leaving her on the streets if that's what she wants, cuffing and spanking her if that's what she wants, putting the collar on him if that's what he wants) is the fundamental principle of SAMOIS's, Ellis's, and Delany's liberalism—the commitment to contract.[34]

But the point for Delany is not just that "you can do S/M by agreement *and* it can still be a turn-on"; his point is that it can be a "turn-on" *only* if you do it by agreement, that the agreement is the turn-on. It's not just that masochism is legitimated by freedom of contract or that masochistic sex is something everyone should be free to engage in. Rather, masochism is itself the love of that freedom; the "tingling" you get when you put the collar on is "the same tingling" (62) you get when you take it off: "Why not call it freedom?" says Gorgik. Masochism in Delany is thus the eroticized form of liberalism. It's as if Delany is here responding to one of the standard critiques of the liberal society—that, with its valorization of individual choice and its privatization of beliefs and desires, liberalism provides no object of affect for its citizens, no sense of a community that can be the object of their loyalty, above all, we might say, no culture. The formal valorization of choice over any substantive good (over what gets chosen) cannot, on this account, provide an adequate basis for a human community. It cannot provide something for the members of that community to love, which is just what culture and cultural identity *do* provide. But if you redescribe the commitment to freedom of choice as sexual masochism, you convert the formal into the substantive. Liberalism here is not the guarantee of your ability to choose what seems to you good, it is itself the good; the masochist doesn't choose what he loves, he loves choosing.

Understood in these terms, masochism is the solution to a problem. During the Cold War, the alternative to liberalism—communism—made freedom loveable and could at least be imagined to make the exercise of that freedom (buying and selling) into an ideologically meaningful activity. But even though this phenomenon made a brief comeback in the months after the attack on the World Trade Center—with the president urging citizens to fight terrorism by shopping and vacationing—the end of the Cold War has mainly left writers from Fukuyama to Slavoj Žižek complaining about what Fukuyama called the "boredom" that must characterize a society devoted above all to "the satisfaction of sophisticated consumer demands" and what Žižek describes as the abandonment of the ambition "to change the world." Instead of seeking to change the world, the "Last Men" (and women) of posthistoricism seek to change themselves, replacing the devotion to a "Cause" with the commitment to "new forms of (sexual, spiritual, aesthetic . . .) subjective practice" (85). But even sex, according to Žižek, isn't any good if it's confined to the private sphere. The "only way," he says, for two people "to have an intense and fulfilling personal (sexual) relationship is not for the couple to look into each other's eyes, forgetting the world around them," but for them "to look together outside, at a third point (the Cause for which both are fighting)" (85). The problem, of course, is to find the Cause. Fukuyama's point was that there weren't any more causes (that's what makes what Žižek calls "our postideological era" postideological), that once socialism ceased to count as a cause, liberalism did too—there could be nothing heroic about fighting for liberalism when everybody was already a liberal. But masochism in Delany makes liberalism heroic again.

What Žižek's lovers can't find in each other's eyes, Delany's lovers—exchanging the gaze of willing submission—can.

Masochism in Delany might thus be understood as an effort both to redeem Žižek's lovers and to supply the intensity that he and Fukuyama miss. The "Lord" and the "slave," the top and the bottom, aren't looking desperately out for socialism; they're looking passionately in at liberalism. More abstractly, they are looking at the transformation of their desire into a politics. Identities, as we have already had occasion to note, have desires in a way that they cannot have beliefs, if only because beliefs necessarily transcend the person who holds them: to believe that something is true is to believe that it is true for everyone and thus only incidentally true for oneself. So Delany's masochists are not only not a people (on the model of Jews or African-Americans); they don't, insofar as they are defined by desires that have been redescribed as beliefs, exactly inhabit a subject position either. If, in other words, identity is the complete triumph of the subject position, and the subject position is defined not only by who you are but by what you want—by everything, in effect, except what you believe—masochism's redescription of desire as ideology makes it the salient alternative. It's as if Delany wanted to put the passion that Fukuyama and Žižek miss back in liberalism by converting it from what it used to be (the alternative to socialism) to what it now becomes (the alternative to identity).

As a strategy for making fun of the identitarianism of writers like Morrison and Spiegelman, this is pretty effective; as a politics—or, at least, as a left politics—it isn't: the absolute commitment to freedom of contract can hardly function as the basis for a critique of economic inequality. On the contrary, it's the mechanism through which the inequality between labor and capital is imagined out of existence. The laborer, as Melville's *Bartleby* made clear long ago, doesn't *have* to sell his labor; he can prefer not to. But, of course, this formal equality—no one has to buy, no one has to sell—may comfortably be accompanied by forms of inequality. In fact, from the standpoint of (a no doubt discredited) Marxism, the contract between buyer and seller is the technology through which inequality is reproduced. If, then, peoples' conviction that they belong to races and cultures (that they have identities) may make them less alert to the disadvantages accompanying the fact that they actually belong to classes, the eroticization of the mechanism through which those classes are established may make even the classes themselves—or, at least, the society they structure—look more attractive than does the structure of inequality on which that society depends.

Delany's characterization of what he calls "sadomasochism" as "marginal" and his interest in what it means for "a middle-class man or woman to desire the lower or marginal classes"[35] is revelatory here. For one thing, as we have already seen, there's no sense in which the masochist's love of freedom is at the margins of liberal society; on the contrary, it's at the center, and this misrecognition of the center as the margin turns what is imagined as the critique of liberalism into a celebration of it. More striking still, however, is his equation of the "lower" with the "marginal" classes. The difficulty here is not just that the lower classes (like the idea of the masochist) are in no sense marginal to capitalism (without them, there would be no capitalism); the problem is rather with the whole apparatus of the center and the margin, and with its commitment to granting the marginal its own status. No doubt masochists (who, unlike the liberalism they epitomize, probably *are* marginal—in the sense, at least, that there aren't so many of them) should not be stigmatized. But the problem of the "lower" classes is not being stigmatized. The problem of eliminating inequality is not the problem of reorganizing the relations between the margin and the center, and the solution to the problem of inequality is not learning to love it.

Forgetting

In Delany's Nevèrÿon, you don't need to remember the history of masochism in order to be a proper masochist. The point can be extrapolated to a higher level: you don't need to know its history in order to love freedom, which is just another way of saying what has already been said—if history isn't able to serve as a source of identity, it isn't needed to serve as a source of ideology. It isn't able to serve as a source of identity because things that didn't happen to us can't count as part of our history. And it isn't needed as a source of ideology because beliefs need reasons rather than sources, and the fact that our (or anybody else's) ancestors believed in, say, socialism, isn't much of a reason for us to believe in it. But, of course, the fact that we cannot derive either an identity or an ideology from our history doesn't mean that we have no history or that the history we have is utterly irrelevant to us. In fact, there is an obvious sense in which we are entirely the product of our histories, the sense in which we are all the end result of a long chain of causes. If, for example, our parents were rich, it may be a significant truth about us that we went to the best schools. If our parents were poor, it may be an equally significant truth that we didn't go to good schools. And while the fact that your ancestors were slaves cannot make you black, it can make you poor.

Hence the comparatively recent intense interest in the history of slavery may be understood not only as the failed effort to explain who we are but also, more successfully, as the effort to explain how we came to be who we are. Indeed, in a text like *The Debt* (2000), Randall Robinson's widely noticed polemic in favor of the idea that the United States should make monetary reparation to the descendants of slaves, both these views are on display. *The Debt*, that is, deploys (more or less interchangeably) both the argument that wrongs done to the slaves are wrongs done to African-Americans today (on the grounds, à la *Beloved*, that the history of slavery is their history) and the argument that wrongs done to the slaves, while they were not done to anyone living now, have nonetheless had effects on people who are living now. *The Debt* is simultaneously committed, in other words, to the view that people are owed reparations because they're black and because of the many injustices that have been visited in the United States on black people, and to the view that people are owed reparations because they're poor and because their poverty is the consequence of an injustice done to their ancestors. And while the difference between these commitments may seem negligible—after all, aren't the two populations, African-Americans and the descendants of slaves, for all practical purposes identical?—it turns out that quite a lot actually hinges on which argument you choose.

For one thing, the claim to racial identity—the claim to reparations in virtue of being black—explicitly produces the metaphysics that the *Beloved*-style appeal to history sought unsuccessfully to bypass. When, for example, Robinson announces that he was born in 1941 but that his

"black soul is much older than that,"[36] he deploys racial identification as
the technology that makes it possible to understand events that apparently happened to other people before you were born as nonetheless
having really happened to you. It's in this sense that a poor young black
girl can, he argues, benefit from the study of American history—she can
learn "what happened to her" (239). So even though Robinson sometimes analogizes race to merely physical characteristics—if "short people
had been enslaved, reviled, kept illiterate" (77), and so on, their test
scores would be as much below those of tall people as blacks are below
whites, he says—he clearly doesn't think that being black is like being
short. There is no short soul. And since he is skeptical also of "the very
ascientific social notion of race" (and rightly so, since the social notion
of race is either entirely dependent on the physiological criteria of descent—black people are people who are descended from other black people—or entirely empty,)[37] what he's left with is a metaphysical instead of
physical entity—the soul.

The advantage of this entity is that it solves the problem of how things
that didn't happen to you can nonetheless be thought of as part of your
history—they *did* happen to you, or at least to your soul. The disadvantage is that it's hard to see why anyone should think there really is such
a thing as a racial soul. It's possible, of course, that Robinson intends the
soul as a kind of metaphor. But the problem then is the same problem
we had with the ghost in *Beloved*—a metaphor for what? The soul can't
be a metaphor for the thing that unites black people today with black
people long ago, since if we believe in the biology of race, that thing is
the very opposite of the soul—it's the body—and if we don't believe in
the biology of race, we need the soul itself to be real, since there's nothing for it to be a metaphor for. But, of course, the argument for reparations needn't depend on the ghost of slavery or the black soul. It needn't
depend on the idea that slavery is ongoing or on the claim that the things
that happened to the slaves are somehow still happening to black people
today. Robinson's entirely plausible insistence that what he describes as
"the socioeconomic gap between the races" in the United States today
"derives from the social depredations of slavery" (173) does not require
a racial soul to identify the descendants of slaves with their ancestors. It
requires only that we accept the idea that the economic disadvantages

under which slaves labored were passed on to their children and that the additional economic disadvantages (the disadvantages produced as well as maintained by Jim Crow) under which the slaves' children labored have been passed on to their children. So the fact that black people today are disproportionately represented in the lowest quintiles of American wealth can be causally linked to the fact that many of their ancestors were the victims of injustice. The history of slavery is relevant here because it is in the best sense a history of the present—as a history of how African-Americans have come to be poor, it is also a set of arguments for why the United States owes them reparations. The debt owed to African-Americans today depends not on them suffering an ongoing injustice (the debt is owed even though slavery is over, and it does not depend on racism continuing—if it did, then the proper response would be not to pay the debt but to end racism) but on them suffering the consequences of a previous injustice. The history of slavery is the history of the poor little black girl whom Robinson imagines destined to failure because slavery is a crucial link in the causal chain that explains how that girl came to be poor and so—since the greatest predictor of economic status for children is the economic status of their parents—of why she is likely to remain so.

The argument for reparations is thus a historical one inasmuch as it involves studying the past in order to explain how the present came to be. But it crucially involves also what Orson Scott Card—in his counterfactual or alternative history, *Pastwatch: The Redemption of Christopher Columbus* (1996)—calls "the unmaking of history."[38] Alternative histories are devoted to imagining what the world would have been like if certain events had turned out differently (What if Hitler had been aborted? What if Castro had signed with the Giants?), and the very idea of reparations is crucially linked to questions of this kind. Thus, for example, Lord Anthony Gifford, in a paper presented to the First Pan-African Congress on Reparations, begins by citing a decision by the Permanent Court of International Justice (the predecessor of the International Court of Justice) which argues that the purpose of reparation is, "as far as possible," "to wipe out all the consequences of the illegal act and re-establish the situation which would, in all probability, have existed if the act had not been committed."[39] What if Columbus had not begun the European colonization of the Americas? What if we could go back in time and induce both him and the "Indians" he encountered to behave very differently? What if we could prevent the conditions that made the market for slaves and hence the slave trade possible? Reparations for slavery require us first to imagine and then to seek to establish the situation that would have existed if there had been no slavery, which is precisely what the historians and time travelers of *Pastwatch* seek to do. Only where real historians must reconstruct how things were and imagine how they might have turned out differently, the historians of science fiction novels (in *Pastwatch* through a machine called the Truesite) actually get to go back to the past, turning you who never was there into someone who might have been there after all, and not only been there but done something about it.

Alternate histories like *Pastwatch* thus take up the Greenblattian project of listening to the dead and push it a little farther; Card's historians spend more time talking to the dead than they do listening, since it's through the talking that they can not only learn about but alter the past. Greenblatt, of course, was already headed in this direction, which is why critics of the New Historicism like Carolyn Porter could accuse him of a kind of "linguistic colonialism" in his essay "Invisible Bullets," claiming that the "potential cultural agency" and ability to "speak for themselves" of the Algonkian Indians were being "eradicated" by Greenblatt's discussion of them.[40] And the implausibility of this accusation—how, with the best will in the world, could Greenblatt silence people who had been dead for over four hundred years?—was somewhat mitigated by Greenblatt's own conception of his vocation. He "began," we remember, "with the desire to speak to the dead," and once you think of yourself as trying to hear the dead speak, you more or less inevitably license others to think of you as trying to shut them up. Either way, listening or interrupting, your conception of your relation to the past has gone beyond just learning about it; the time-traveling historians of Card's *Pastwatch* are only literalizing a condition that both the New Historicism and its critics had already envisaged and on which the reparations movement has constructed itself.

In the reparations movement, of course, it is money (rather than Greenblatt's middle-class shamanism or Orson Scott Card's Truesite) that functions as the technology for undoing history. But the questions raised about the relation between past and present, in particular the question of what the consequences for the present would be if we could indeed make it as if there had been no slavery, remain central and unresolved. *Pastwatch* insists that the most obvious consequence of retroactively eliminating slavery (or, for that matter, of changing the past at all) would be to eliminate the present we have—there would, to begin with, be no descendants of slaves—and it understands both the history and the legacy of slavery as so unacceptable that its historians are willing to take that step. But the actual descendants of slaves are bound to have a different view. The heroine of one of Octavia Butler's first novels, *Kindred* (1976), for example, is a woman descended from both slaves and slaveholders who keeps being called back to the past to rescue first the white man and then the black woman who will become her ancestors—if she fails, there will be no present to which she can return.

From the standpoint of reparations, obviously, this is a skeptical position, since the story makes at least this one descendant of slaves the grateful beneficiary of (and reluctant contributor to)[41] their ability to survive hardship. It's a version of David Horowitz's argument—expressed in his "Ten Reasons Why Reparations for Blacks Are a Bad Idea for Blacks"—that black as well as white Americans are better off because of slavery, since, without slavery, African-Americans would just be Africans and would, he claims, have average per capita incomes considerably smaller than the ones they have now.[42] Butler casts no aspersions on Africa, but she too is committed to the idea that, as bad a thing as slavery was for the people who experienced it, it was a good thing for their descendants, and not only for the white ones—causal gratitude to the brutal white slaveowner who raped your great-grandmother more or less inevitably trumps moral disapproval of him.[43]

But Horowitz's point—that African-Americans, who owe their very existence to slavery, are better off than Africans—doesn't get at the core claim of the reparations movement, which is that white Americans today are disproportionately better off than black Americans, and that the comparative disadvantage of blacks can be attributed to slavery and past racism. No one, including right-wing polemicists like Horowitz and Dinesh D'Souza, denies, what I've already noted, that blacks are overrepresented at the lower levels of American wealth. And it's hard to see how this fact can be explained without recourse to the history of slavery and racism. Even D'Souza's notorious invocation of the "pathology" of black culture must rely on some such historical explanation, for the culture that supposedly keeps blacks from attaining economic equality with whites is a product of the same history that Robinson and the advocates of reparation invoke.[44] Whether we blame the failure of Robinson's emblematic nine-year-old on her poverty or on the "pathology" of her culture, we can't possibly blame it on her—the cause in either case is a situation over which she has no control that is itself the product of a series of events that were over before she was ever born.

And it is, of course, precisely this fact that makes the project of undoing history so attractive. If we could create a world in which there had been no slavery and somehow limit the effects of that change to the disadvantage suffered by the descendants of the slaves, the "yawning economic gap between whites and blacks in this country" would disappear: blacks would be proportionately represented (13 percent) at every level of American society. Where, in other words, blacks currently make up a disproportionately large segment (around 20 percent) of the population with a household income under $15,000, they would, if we could undo the effects of slavery and racism, make up only 13 percent. And where they now account for only about 7 percent of the households earning above $75,000, they would, once history was undone, make up 13 percent of that group, too.[45] This wouldn't, of course, eliminate economic inequality. But while the gap between the rich and the poor would remain, the gap between black and white would disappear; inequality would no longer be racialized.

To put the point in this way, however—to describe the goal of reparations as a racially proportionate redistribution of wealth—is immediately to invite the objection that it's hard to see how leaving the economic inequalities of American society intact while rearranging the skin color of those who suffer from and those who benefit from those inequalities counts as progress. And, if what we are seeking is economic equality, it doesn't. What drives the reparations movement, however, is not the mere fact of economic inequality—"Lamentably," Robinson says, "there will always be poverty" (8). The point of reparations is not to eliminate poverty but to compensate those whose poverty "derives from the social depredations of slavery" (173), whose poverty is an effect of the great crimes committed by an unjust social system. Once not only the social system but also its consequences have been destroyed, whatever economic inequality survives may be, as Robinson says, "lamentable," but it won't be unjust. If, in other words, some or even many people still become poor, from the standpoint of the logic of reparations, we will want to argue that their poverty is their problem—that poverty is acceptable (i.e., not compensable) as long as it's not the product of injustice, as long as the people who are poor are poor because of what they themselves have or have not done rather than because of what has or has not been done to or for them.

This is, of course, a familiar position, if not exactly a familiar left position.[46] And, if we can imagine a world in which everyone really does begin with an equal opportunity to achieve the various forms of success, it is, at least, a defensible one.[47] If reparations were paid to the African-American population, perhaps those African-Americans who still—despite the reparations—ended up poor could be said to deserve their poverty. But it's hard to see how the children of these deserving poor would deserve *their* poverty. More generally, it's hard to see how children raised in poverty can be held responsible for that poverty whether or not their parents were the victims of an unjust social system. Shouldn't they be given an equal opportunity regardless of how their poverty was produced? Why does the cause of their poverty matter, as long as they are not themselves its cause? Hence, and still more generally, why should this policy of reparations apply only to African-Americans? Everybody's poverty is the result of some cause; every child's poverty is the consequence of some event in which that child was not involved. Why should slavery and apartheid be compensable while, say, free but poorly paid labor is not? Or—more to the point—why should any particular narrative, any particular history of the events that culminate in some child having less of an opportunity to succeed than some other child, matter? If I'm born in poverty, what does it matter whether my father was an exploited slave or a spendthrift playboy? The money, after all, is going to me, not to my ancestors; it is my victimization, not theirs (they're dead), for which reparation must be made.

The point here is not that our sense of whose histories need to be taken into account must be extended; it is instead that no one's history need be taken into account, that the recognition of inequality makes the history of that inequality irrelevant, and that the question of past injustice has no bearing on the question of present justice. The "blameless" but poor and hence "embattled nine-year-old" (239) who is Robinson's emblematic victim of the history of slavery and discrimination would be just as blameless if her great-great-grandfather had been Simon Legree. Every nine-year-old is blameless; what a just society owes them is not reparations for bad things that were done to their ancestors but an opportunity equal to that of all the other nine-year-olds. So what's relevant is never any particular account of why some child has been impoverished but only the recognition that, whatever the account is, the child cannot be understood to deserve his or her impoverishment. Our schools could stop teaching the history of slavery and of the wrongs done to the native population and of the exploitation of immigrant labor—our schools could stop teaching any history—and our sense of what's owed to the children attending those schools would be utterly unaffected. If no one knew anything about American history, the world would be more ignorant but not less just. Which is only to say that the knowledge that each student's poverty has a cause is crucial to justice; the knowledge of what that cause is is not.

The Debt begins by asking why "African-Americans lag the American mainstream in virtually every area of statistical measure" and by claiming that the "answer can be found only in the distant past." Its historicism consists first of all in its interest in the causes of contemporary conditions. But, of course, Robinson is interested not only in the essentially academic question of how current conditions have come to be but especially in the ways in which the knowledge of how things have come to be can alter the way they are. This alteration takes at least two forms: self-knowledge (which involves racial self-knowledge and hence the racial soul—knowing what happened to your ancestors is knowing what happened to you) and compensation (which doesn't, strictly speaking, involve the notion of race at all—the relevant group is the group of people who have inherited the harm). Both these interests (history as self-knowledge, history as causal account of our current situation) are today widespread; they are what people have in mind when they say that we can't know who we are without knowing our history, that history is what makes us who we are. But I have tried to suggest that both these interests are, in different ways, misplaced.

The first—history as self-knowledge—is based on a mistake, the mistake of thinking that things that didn't happen to us can nonetheless be understood as part of our history. But the knowledge of things that didn't happen to us is precisely not *self*-knowledge, and the effort to imagine things that happened to other people as having happened to us too (as being part of *our* history) requires racialized fantasies that their own proponents are not prepared to defend. Does Randall Robinson really believe in the racial soul he begins by invoking? If he doesn't, if the racial soul is really another name for the racial body, then he needs an account of how things that happened to people with bodies like mine can be bootstrapped into things that happened to me. Or if the racial soul is really just a metaphor for nonbiological historical continuity, then he needs an account of what it is that's nonbiologically continuing. Which is just to say that he needs the soul.

The second interest—in the history that makes us who we are—is not based on a mistake: it's true that history makes us who we are, but it's also, for the purpose of making our society more just—at least if we identify justice with equal opportunity—irrelevant.[48] What we owe the victims of injustice is justice, not a causal account of how they came to be victimized. If, however, we don't identify equal opportunity with justice, if we think that the diminished access of some nine-year-olds to the opportunities our society makes available to some other nine-year-olds is not in itself unjust, then, of course, history does become crucial. For if inequality can be justly inherited, it's only history that will be able to tell us which children have been the victims of injustice and which ones haven't, which ones have been deprived of their inheritance and which ones have no inheritance to be deprived of. The proper use of history, in other words, will be to legitimate (at least some) inequality. But if you're not interested in legitimating some inequality, if you think that equal opportunity is a right, not an inheritance, then the causal account of how our inequalities came into being can have only an antiquarian interest. Not that there's anything wrong with that. Nothing I've said here is meant to count as an argument against antiquarianism. My point is only that the interest in the past shouldn't be mistaken for an analysis of or an attempt to deal with the problems of the present. It's one thing to celebrate Black History Month; it's another thing to redistribute wealth. And, in fact, the two things are not only different, they are, in crucial ways, opposed: reparations and the celebration of a history involve the respect for identity and for inheritance, which is to say, the respect above all for property, whether it takes the form of cultural heritage or of money. History here is a technology designed not to produce equality but, like the lawsuits brought by victims of the Nazis, to return to people the things they own. Redistribution of wealth, however, involves a certain skepticism about ownership, matched by indifference to inherited identity and hostility to inherited property.

CODA

Empires of the Senseless

"You make a mistake," says Adolf Hitler in one of the opening epigraphs to Bret Easton Ellis's *Glamorama* (1998), "if you see what we do as merely political."[1] In *Glamorama*, however, it's hard to see "what we do" or what anyone else does as at all political, much less merely political. *Glamorama* is about models and terrorists—about model-slash-terrorists—and the acts of destruction its model/terrorists perform are unlinked to any particular political program, while the terrorists themselves belong to rival "factions" whose differences are equally unlinked to politics. In an earlier terrorist novel, Don De Lillo's *Mao II* (1991), the terrorists are at least supposed to represent a "new communist element," "an assertion that not every weapon in Lebanon has to be marked Muslim, Christian or Zionist."[2] But even *Mao II* isn't early enough to make the appeal to communism anything more than a gesture of posthistoricist nostalgia; by the time it was published, there were hardly any communists in Russia, much less in Lebanon. And *Glamorama*, whose terrorists have allies in Dublin and Virginia as well as in Beirut and Baghdad, can't work up any more interest in their religion or nationality than it can in their ideology.

But then this presumably is part of Ellis's point—that terrorism cannot be linked to any particular political position. And even if such a judgment seems at best a little premature—even if those who currently commit acts of terrorism may still be able to articulate a connection between their acts and some identifiable political goal—it is certainly true that our "war on terrorism" is rigorously indifferent (one might say, indifferent in principle) to the reasons terrorists might give for their acts. Indeed, although the war on terrorism is not exactly unprecedented—it has been anticipated, even prepared for, by wars on poverty, crime, and drugs—it is nevertheless importantly new, since like the Cold War, the war on terrorism is not a war against some nation (say, Germany or Japan), but unlike the Cold War, it is not a war against some ideology (say, communism) either. Terrorism is like communism in that we are at war with it and only incidentally at war with some nation; just as Russia was an enemy only insofar as it was the site of communism, nations like Afghanistan matter only insofar as they harbor terrorists. But if communism had only an incidental relation to a nation, it had an essential relation to an ideology—it *was* an ideology. Terrorism, however, is not. So the question of what terrorists believe is made as irrelevant as the question of what nation they come from.

And this irrelevance of belief puts both terrorism itself and the war against it on firm and familiar postmodernist ground. Imagine that the terrorists who destroyed the World Trade Center had been communists; the ensuing war against them would have been a war between liberal capitalism and socialism, a war produced by fundamental political disagreement. Imagine, even, that we took the terrorists who attacked New York to be Muslims, representing not what we quickly learned to call a perversion of Islam but a particular form of it; the ensuing war would be between liberalism and Islam. But virtually no one in the United States understands the war against terrorism as a war against Islam; indeed, no one really thinks of Islam, or any other religion, as a set of beliefs in the same way that communism was. We treat religion on the model of a culture, which is to say, we treat people who belong to other religions not as if they have false beliefs but as if they have different identities. Religious belief *as belief*—which would require a commitment on the part of people who didn't believe in Islam to the idea that people who did believe in Islam were mistaken—is replaced by religion as a kind of identity, from which standpoint, people who *believe* differently are treated as people who *are* different.[3] Their religious convictions are redescribed as expressions of their culture, like an ethnic cuisine or, if we want a less trivial but equally disabling example, like a language.[4] Languages are neither true nor false, and if we treat religions like language, then we will regard them too as neither true nor false, just different.

Hence, in the immediate wake of September 11, the familiar, comforting, and largely successful reminders (from the Right as well as the Left) to respect difference. (Imagine again that the attackers had been communists—would they have been allowed to continue their activities? Would it even have made sense to allow them to do so?) And hence also the characterization of the terrorists as people who, having failed to respect (our) difference, have forfeited the respect owed to (their) identity. As the question of what people believe becomes irrelevant, the fact of who they are becomes crucial, but where we reject the value of different beliefs (that's just what it means to think of them as mistaken), we appreciate different identities. So just as terrorists are understood to leave their politics behind when they become terrorists (in the sense that their motives are no longer allowed to matter), they must leave their identities behind as well. And just as we invent an Islam that demands our respect only insofar as we can think of it as a culture rather than as a collection of what must seem to us, if we are not Muslim, false beliefs, we must also invent a perversion of Islam which we don't agree or disagree with either (since it isn't a system of belief) but which we also (since it isn't an identity) don't have to respect. If, in other words, the war on terrorism isn't (like the Crusades or the Cold War) a war between ideologies, it isn't a war between identities (even cultural identities) either.

For if, according to Fukuyama's *End of History*, the end of the Cold War was the end of ideological conflict, and if, according to Hardt and Negri's *Empire*, the rise of Empire is the end of national conflict, the "enemy" now, whoever he is, can no longer be ideological or national. The enemy now must be understood as a kind of criminal, as someone who represents a threat not to a political system or a nation but to the law. This is the enemy as terrorist. Insofar as he is regarded as a criminal, he testifies to the existence of laws that would govern not just one nation but the entire world, and thus to the triumph (imagined if not yet consolidated) of world citizenship. From this perspective, the war on terrorism is the internationalization or, rather, globalization, of previous wars, like the ones on drugs and crime. Terror is not a nation, and the enemies in

such wars are not nations; that is why any nation, simply by repudiating
terrorism, can become our ally. And that is why any nation, even nations
as ideologically different as Iran and North Korea, can, if they are seen
to embrace terrorism, become our enemies.[5] In this sense, the point of
the war on terrorism is to imagine a world no longer divided by the
conflicting beliefs of ideologies or conflicting interests of nations, but a
world in which enemies are always outlaws, a world divided into those
who follow the law and those who break it. If, in other words, what we
did with our enemies in the old days was defeat them, what we do with
them now is bring them to justice (a maneuver we spent several months
practicing in the Clinton impeachment trial). And from this perspective
the quarrel between those (on the human rights Left) who wanted to
try terrorists in an international court and those (on the right) who
wanted to try them in American courts was merely jurisdictional, like
the question of whether someone should be tried in a state or federal
court. Perhaps one should say that those who wished to try them in
international courts represent the avant-garde of posthistoricism or of
Empire. They treated the attack on the World Trade Center not as an
attack on the United States or on capitalism, but on law itself.

Hardt and Negri get this absolutely right when they say that in the
"new order that envelops the entire space of . . . civilization," where conflict between nations has been made irrelevant, the "enemy" is simulta-
nously "banalized (reduced to an object of routine police repression) and
absolutized (as the Enemy, an absolute threat to the ethical order")."[6] The
way we would put this today would be to say that the banalized enemy
is a criminal, the absolutized enemy, an "evildoer." The criminal belongs,
for all juridical purposes, to the same nation that we belong to and also,
as a criminal, to the same "ethical order" we belong to, or rather, given
the universalization of ethics imagined through international law, to the
ethical order as such. That's what makes the terrorist an "evildoer." Terrorism rejects the ethical order, which is to say that just as the understanding of the terrorist as criminal repudiates the idea of other nations, the
understanding of the terrorist as evildoer repudiates the idea of other ethical systems. So the war on terrorism puts into place—as the condition of
its possibility—not only a global citizenship but a global ethics. The criminal does what he does even though it's wrong; the evildoer does what he
docs because it's wrong: either way, he makes no claim to be right.

This is why what *Glamorama*'s terrorists like best about their new re-
cruit is that he doesn't "have an agenda" (327), by which they mean that
he doesn't have any political beliefs. They don't either. And that's why
Mao II's novelist and its terrorist have "no deep disagreements at the
level of ideas" (157); neither one of them has any ideas. Indeed, it is the
irrelevance of political beliefs or ideas and their replacement by what
(thinking to follow Foucault) Hardt and Negri call the "biopolitical," that
mark the special contribution of the discourse of terrorism, which we
might more generally call the discourse of globalization. Biopolitical
"struggles," say Hardt and Negri, are "struggles over the form of life"
(56), and struggles over the form of life are "ontological" rather than
ideological; they have nothing to do with the question of what is believed
and everything to do with the question of what is.

For Hardt and Negri, of course, Empire is what is, and in their efforts
to imagine "resistance" to it, they are as skeptical of political alternatives
as Ellis or De Lillo or, for that matter, George W. Bush. Just as the point
of the war on terrorism is to insist that there is no alternative ethico-
legal order (you either follow the law or break it), the point of Empire
is that it, too, is "total" and that resistance to it can only take the form
of negation—"the will to be against." So if political conflict may be imagined as conflict between two competing commitments to what's right,
biopolitical conflict appears as conflict between what is and what isn't,
or (in its more forward-looking mode) between what is and what will be:
"Those who are against . . . must also continually attempt to construct a
new body and a new life" (214). In ideological struggles, victory is imagined as the triumph of one political and economic system over another;
no new bodies are required. In ontological struggles, victory is the defeat
of one body by another; in the ontological struggle not against some
other body but against what *is* (hence against even one's own body),
victory will be "change," the destruction of what is and its replacement
by something "new." (The word "new" appears some twenty-five times
in the three pages Hardt and Negri devote to this discussion.) Hence the
vision of a future inhabited by people with different bodies rather than
different beliefs and the transformation in *Empire* of political science into
political science fiction, complete with hopeful gestures in the direction
of the cyborg, even if they must be accompanied by regretful acknowl-

edgments that the cyborg is just a "fable" (218). And hence, in *Glam-orama*, a novel of manners more alert to the technologies of self-transfor-mation (from the personal trainer to the cosmetic surgeon) that our society has already put into place, an even more sanguine assessment of the possibilities available to anyone willing to take advantage of them. What the model Victor's terrorist handlers like about him is not only that he has no beliefs ("no agenda") but that he's "not afraid to try things": "Everybody's afraid of changing," the terrorist leader, Bobby, says to Victor. "But we don't think you are" (326).

Thus Hitler's suggestion that what the Nazis do should not be under-stood as "merely political" is echoed in *Glamorama* by Victor's assertion that he is "not . . . political" and explained rather than contradicted by Bobby's response—that "everyone" "is political," that "it's something you can't help" (358). The "merely political"—which would be some-thing you could help—would involve taking one political position instead of or as opposed to another, but no one in either *Empire* or *Glamorama* is political in that way. The politics you can't help is biopolitical rather than political; it's the politics of being who you are, and the revolution it imagines involves becoming "whatever you're not" (327). In *Empire*, becoming what you're not is imagined (with a kind of Harawayesque boosterism) on the model of an "ontological mutation," which, replacing the old bodies with new, makes the "political" (what people believe) "yield to love and desire" (388) (what they want). This is what it means to think that "every metaphysical tradition is now completely worn out" and that the "solution" must be "material and explosive" (368). Ellis's commitment to love and desire is a little less ingenuous: "I had done so many shows . . . but I was still mid-level," says one of his model/terror-ists. "I wanted something else." But the process is just as evolutionary—"and then there was what Bobby wanted . . . and . . . I . . . evolved" (352)—and the outcome is just as material and explosive. The "point," he says, "is the bomb"; "that's the statement" (337), except that it's not exactly a statement because in Ellis no one is interested in what you say. You don't really say things; "you show the world things and in showing the world you teach it what you want" (353).

Showing rather than telling is, of course, one of the traditional respon-sibilities of the novelist, and although characterizing a terrorist act as "the biggest work of art" got Karlheinz Stockhausen into a lot of trouble after the attack on the World Trade Center, the idea of a "knot that binds novelists and terrorists" (41) is fundamental to *Mao II* and to the literature of terror more generally. Indeed, De Lillo's novelist worries that terrorism has essentially replaced the novel in its ability "to alter the inner life of the culture," while at the same time he understands the act of writing as already what Hardt and Negri would call a biopolitical activity, as, in effect, biowriting: the text is a "pale secretion," "bits of human tissue sticking to the page" (28). The tissue that sticks to the page is material in that it's a piece of your body rather than a representation of it, and this disarticulation of writing from representation is fundamental to the literature of terror—from Kathy Acker's redescription of writing as bleeding in *Empire of the Senseless* to Richard Powers's invocation of "the word made flesh" in *Plowing the Dark*.[7] If when I write "my blood shoots into your face," it's not the meaning of my words but the touch of my body that matters—that's why Acker's is the "empire" of the "senseless" (and that's also why it's an empire).[8] And when, like Powers's poets turned computer programmers, I produce "images" so "real" they become the things "they once represented" (67), the meaning of what I write is equally irrelevant; because, "with software," "the thing and its description are one and the same" (307), what I mean is always and instantaneously replaced by what I make. The poet who stops writing poetry and starts writing code is still trying to fulfill a poet's ambition, to make something that will be rather than mean, and it's only insofar as he doesn't mean anything that the writer can become a figure for the terrorist who doesn't believe anything.

Or, for that matter, for the Rortyan pragmatist-slash-patriot, whose beliefs still seem to him "worth dying for" even if, or rather (as I have argued) just because they don't seem to him true. It's the irrelevance of reasons that requires acting rather than arguing, and terrorism is our current name for political acts that seem to us to render whatever reasons might be given for them irrelevant, to turn, as Rorty would put it, reasons into causes. Thus we find Slavoj Žižek (in *Welcome to the Desert of the Real*, published on "the first anniversary of the attacks on the World Trade Center and the Pentagon") just as keen on the importance of the "Act" (152) as he is on the "Cause," and precisely in a way that reduces the

"Cause"—the reason for which the "Act" is committed—to a cause, what Rorty would call a "contingent historical circumstance." "What makes life worth living," Žižek says, is "the awareness that there is something for which one is ready to risk one's life"; what that "something" is seems to him an essentially secondary concern, since, whether we call it "free-dom," "honour," or "autonomy" (his suggestions), what it really is is "the very excess of life" rather than any particular set of beliefs or values.[9] Once the Cause has been turned into the excess of life, it no longer mat-ters whether your beliefs are true or even what they are; it no longer matters what the Cause is; all that matters is that you're ready to die for it. From this standpoint terrorists (especially suicide bombers) are to be envied because they are "more alive" than we are, and the way to combat terrorism is to become as alive as they are—hence, despite his conviction that torture is wrong, Žižek argues that, "confronted with the proverbial 'prisoner who knows' and whose words can save thousands," we should, in the "brutal urgency of the moment, . . . simply do it" (103).[10]

The point here is not, of course, that Rorty, Žižek, or anybody else I've been writing about means to endorse either terrorism or the war against it. The point is, rather, that the terms in which terrorism and the war against it have been conceived are the terms in which the question of whether we are doing the right thing has been redescribed as the question of whether we are living our lives to the fullest (whether we're as alive as the suicide bombers), while at the same time the question of what a text means has been redescribed as the question of what it is (and hence of how it looks to us). Writing, in other words, is ontologized in the way that politics is in *Empire* and for the same reason: insofar as people's beliefs have been replaced by their "needs and desires" (49) and their ideas replaced by their bodies, the whole project of what Hardt and Negri call "representation" becomes irrelevant. What this means in writing is a commitment to the transformation of the text into a thing, either (as in Powers) into the thing it seeks to represent (the word made flesh) or (as in Acker) into the thing that replaces the representation (the bleeding that replaces writing). The point both times is to turn a meaning that might be understood into an object or event that will be experi-enced. When, as Powers says, the "weather-map" becomes "the weather," you really *don't* need a weatherman to tell which way the wind

blows. What it means in politics is a commitment to new subject positions instead of to more just societies. Or, rather, that's what it means
to a Left politics. The Right can understand the fact that no one has any
better ideas about how society might be organized as a tribute to the
way things are. The Left must make up for its refusal of better ideas by a
demand for better bodies, for what Hardt and Negri call the "ontological
constitution" of a "new proletariat" (402). Just as the literary critique of
representation substitutes the ontology of the text (what it is) for what
it means, the political critique of representation substitutes the ontology
of the subject (who we are) for what we believe.

The discourse of terrorism, then, is the discourse of the replacement
of ideology by ontology, and of the universality intrinsic to ideas by the
universality available to bodies. Another way to put this would be to say
that the discourse of terrorism is the discourse of empire—Acker's or
Hardt and Negri's—insofar as both Acker and Hardt and Negri understand empire as the moment in which the old political struggles (between
nations, between political theories) have become irrelevant. We are all,
Acker says, "world citizens" (39), and we should stand prepared to assert
our demand for "global citizenship" (400), say Hardt and Negri, by dem-
onstrating our capacity to move around the world. Because the ability
to be wherever we want to be anywhere in the world is the first step
toward a distinctly ontological—as opposed to metaphysical—universality, "circulating," according to them, "is the first ethical act of a counterimperial ontology" (363). If, in other words, from the standpoint of a
metaphysical universality, it doesn't matter where we are, for Hardt and
Negri what matters is that we can be everywhere. This is what the transformation of politics into biopolitics, of what we believe into what we
are, requires. If our beliefs are true, they are true for everyone everywhere; that's what's meant by their universality. But the whole point of
the notion of empire at work in the texts I have been examining and
in the logic of the response to terrorism (i.e., in our commitment to
understanding the course we're embarked on as a war on terrorism) is
to render the question of what people believe irelevant and therefore
to redescribe the "universal" not as the irrelevance of the subject (an
irrelevance built into the very concept of belief) but as the achievement
of a global subjectivity.

One might say, in the terms they derive from Deleuze and Guattari, that Hardt and Negri treat "nomadism" and "deterritorialization" as equivalent technologies of the "universal" when in fact they involve two very different accounts of universality. Nomadism and the "power to circulate" imagine the universal as the global—a place (or territory) so big that it is everywhere (like the world seen from the Concorde in Ellis, the "curvature of the earth" that makes the model / terrorist Jamie "break down" or "freak out" [354]). Circulating is "the first ethical act of a counterimperial ontology" precisely because it requires no transcendence of the subject position but only the subject's ability to move around. And the commitment to the global, as opposed, say, to the local—think of the debates, for example, over whether various national or cultural liberation movements are or are not "merely" local—is a commitment to calibration, to the idea that size, big or little, matters. Deterritorialization, however, involves a universality that makes no reference to even a very big place, much less to the subject's position in that place. Unlike "needs and desires," which achieve universality only if everyone has them, beliefs are intrinsically universal: true (if true) whether or not everyone believes them, false (when false) even if everyone believes them. And it is the potential universality of desire rather than the intrinsic universality of belief that *Empire* calls upon. Thus, what looks like the critique of identity in "Workers of the world unite!—not on the basis of national identities but directly through common needs and desires, without regard to borders and boundaries" (46)—is really just a relocation of identity; it is the "needs and desires" of workers rather than of Germans or Englishmen that matter. *Empire*'s appeal is to what the workers want rather than to what they believe, to what one could properly call the global rather than the universal.

Hardt and Negri are not, of course, alone in their identification of universality with what Judith Butler calls "commonality"; on the contrary, it is this identification and the problems that accompany it—above all the problem of exclusion—that constitute the ground for the recent effort on the part of what might be called the deconstructive (or, in a more catholic vein, the poststructuralist) Left to address what it takes to be the particularist failures of identitarianism. Thus Butler, in an essay called "Competing Universalities," sees her task as finding "what basis of

commonality there might be among existing movements" while making
no appeal to "transcendental claims" and then "establishing *practices of
translation*" among these movements. The idea of the universal here is
the idea of a universal language, a language that everyone speaks, and
the commitment to translation is a commitment to establishing the con-
nections between the languages without destroying the difference between them—this is what Butler calls "an active engagement with forms
of multiculturalism" that does not "reduce the politics of multiculturalism to the politics of particularity" (169). But, as we have already seen,
people who have different beliefs (different ideologies) cannot be understood as people who speak different languages. People who speak different languages, like people who have different interests or who desire
different things, need never make any transcendental claims. They need
never, that is, imagine that everyone should speak the language they
speak or want what they want. But all beliefs always involve "transcendental claims"; the claim that something is true (even if the claim itself
is mistaken) is always a claim that it is true for everyone, whether or not
everyone believes it.

Butler's universalism is thus a form of the identitarianism she imagines
herself to critique, a commitment to the subject position every bit as
complete as those whose conception of the subject is supposedly more
naive. The language I speak, after all, is just as much a fact about me as
the structure of my body. But the truth (or falsehood) of the things I say
in that language and with that body necessarily transcends them both.
And it is Butler's effort to avoid this transcendence, like Hardt and
Negri's effort to deny the "metaphysical," that commits her and them
to refining rather than repudiating the posthistoricist commitment to
difference and identity. Indeed, Hardt and Negri may best be understood
not only as refining it but as extending it. The problem, as they see it, is
that "postmodernist authors" have neglected the one identity that should
matter most to those on the left, the one we have always with us: "The
only non-localizable 'common name' of pure difference in all eras is that
of the poor" (156). If the value of cosmopolitanism's traveling subjects
is that they can see things from a perspective wider than those who are
physically and spiritually stuck in one place, the poor make even better
traveling subjects than the cosmopolitans, since they don't actually have

to go anywhere—they're already everywhere. And they're at least as good at embodiment as the terrorists; in fact, they embody embodiment: only the poor, Hardt and Negri say, "live radically the actual and present being" (157). So even though multiculturalists don't care about them, and even though "the dominant stream of Marxism" has "always hated" them (157), the poor are as much the heroes of *Empire* as terrorists are of *Glamorama*, or novelists of *Mao II*, or computer programmers of *Plowing the Dark*.

From the standpoint of a more traditional Marxism, or at least of its "dominant stream," it may, of course, be a little hard to see how appreciating the poor—as opposed to, say, eliminating them—can count as a contribution toward progressive politics. From the standpoint of that Marxism, capitalism is understood to need the poor, whether or not anyone likes them, and the end of capitalism is supposed to be the end of poverty—or, at least, the end of the difference between the poor and the rich. It's as if Hardt and Negri have missed the point of Hemingway's famous reply to Fitzgerald—"Yes, they have more money"—and have thus transformed the thing that makes the poor different from you and me (they have *less* money) into the "pure difference" of unassimilable being. They have begun, in other words, to treat poverty as if it were an identity, or, more precisely, as if it were identity itself ("all of being and nature" [413]), which is only, after all, what's required by their commitment to ontologizing politics. So instead of seeking an alternative to postmodernism's valorization of difference, they turn out to be committed to producing that valorization in its most radical form. For if "postmodernist authors" have, in their attention to racial, cultural, and sexual difference, neglected class difference, they have surely done so because class difference—more or less money—has always seemed an implausible candidate for promotion to the status of a subject position that we must respect. Writers whose model of "oppression" is "marginalization" have, in other words, had a hard time thinking about economic inequality, since the problem of the poor is not the problem of a minority and is not the problem of the subject articulated through its relation to an oppressive norm (a median income, unlike, say, heterosexuality, is not a norm). And because the poor are not marginalized, and because they are victimized by capitalism rather than by "oppressive definitions of the

subject," writers committed to Butler's version of "a Left political project" have tended more or less to ignore them. The great merit of Hardt
and Negri is thus to reclaim the poor for the Left, and their great ingenu-
ity is to do so by ontologizing poverty, treating it as if it were not so
much a lack of money as a way of being. It's no wonder, then, that Saint
Francis emerges as the "communist" hero of *Empire*; he turns the project
of getting rid of poverty into the project of becoming poor.[11]

Or, perhaps more precisely, into the project of outing ourselves as the
poor people we all potentially are. For once we turn poverty into a structure of identification, a relation to identity rather than to money, we can
begin to think that our problem is that we're all insufficiently "poor."
It's for this reason that Žižek, as hostile to the usual forms (cultural,
national, racial) of identitarianism as Hardt and Negri, nonetheless finds
himself reproducing their ontologizing commitments, lamenting the
plight of the "New York yuppie jogging along the Hudson River" and of
all the other Last Men "having a good time" while losing "life itself" (88).
What's wrong with capitalism on this account is that it produces DVD
players and TIVO, not that it produces inequality. And its true victims
are people who waste their lives trying to stay in shape. Žižek, we might
say, has the sentimental reading of *American Psycho*—it's Bateman ("All I
seem to want to do now is work out" [300]) who's the victim. More
generally, we might say that *we*—the middle class, not as alive as Saint
Francis, not as alive as Palestinian suicide bombers—are the victims. And,
more generally still (but this is a slightly different topic), we might also
say that the Left today obsessively interests itself in a set of essentially
liberal issues—from racism to gay marriage—as a way of not interesting
itself in the problem of economic inequality.

But if there's a more local political point here, it's that the attack on
the World Trade Center—redefining the political world into those who
are for terrorism and those who are against it—only confirmed the onto-
logization of the political that had already taken place. Although a good
many people described the attack as marking the end of what they called
postmodernism—claiming that, in its face, no one could remain a postmodernist—the truth is that the response to it marked the complete
triumph of postmodernism or, as it should, perhaps, in its most purely
theoretical form, be called, posthistoricism. Conflict in posthistoricism

is between subject positions, not ideas, between what is and its negation, between people who aren't afraid of change and people who are. This is biopolitics instead of politics—it is, as Acker makes Henry Kissinger say, "not ideological" (144), and, as we have already begun to see, it is matched in literary production by a kind of biowriting, which is why Acker's Abhor writes "Empire of the Senseless" with blood instead of ink and traces "rather than" draws "her own" heart. Where the drawing is a representation of the heart, the trace is a remnant of it, and the words you write with your own blood testify to your presence without needing to signify it: "hearts" are "applicable," as Abhor says, because they are "senseless" (204). The literary historical point, then, to accompany the political one is that the fantasy of the senseless (writing without meaning) has taken its place alongside the fantasy of Empire (politics without believing) in, or rather as, the discourse of terrorism. History, as of this writing, is still over.

Notes

Introduction: The Blank Page

1. Susan Howe, *The Birth-mark* (Hanover, N.H.: Wesleyan University Press, 1993), 57, 59, 58.

2. Susan Howe, *My Emily Dickinson* (Berkeley: North Atlantic Books, 1985), 35.

3. The point is a general one, by which I mean that I am not arguing here for any particular account of what makes the crucial features crucial but only for their reproducibility. If, in other words, you think that the crucial features of a work of art are not reproducible (are lost in reproduction), you must also think that there can be no edition of that work. So the question of whether Dickinson's poems should be understood as drawings is a question about whether published versions of them will have the status of, say, the copy of Fra Angelico's *Annunciation* that you have on the wall or the copy of Whitman's *Leaves of Grass* that you have on the shelf.

4. Paul de Man, *Aesthetic Ideology* (Minneapolis: University of Minnesota Press, 1996), 81.

5. Andrzej Warminski, " 'As the Poets Do It': On the Material Sublime," in *Material Events: Paul de Man and the Afterlife of Theory,* ed. Tom Cohen, Barbara Cohen, J. Hillis Miller, and Andrzej Warminski (Minneapolis: University of Minnesota Press, 2001), 18.

6. Many of de Man's commentators (Warminski would be an important exception) treat these two phenomena (the text that has many meanings/the text that has no meaning) as if they were the same. This is in one sense a mistake but in another sense accurate; part of the point of this book will be to try to show that the apparently uncontroversial, even commonsensical, notion that texts can have more than one meaning (in the sense that they can mean something more than their authors intend) is really just a disguised form of the much more implausible idea that texts do not mean at all.

7. The difference between marks that function as evidence and marks that mean is just the difference between the physical trace left by the body and the representation made by the body: my footprints in the sand are evidence of where I was; the words that I write in the sand ("I was here") are not only evidence of where I was but also a statement about where I was.

8. The authors of the preface to *Material Events* (Tom Cohen, J. Hillis Miller, and Barbara Cohen) deny the relevance of experience to de Man and, in fact, associate it with the post–de Manian "relapse" into aesthetic ideology that they argue has characterized literary theory over the last twenty years; "rhetorics of historicism, . . . of practicality (neo-pragmatism), of descriptive forms and empiricisms, . . . retrohumanist appeals to representation, the subject (identity politics), or experience more generally . . . are examples of this relapse" (xi). But my point here is that de Man's commitment to what he calls "sensory appearance," to "the eye" which, "left to itself," "ignores understanding" and "notices appearance" (127) has the appeal to experience (and hence also to the subject) built into it.

9. Francis Fukuyama, "The End of History?" in *The New Shape of World Politics*, edited with an introduction by Fareed Zakaria (New York: Norton, 1997), 2. The original essay was published in the summer 1989 issue of the *National Interest*.

10. This is why, to get a bit ahead of the argument, the critique of identity that takes the form of suggesting that we "supplant the language of 'being'—with its defensive closure on identity, its insistence on the fixity of position, its equation of social with moral positioning—with the language of 'wanting, ' " with its potential to "destabilize the formulation of identity as fixed position," actually functions as a refinement rather than a critique of the primacy of the subject position (Wendy Brown, "Injury, Identity, Politics," in *Mapping Multiculturalism*, ed. Avery F. Gordon and Christopher Newfield [Minneapolis: University of Minnesota Press, 1996], 163–64). The relevant alternative to being is believing, not wanting.

11. Craig Owens, *Beyond Recognition* (Berkeley: University of California Press, 1992), 110. The essay in which this remark appears was originally published in 1982.

12. On the one hand, then, I understand the end of the Cold War—or, rather, the description of the end of the Cold War as the end of history—as an occasion to assert at the level of politics what literary theorists of the text and social theorists of identity have also been asserting: the end of or the irrelevance of or, in its purest form, the impossibility of disagreement. On the other hand, I am not arguing and I do not in fact believe that while the Cold War was ongoing everyone was really much more interested in ideological disagreement than in identitarian difference (how then explain, just for starters, the House Un-American Activities Committee?). And I obviously do not believe that the currently widespread effort to redescribe

all differences as identitarian is itself undisputed. What I believe instead is that the set of debates around identity and ideology have—albeit in different forms and with different stakes and different consequences—been constitutive of the modernist problematic, and that what we call modernism and postmodernism are different ways of negotiating that problematic.

13. It can also be posed in such a way that the reciprocity—the way in which a certain account of the object calls for a certain account of the subject and vice versa—gets obscured. Thus, for example, Clement Greenberg's foundational account of modernism as the requirement that "each art" "determine, through its own operations and works, the effects exclusive to itself" and his claim that the "flatness of the surface" emerged as essential to the "medium" of painting ("Modernist Painting," in *The Collected Essays and Criticism*, ed. John O'Brian [Chicago: University of Chicago Press, 1993], 86) might be described as entirely concerned with the question of the ontology of painting and at the same time as almost completely uninterested in the relation between the painting as an object and the subject who beholds it. It's as if his interest in painting as a medium misdescribes for him his interest in paintings as objects and as if his orientation toward the relation between painting and the other arts directs him away from the problem of the painting's relation to the beholder—the problem that Minimalism would make crucial for Fried.

And Fredric Jameson's equally brilliant and important account of postmodernism performs this operation in reverse. If, in other words, Greenberg renders invisible the degree to which the problem of the subject is foundational for modernism, Jameson makes the problem of the object in postmodernism equally invisible. One need here think only of the pride of place conferred by *Postmodernism* on architecture, which not only is at the cutting edge of the integration of "aesthetic production" into "commodity production" (5) but also is paradigmatic in its ambition to create a "new" kind of "space," a "new mode in which individuals move and congregate" (*Postmodernism* [Durham, N.C.: Duke University Press, 1991], 5, 40). Here the question of the reader's or the beholder's experience is paramount except, of course, that the moving and congregating individuals aren't really readers or beholders—they don't interpret the building, they use it. So if the question about the ontology of the text in Howe, for example, is a question about whether it matters where you are when you read or see it, there is no equivalent problem about buildings—it always matters where you are. One way, then, to describe architecture is as exemplary of the postmodern because it requires the participation of the subject, but a better way would be to describe it as neither modern nor postmodern for the same reason—it requires the participation of the subject. Because the building can't ignore the subject, it can't acknowledge the subject either. There is thus no problem about the ontology of buildings, and modernism and postmodernism in architecture are essentially questions of style.

My point here is not, of course, to denigrate architecture, or even to insist on the impossibility of making the ontological status of the building into a problem. It is only to suggest that the commitment to the organization of space isn't enough for postmodernism, any more than the commitment to the medium is enough for modernism. I want, in other words, to insist on the specificity of the ontological problem as a problem about the object and for the subject.

14. Robert Smithson, *The Collected Writings*, ed. Jack Flam (Berkeley: University of California Press, 1996), 85.

15. Slavoj Žižek, "Class Struggle or Postmodernism," in Judith Butler, Ernesto Laclau, and Slavoj Žižek, *Contingency, Hegemony, Universality* (London: Verso, 2000), 130.

16. The relevant point here is that the logic of class is just as incompatible with the logic of identity as the logic of belief is. For accounts of why class is not an identity, see, among others, John Guillory, *Cultural Capital* (Chicago: University of Chicago Press, 1993); and Walter Benn Michaels, "Autobiography of an Ex-White Man: Why Race Is Not a Social Construction," *Transition* 73, 7 (1998): 122–43, reprinted in *The Futures of American Studies*, ed. Donald E. Pease and Robyn Wiegman (Durham, N.C.: Duke University Press, 2002), 231–47. It should be obvious here that I am not using the term "ideological" in its Marxist sense; if I were, then ideology and class position would, of course, be inextricably connected.

17. For discussion of Žižek's own rather complicated relation to this project, see the "Coda."

One: Posthistoricism

1. Francis Fukuyama, "Second Thoughts," *National Interest*, summer 1999, 16.

2. The point here is that the recent redeployment of the example of the Cold War in the form of the war against terrorism makes sense along Fukuyama's lines not only because terrorism, unlike socialism, is not an ideology but also because the idea that the terrorism might be motivated by an ideology is denied by a discourse that understands the terrorists only as criminals, motivated only by a "perversion" of an ideology (Islam) or essentially unmotivated (i.e., "evil").

3. This particular formulation is Judith Butler's ("Competing Universalities," in *Contingency Hegemony, Universality,* 178), and, since the body is here invoked in the context of writing ("It is not easy, as a writer, to put one's body on the line, for the line is usually the line that is written, the one that bears only an indirect trace of the body that is its condition"), it points not only toward the political eagerness to give up their bodies that we will see in Arthur Schlesinger Jr., Richard Rorty, and Slavoj Žižek but also to their literary equivalent—the imagination of writing as above all the trace of the body—in Howe and in Kathy Acker or even Don DeLillo.

4. Arthur Schlesinger Jr., *The Disuniting of America* (New York: Norton, 1992), 9–10.

5. Leslie Marmon Silko, *Almanac of the Dead* (New York: Penguin, 1991), 513.

6. Fukuyama's views are here identical to Randall Robinson's (in *The Debt: What America Owes to Blacks* [New York: Plume, 2000]) and to those of the reparations movement more generally. For a critique of those views, see the section "Forgetting" in chapter 3.

7. Michael Lind, *The Next American Nation* (New York: Free Press, 1995), 3.

8. Thus, although the best writers on Silko, Caren Irr and Sharon Holland, emphasize what Holland calls "her challenge to existing paradigms" of "narrative, memory, history" (Sharon Patricia Holland, *Raising the Dead* [Durham, N.C.: Duke University Press, 2000], 98), my own reading emphasizes her participation in the formation of those paradigms.

9. This commitment to seeing Marx as above all a Jew is anticipated in William L. Pierce's *The Turner Diaries* (Arlington, Va.: National Vanguard Books, 1978) and his later, less influential (i.e., Timothy McVeigh never read it) *Hunter* (Hillsboro, W.V.: National Vanguard Books, 1989) (both published under the pseudonym Andrew Macdonald). In both texts, Jews are characterized à la Silko as "a notoriously tribal people" (*Hunter*, 100). But where Silko distinguishes between Marx's Jewishness and his communism, Pierce treats the communism as irrelevant, a mere ploy: "the whole communist movement was simply a Jewish power grab" (125). For Pierce, the fundamental opposition is between identities (Jews and whites), not ideologies (communists and capitalists) or even nations (Russia and the United States); in fact, *The Turner Diaries* refers to Russians as "racial kinsmen" (191). Inasmuch as communism had stopped worrying Pierce and his colleagues long before the "Evil Empire" stopped worrying Fukuyama, the radical Right ought to be understood as early adopters of posthistoricist identitarianism.

10. Howard Winant provides a more programmatic statement of this position in *Racial Conditions* (Minneapolis: University of Minnesota Press, 1994) when he criticizes the "subordination of race to class" and insists that the goal of a truly "radical democracy" should be to attack racism not by attacking the reality of race but by "accept[ing] and celebrat[ing]" "racial difference" (31).

11. Samuel P. Huntington, "The Clash of Civilizations?" in *The New Shape of World Politics*, with an introduction by Fareed Zakaria (New York: Norton, 1997), 69.

12. Orson Scott Card, *Speaker for the Dead* (New York: Tom Doherty Associates, 1986), 3. The other volumes of the quartet are *Ender's Game* (1985), *Xenocide* (1991), and *Children of the Mind* (1996).

13. George Kennan as Mr. "X," "The Sources of Soviet Conduct," *Foreign Affairs* 25 (July 1947): 567.

14. I don't mean to suggest here that the Cold War was invariably thought of as ideological; indeed, as my later discussion of the imagination of nuclear holocaust indicates, I don't believe that it was. But, although sustained attention to the representation of conflict in the period itself would doubtless reveal many fascinating variations, my focus here is only on representations of Cold War conflict at what was announced as its end. The idea, in other words, is that, whatever the Cold War actually was, its end became the occasion for announcing the end of ideological conflict.

15. Thus Judith Butler comments on the difficulty of grounding "a theory or politics" in a "subject position which is 'universal,' when the very category of the universal has only begun to be exposed for its own highly ethnocentric biases" (*Feminists Theorize the Political*, ed. Judith Butler and Joan Scott [New York: Routledge, 1992], 7). There are two mistakes here, or perhaps two versions of the same mistake: the universal cannot function as a ground (even the "permanently open, permanently contested, permanently contingent" [8] ground that Butler hopes for), and it is not a kind of subject position. Universality cannot be invoked to ground our theories because the claim to universality is built into the very possibility of having a theory, and, rather than being a kind of subject position, it marks the irrelevance of the subject position—to disagree with someone is to think that the truth or falsehood of our theory has nothing to do with the fact that it is ours.

16. The point, in other words, is not the Habermasian one that "what we hold to be true has to be defendable on the basis of good reasons . . . in all possible contexts, that is, at any time and against any one" (Jürgen Habermas, "Richard Rorty's Pragmatic Turn," in *Rorty and His Critics*, ed. Robert Brandom [Oxford: Blackwell, 2000], 46). It is instead, if we are citing philosophical authority, the Davidsonian one that "it is possible to have a belief only if one knows that beliefs may be true or false" and that the truth of my belief "does not depend on whether I believe it, or everyone believes it, or it is useful to believe it" (Donald Davidson, "Truth Rehabilitated," in *Rorty and His Critics*, 72). The idea that our beliefs are true or false regardless of whether we believe them is not an "ideal" toward which some of us strive but a presumption to which all of us are already committed. And it may also be worth pointing out that my interest in argument, here and later, does not involve a commitment to rationality on the model of what Habermas calls "good reasons." Our reasons always seem good to us; that's what makes them our reasons. My commitment is, rather, to the difference between those things (beliefs, interpretations) that seem to us true or false and for which we can give some reasons and those things that seem to us to require no justification

17. Stanley Fish, *Is There a Text in This Class?* (Cambridge, Mass.: Harvard University Press, 1980), 169. We read different poems, Fish writes, because we belong to different "interpretive communities," which is to say, we have "different strategies

not for reading (in the conventional sense) but for writing texts, for constituting their properties and assigning their intentions" (171). In his subsequent writings, however, the idealism of this account gives way to a more sociological approach; the effort to explain different interpretations is disarticulated from the claim that the interpretations create the text.

18. Hence the difference between losing a game and losing an argument: you don't lose at chess when you are convinced that you cannot move your king out of check; you lose when, whatever your views, you cannot, within the rules of the game, move him. The point can be put more generally by saying that in any game the players' moves have a force that is utterly undetermined by their beliefs about them. Beating someone at chess has nothing to do with changing his or her mind. And it can be put more generally still by saying that just as two players in a game cannot be described as disagreeing, two players playing two different games can't be described as disagreeing either, not because they have the same beliefs but because, once again, their beliefs are irrelevant. Chess isn't a set of beliefs; it's a set of rules. That's why the redescription—in philosophers like Richard Rorty and Jean-François Lyotard—of people who have different beliefs as people who are playing different "language games" amounts to a repudiation of the idea that people actually have any beliefs. The point here is not a skeptical or even a relativist one about the possibility of having *true* beliefs; postmodernism, properly understood, is required to be just as skeptical about the possibility of having false beliefs as it is about the possibility of having true ones.

And the analogy of the game is just as problematic for language as it is for ideology. No one cares what you meant by moving your rook four spaces to the left—you don't need to mean to checkmate your opponent in order to do it. (You can just as effectively, although not just as easily, do it by accident.) And if the meaning of your move is irrelevant to the question of whether your opponent has been checkmated, your opponent's understanding of the meaning is equally irrelevant. Indeed, this point can be put more generally just by saying that the moves in a game don't have any meaning. Which is just to say, what I've already said, that they have force. So redescribing ideologies as language games makes the mistake of leaving out beliefs, and redescribing speech acts as moves in a language game makes the mistake of leaving out meaning. Lyotard's *Postmodern Condition*, a classic, makes both these mistakes.

19. Differences in height and weight are not, of course, intrinsically insignificant; in fact, for many purposes they are crucial. It is only with respect to the determination of identity that they don't matter. Which is why, absent some appeal to utility or aesthetics, no one is committed to appreciating differences of height and weight. Of course, in a society as committed to the production of identity as ours is, there

have been efforts to treat these physical features along the lines of skin color and thus turn them into markers of identity. But, as I have argued elsewhere ("Autobiography of an Ex-White Man: Why Race Is Not a Social Construction"), identity on the model of race (or culture) requires that our bodies (or beliefs and actions) represent rather than constitute our identity, and while it's easy to see how having a certain skin color can represent (or misrepresent) your race, it's hard to see how the height you are can be thought of as representing (or misrepresenting) rather than simply determining your tallness.

20. Octavia Butler, *Dawn* (New York: Popular Library, 1987), 36–37, 6. The succeeding volumes of the trilogy are *Adulthood Rites* (1988) and *Imago* (1989).

21. In this sense, there is something a little misleading about my description of nuclear holocaust fantasies as characteristic of the Cold War. It would be more accurate to insist on a certain tension between that war and the technology that was imagined as its most likely end. For although the war might be understood to be about ideology, its nuclear climax would involve not the defeat of one ideology by another but the defeat of humanity itself, Butler's "humanicide." The nuclear scenario thus functions to make a war between ideologies into a war against humanity—against, that is, an identity.

22. Dershowitz tends to describe the difference as that between Jews "as *individuals*," who have never been better off, and Jews "as a *people*" who "have never been in greater danger" (*The Vanishing American Jew* [New York: Little, Brown, 1997], 1), but this somewhat misrepresents his point. The relevant opposition is not between Jews as individuals and Jews as a group but between Jews and their Jewishness.

23. Octavia Butler, *Adulthood Rites* (New York: Warner Books, 1988), 80.

24. Donna J. Haraway, *Simians, Cyborgs, and Women: The Reinvention of Nature* (New York: Routledge, 1991), 226.

25. In this connection, it's probably worth pointing out that the recent interest in cosmopolitanism as (alongside hybridity) a kind of corrective to what are understood as the excesses of identitarianism is just another way saving the primacy of the subject position. Universalism makes the subject irrelevant; cosmopolitanism just makes her more widely traveled.

26. Kim Stanley Robinson, *Blue Mars* (New York: Bantam, 1996), 23, 3. *Blue Mars* is the third volume in the trilogy; it's preceded by *Red Mars* (1993) and *Green Mars* (1994). The Mars trilogy as a whole is, among other things, a tribute to the success of postcolonial studies and, more generally, to the replacement of oppositions like true/false, just/unjust with self/other and same/different. The idea, of course, is that peoples' beliefs about what is just are really just expressions of their identity; the problem with the idea is that it confuses the conditions under which people come to believe something with their reasons for believing it. For a non-Martian

equivalent, see Richard Rorty's *Achieving Our Country*, with its hope for "suggestions about how to make us wonderfully different from anything that has been" (Rorty, *Achieving Our Country* [Cambridge: Cambridge University Press, 1998], 24).

27. It's striking that the characters of the Mars trilogy understand themselves as inhabiting "the postcapitalist era" (77), that the trilogy attempts to imagine postcapitalism at the moment when Earth is beginning to understand itself as postsocialist. In fact, however, Robinson's postcapitalism looks a lot like postsocialism—everything is corporations, everything is private property, it's just that corporations are "employee-owned." And this appeal to corporate difference is widespread in the science fiction of the period. Sometimes it takes the form of analogizing corporations to countries; sometimes it takes the form of replacing countries by corporations. Both forms, however, make possible the rewriting of political difference as economic competition, and hence the transformation of social visions into corporate interests. Corporations, in other words, are more like bodies and cultures than like ideologies; their competition involves only the question of who is stronger or more successful, not the question of who is right. At the same time, however, there is something weirdly postcapitalist about the corporate world imagined in posthistoricist science fiction—it also seems to be posteconomic; it's impossible to tell in these novels how the corporations make their money or even what they produce. Instead of nation-states being imagined as corporations, the corporations are imagined as nation-states. Various economists have criticized the analogy between the corporation and the state on the grounds that the state has no product to sell; posthistoricist science fiction replaces the state with the corporation by imagining the corporation as if it were a state, by imagining it without any commodity to sell. And even when this effort to imagine corporations as if they were states is compromised by the appearance of some product, the product turns out to be something to which the state is more likely to be committed than is any corporation—the antiracist black skin dye marketed by the good corporation in Bruce Sterling's *Islands in the Net* is more like an antidiscrimination law or affirmative action program than a commodity.

28. Native American Council of New York City, *Voice of Indigenous Peoples*, edited by Alexander Ewen, with a preface by Rigoberta Menchu and a foreward by Boutros Boutrous-Ghali (Santa Fe, N.M.: Clear Light Publishers, 1994), 21, 19.

29. The fact that we can sometimes replace blood ties with legal ones—say, by adoption—doesn't really alter the point. The idea of the nation as family is meant to capture your ties to people whom you don't actually know but who nonetheless have some privileged relation to you. But however intense your feelings might be for the sister you never met, it's hard to imagine feeling very strongly about the adopted sister you never met.

30. Richard Rorty, *Contingency, irony, and solidarity* (Cambridge: Cambridge University Press, 1989), 5.

31. Walker Connor, *Ethnonationalism* (Princeton, N.J.: Princeton University Press, 1994), 203.

32. Charles Taylor, *Muticulturalism and "The Politics of Recognition"* (Princeton, N.J.: Princeton University Press, 1992), 40.

33. Will Kymlicka, *Multicultural Citizenship* (Oxford: Clarendon, 1995), 36.

34. Ibid., 105. Yael Tamir makes this point with precision, as Kymlicka notes, when she describes cultures and national communities as being "outside the normative sphere" (Yael Tamir, *Liberal Nationalism* [Princeton, N.J.: Princeton University Press, 1993], 90). It's for this reason that, as Tamir says, such groups can "accommodate normative diversity"—since membership is not determined by values, people with very different values can be members. But it's for this same reason, of course, that membership can neither require nor justify normative diversity. Cultures, according to Kymlicka and Tamir, are entitled to respect; values, insofar as they have been disconnected from cultures, are not.

35. Kymlicka is explicitly opposed to the idea that the "national groups" whose rights he means to defend can be "defined by race or descent" (22); he insists rather that "national membership should be open in principle to anyone, regardless of race or colour, who is willing to learn the language and history of the society and participate in its social and political institutions" (23). But, with respect at least to minority rights based on past treaties, descent is clearly essential (people can't *become* aborigines). And it's hard to see how learning its history can make you a member of the culture whose history you're learning; knowing the history of Quebec doesn't make you Quebecois. For that matter, knowing the history of Quebec and also being able to speak the language of Quebec doesn't make you Quebecois. What's left, then, is the participation in the social and political institutions. But the commitment to political institutions seems problematic from the standpoint of multiculturalism. The whole idea of one country with different cultures (i.e., the whole idea of multiculturalism) seems to rest on the political institutions not being distinctive—if they are, then what's separate isn't merely the culture but the state.

36. John Edwards, *Multilingualism* (London: Penguin, 1995), 90, 92.

37. We might, of course, think of ourselves as wanting our language to survive because of the great works of literature that have been produced in it. If, however, this is our reason, then we've actually lost our interest in the survival of languages as such and become interested instead in the survival of great works of literature. And this interest would not, of course, commit us to the survival of those languages in which we thought there were no great works. Or we might be interested in preserving languages as objects of antiquarian interest, for linguists to study. But it

wouldn't matter for this purpose whether anyone actually spoke the language; a dictionary and a grammar would suffice, or a tape made by the last speaker. In fact, the most common arguments for the survival of languages rest on an analogy between languages and species. For example, Daniel Nettle and Suzanne Romaine (in *Vanishing Voices: The Extinction of the World's Languages* [Oxford: Oxford University Press, 2000] describe a language called Taiap, spoken only by about one hundred people in Papua New Guinea and apparently, since the children of Taiap speakers now tend to speak Tok Pisin (pidgin English), on the verge of dying out. "If Taiap were a rare species of bird," say Nettle and Romaine, people would be "concerned." "Yet in Papua New Guinea and all over the world, many unique local languages are dying at an unparalleled rate," and "few people know or care" (13–14). The question of why people should care about the extinction of the rare bird is, of course, itself a complicated one—answers tend to oscillate between the anthropocentric instrumentalist (extinction of other species is bad for *us*) and the deeper ecological (extinction of other species is bad for *them*). But it's notoriously hard to see why we should feel any moral obligations to the abstract entity that is a species: as Joel Feinberg (quoted in Eric Katz, *Nature as Subject* [New York: Rowman and Littlefield, 1997]) puts it, "A whole collection, as such, cannot have beliefs, expectations, wants or desires . . . individual elephants can have interests, but the species elephant cannot" (20). And it's that much harder to see how languages can be worthy of moral consideration, since a language is not only not itself a living entity, it's not even (like a species) a collection of living entities. We can at least feel bad about the rare birds that we imagine dying as the species dies out, but it's pretty hard to feel sorry for Taiap, which was never alive and didn't really die—it just stopped being used.

38. Gordon and Newfield, "Multiculturalism's Unfinished Business," 80, 86, 84.

39. I recognize that this is exactly the kind of formulation that will lead some readers to complain (as some readers of my earlier work already have) that my characterizations of what people can and cannot coherently care about miss what Douglas Mao calls "the crucial point that we don't live in a world in which all parties exercise reason all the time" ("Culture Clubs," *Modernism/Modernity* 8 [2001]: 1710). Such complaints seem to me, however, to rely on a mistaken idealization of "reason," what might be described as the elevation of reason over reasons. The fact that people have lots of false beliefs and do lots of stupid things based on those false beliefs doesn't mean they don't have any reasons—it just means they have bad reasons. And having bad reasons is one way (having good reasons is the other) of exercising reason. So if my argument against caring about the culture of our descendants fails to convince people, it's not because the question of whether we should care about their culture is somehow immune to (above or below) reason; it's because my reasons don't seem good enough.

40. Ben Bova, *Mars* (New York: Bantam, 1992), 11.

41. Ibid., 107, 247, 12.

42. William M. Ferguson and Arthur H. Rohn, *Anasazi Ruins of the Southwest* (Albuquerque, N.M.: University of New Mexico Press, 1987), 1.

43. The locus classicus would be Willa Cather's extraordinary novel *The Professor's House*. For an account of this and related texts, see Walter Benn Michaels, *Our America* (Durham, N.C.: Duke University Press, 1995).

44. The point here is not to identify indigenous peoples with nature as opposed to culture but to imagine instead that nature has a culture and, identifying the cultures of indigenous peoples with nature's culture, to make the commitment to the cultural rights of indigenous people identical to the commitment to preserving nature.

45. As Robert Markley's exceptionally informative essay, "Falling into Theory: Simulation, Terraformation, and Eco-Economics in Kim Stanley Robinson's Martian Trilogy," *Modern Fiction Studies* 43 (1997): 773–99, makes clear, however, Robinson's interest in Mars is at least as much a function of the new knowledge generated by the *Mariner* voyages and of the late 1980s and early 1990s scholarly debates about the possibility and/or desirability of remaking the Martian atmosphere to support human life. My point here in emphasizing the Columbus quinquecentennial is just to highlight the way in which questions about what to do with Martian nature get rearticulated as questions about what to do with Martian culture.

46. Native American Council of New York City, *Voice of Indigenous Peoples*, 9. Many of those involved in the project had wanted 1992 to be the International Year of the World's Indigenous Peoples, but, according to the anonymous authors of the introduction to *Voice*, "pressure from Spain, Brazil, and the United States, among others" (21), made that impossible.

47. Ibid., 26, 115, 60, 115.

48. David Abram, *The Spell of the Sensuous* (New York: Vintage, 1996), 80–81.

49. It is, of course, possible to articulate a commitment to rights independent of the question of language, and at least one important strain of deep ecology—that represented, for example, by the legal writer Christopher Stone—has been interested in the "legal rights" of what he calls "natural objects" without being interested in their language or, for that matter, even feeling compelled to assert that they speak a language (Stone, *Should Trees Have Standing?* [Dobbs Ferry, N.Y.: Oceana Publications, 1996], 1). Subsequent references to Stone's writings are to this book and are cited in parentheses in the text. Stone's original essay ("Should Trees Have Standing? Toward Legal Rights for Natural Objects") was published in 1972; perhaps, putting the point a little too crudely and anticipating an argument that will need to be made at greater length, one could say that as deep ecology's interest in

the natural world has modulated from an interest in respecting the rights of objects to an interest in respecting their differences, it has made the question of language increasingly central.

50. Bova, *Mars*, 272, 245, 258, 247.

51. Also on Richard C. Hoagland's Mars. Hoagland thinks there is a "bizarre object" on Mars that he and other believers call the "Face" and that, they say, could not have been caused by either "wind" or "tectonics" (Hoagland, *The Monuments of Mars* [Berkeley: North Atlantic Books, 1992], 8). Their updated version of Lowell's canals is no doubt mistaken, but their theoretical position has a certain force: "There is no middle ground" about the Face, Hoagland says. "It either is or is not artificial," and "If it's not, it is not worth worrying about" (16).

52. Steven Knapp and Walter Benn Michaels, "Against Theory," *Critical Inquiry* 8 (summer 1982): 728.

53. John R. Searle, "Literary Theory and Its Discontents," *New Literary History* 25 (summer 1994): 649–50.

54. Abram, *Spell of the Sensuous*, 95.

55. In response to an earlier version of this argument, Searle suggested that, confronted with such departures from "orthographic norms," one would "appeal to the producer of the sentence to find out what he or she intended" ("Literary Theory and Its Discontents," 680). But if the letters have been produced by natural accident, then, of course, there is no possibility of such an appeal, and, more important, if the letters are defined as purely formal entities, there can be no point to such an appeal. For to define them purely formally is to define them without reference to any particular account of how they were produced. So if the letters really are purely formal entities, which is to say, if they are whatever letters they are independent of any causal account of their production, what good will it do to appeal to the person who produced them? She can, at best, tell you what letters she was trying to write, not what letters she has actually written.

56. For a powerful and sustained account of the empiricism of deconstruction's relation to the materiality of the signifier, and especially of what she calls its commitment to "the prelinguistic rather than the linguistic" (170 n. 7), see Frances Ferguson, *Solitude and the Sublime* (New York: Routledge, 1992).

57. Ibid., 159, 165.

58. Jacques Derrida, *Limited Inc*, trans. Samuel Weber (Evanston, Ill.: Northwestern University Press, 1988), 66. Derrida couples the substitution of the mark for the sign with the "substitution of intentional effect for intention," and although a fuller discussion of the notion of effect in deconstruction will follow, it may be worth noting here the appeal to the subject position intrinsic to it: the meaning of a sign will not depend on its readers; the effect of a mark will.

59. Judith Butler, *Excitable Speech: A Politics of the Performative* (New York: Routledge, 1997), 40.

60. Actually, this formulation is a little unfair to Fukuyama, since his point, of course, is that the end of contradiction (aka the triumph of liberalism) marks an end to politics. Butler's particular contribution is to turn the end into the beginning.

61. The thing there can be a right (or, for that matter, wrong) answer about is what someone means by it, which is why the argument for intentionalism here is just that it is the only way of accounting for conflicts that really are conflicts of interpretation.

62. Haraway, *Simians, Cyborgs, and Women*, 154.

63. Native American Council of New York City, *Voice of Indigenous Peoples*, 13, 15.

64. Derrida, *Limited Inc*, 61.

65. Ibid., 91.

66. Bret Easton Ellis, *American Psycho* (New York: Vintage, 1991), 112.

67. Kathy Acker, *Empire of the Senseless* (New York: Grove, 1988), 210.

68. And not quite even in the way that the condemned men of Kafka's *In the Penal Colony* understand the judgments inscribed on their bodies by the writing machine. The condemned man "deciphers" the "script" "with his wounds" (Franz Kafka, *The Great Short Works*, translated Joachim Neugrochel [New York: Simon and Schuster, 2000], 205), but it's precisely this deciphering that Ellis's and Acker's notions of writing (not to mention Stephenson's notion of code) will make irrelevant. Their readers will not exactly need to know the meaning of the texts they feel.

69. Neal Stephenson, *Snow Crash* (New York: Bantam, 1992), 395.

70. Richard Powers, *The Gold Bug Variations* (New York: HarperCollins, 1991), 86.

71. Ibid., 518.

72. The equivalent in *Empire of the Senseless* is the tattoo that counts for Acker, as Patrick O'Donnell rightly says, as "a force in the war on representation because it is a 'direct' writing . . . that cuts out the representational middleman" (*Latent Destinies* [Durham, N.C.: Duke University Press, 2000], 106). Once, however, you cut out the "representational middleman," what you get is not direct writing but no writing at all.

73. Which is to say not that pain can't be faked but only that it's impossible to think of someone being shot by a nail gun as faking.

74. The difference between the two texts would be that Butler celebrates her aliens' integrity while Bateman's demands for honesty are obviously a little over the top.

75. A corollary would be that it doesn't make sense to think of understanding a text as sharing the experience of the person who wrote it. Butler is fascinated by the idea of the empath, and her *Parable* series (written after *Xenogenesis*) is built around someone who can feel people's pain (or their pleasure) just by looking at them. Thus the "sharer" heroine of *Parable of the Talents* (1998) is tortured by the sight of a rape because she experiences both the pain of the victim and the pleasure of the rapist, an experience that is made even more disconcerting when Butler ingeniously (albeit creepily) makes the empath herself the victim. But where in science fiction it is seeing people rather then understanding them that sets the empath off, in literary criticism it works a little differently. In Cary Nelson's *Repression and Recovery: Modern American Poetry and the Politics of Cultural Memory*, for example, the difference between experiencing and interpreting is completely elided. For Nelson, understanding what people mean is above all a matter of feeling what they feel, so readers who completely understand, say, Ezra Pound's "economic and social views" are imagined as being "fully at one" with them (*Repression and Recovery* [Madison: University of Wisconsin Press, 1989], 140). And if this were true, it would certainly make one nervous, as it makes Nelson nervous, about intentionalist readings of literary texts. "It is worth recognizing," he remarks, "just how appalling it would be to recover such authorial intentionality so thoroughly as to lose ourselves in it." But, of course, it isn't true; understanding what people mean is not the same as feeling what they feel, much less becoming who they are. That's the difference between the empath and the literary critic. The empath will surely find the "subject position" of the rapist "intolerable"; the literary critic runs no risk of losing herself in the world of even the most obnoxious author—since understanding what people mean has nothing to do with occupying their subject position. It's only the empath who starts to shiver when she hears you say you're cold.

76. W. K. Wimsatt and Monroe Beardsley, "The Affective Fallacy," in *The Verbal Icon: Studies in the Meaning of Poetry*, ed. W. K. Wimsatt (Lexington: University of Kentucky Press, 1954), 27. Their assessment of Coleridge's and the tourist's response is, as they point out, derived from C. S. Lewis, and it should be clear that what matters to their argument (and to mine) is not the accuracy of his understanding of the sublime but the inevitability of his distinction between feeling bad and being mistaken.

77. Why isn't the meaning of the text just the intended effect, its making you think of what the producer of the text wanted you to think of? If this were true, then the opposition between the normal and the normative would be irrelevant, since it would be turned into the difference between what people mainly did and what someone wanted them to do. But insofar as we could (only) disagree about what someone wanted us to do, the idea of the desired effect restores normativity.

It is, in other words, the possibility of being mistaken (as opposed to being, say, unusual) that is crucial here.

78. The point here is not that there's anything wrong with talking about the effects that texts have on their readers—there's nothing problematic about describing Acker's depiction of Thivai's love for Abhor as, say, deeply moving. Just as there's nothing problematic about someone agreeing with you that the text does indeed depict Thivai's love for Abhor but recording that he or she is not deeply moved by it. The effect here is a consequence of the meaning but is separate from it. The problem is, rather, when the effect is conflated with the meaning. And the minute you deny that an interpretation of a text can be—must be—accurate or inaccurate, the sort of thing two readers could disagree about it, you replace the meaning of the text with the effect it has on you.

79. Rorty's own version of this point is that he is "happier with uses than with meanings" (*Rorty and His Critics*, 74), a way of putting it that is admirably consistent but hard to believe, since in order for uses to make you happier, you have to understand the difference between them and meanings, and if you do understand the difference between uses and meanings, you've already chosen meanings. From this perspective, however, it is at least easy to see why criticisms of Rorty as a kind of skeptic, denying the possibility that we can have knowledge of the world in the sense of having true beliefs about it, completely miss the mark. What he's denying is not that we can have true beliefs and true interpretations but that we do things like believing and interpreting. And, more generally, we might say that neither postmodernism nor poststructuralism should be understood—even when this is their self-description—as challenges to the independent reality of an external world. What they are instead is a particular description of the way that world affects us— as events that have effects rather than as texts that have meanings.

80. Thus David Palumbo-Liu gets it exactly wrong when he claims that "the key move" in Rorty's recent work, "the move from *contingency* and *poeisis* to an *ethnos* that is stratified precisely as 'American,' " involves a lapse "from his antifoundationalism"—it *is* his antifoundationalism (Palumbo-Liu, "Awful Patriotism: Richard Rorty and the Politics of Knowing," *Diacritics* 29 [1999]: 49, 45). The mistake is, of course, a plausible one; there isn't, as Palumbo-Liu rightly observes, a lot of enthusiasm for "new vocabularies" in *Achieving Our Country*. But Rortyan antifoundationalism doesn't really require enthusiasm for new vocabularies; it just requires that the relevant choice be between vocabularies (rather than beliefs) and that whatever you're enthusiastic about, you be enthusiastic about it because it's new or old (rather than true or false). And the fact that Palumbo-Liu likes the "new voices" where Rorty likes the old ones doesn't make much difference between them. It is true, however, that Palumbo-Liu is more consistent than Rorty; where Rorty

occasionally does lapse into worrying about issues that are not structured on the vocabulary/identity/culture model—like economic inequality—Palumbo-Liu converts that very worry into the expression of an identity: it's the sort of thing that "heterosexual, white, middle-class male progressives" (50) resort to.

81. Neal Stephenson, *Cryptonomicon* (New York: HarperCollins, 1999), acknowledgments.

Two: Prehistoricism

1. J. G. Ballard, *The Best Short Stories of J. G. Ballard* (New York: Holt, 1995), 244, 97.

2. Michael Fried, *Art and Objecthood: Essays and Reviews* (Chicago: University of Chicago Press, 1998), 151.

3. Donald Judd, *Complete Writings 1959–1975* (Halifax: Press of the Nova Scotia College of Art and Design, 1975), 184.

4. Fried puts this point as criticism when he says of works by Judd and Larry Bell that they "cannot be said to acknowledge literalness; they simply *are literal*" (88). More generally, the point would be that for Fried, as for Smithson, there can be no such thing as abstract painting, a point that will become crucial in the next generation when the photographer James Welling, characterizing abstraction as "too hard" for painting, comes to see it as "built into" photography.

5. Hal Foster is thus at least partially right when he describes Fried's turn to conviction as an effort to counter Judd's "subjectivism" with "an appeal to quasi-objective standards of taste" and when he, in effect, criticizes that appeal by historicizing it, linking it to the "disciplinary underpinnings" of "Greenbergian formalism" (Foster, *The Return of the Real* [Cambridge, Mass.: MIT Press, 1996], 52, 57). The problem, obviously, is that our thinking a work of art good may well seem as subjective as our finding it interesting. Insofar, however, as Fried is asking not simply whether the work of art is good but also whether it really is a work of art, the situation is somewhat different; the kind of mistake we might make in taking nonart for art is not the same as the kind of mistake we would make in taking a minor work for a masterpiece. One of the great complications of Fried's writing in this period is its persistent imbrication of the question about whether something is art with the question about whether it is good art. But while the overlapping of these questions is certainly an important moment in the history of art, the questions can still be separated; otherwise there would be no such thing as bad art.

6. Because they are designed to do only what they (what all objects) already do.

7. It's often said the impulse to site specificity was motivated by the desire to resist commodification, to resist, that is, the production of works of art that could

be bought or, in the more sophisticated variant of this argument, consumed. Thus Douglas Crimp says that "the whole point" of Richard Serra's sculpture is to defeat the "consumption of art, indeed to defeat consumption altogether and to replace it with the experience of art in its material reality" (Crimp, *On the Museum's Ruins* [Cambridge, Mass.: MIT Press, 1993], 167). But it's hard to see how the commitment to the primacy of experience can in itself count as resistance to commodification and consumption—what else is the tourist industry?

8. It might be argued that the idea that the meaning of a text can change was already a consequence of New Critical theory, even though it was not a consequence the New Critics recognized or that, in the main, they would have welcomed. And, along the same lines (as will become clear), it might be argued (in fact, I will argue) that theorists who do think of themselves as committed to the idea that the meaning of a text can change are in fact committed to the idea that texts have no meaning. Or, to put it another way, that theorists who think there can be many (correct) interpretations of the same text are in fact committed to the idea that there can be no correct interpretations of the same text and, indeed, to the idea that there is no such thing as interpretation. When I say, "in fact committed," I do not mean, of course, that these commitments are the hidden meaning of the theoretical texts I discuss: to say that an argument has consequences different from those its author intends is not to say that it has a meaning different from the one its author intends. My point will be, rather, that if you set out to imagine a text that can mean something other than what its author intends, you will end up (whether you mean to or not and whether you realize it or not) imagining a text that means nothing—that isn't a text.

9. Thus Smithson will describe the *Non-Site* as a "three dimensional logical picture," both representational and abstract—the technology through which "one site can represent another site which does not resemble it—thus *The Non-Site*" (364).

10. The following discussion is about the practice of straight photography, since it's only straight photography that has this particular ontological interest.

11. Kendall Walton, "Transparent Pictures: On the Nature of Photographic Realism," *Critical Inquiry* 11 (December 1984): 246–77.

12. Robert Demachy, "On the Straight Print," *Camera Work*, July 1907, reprinted in *A Photographic Vision: Pictorial Photography, 1889–1923*, ed. Peter C. Bunnell (Salt Lake City, Utah: Peregrine Smith, 1980), 172.

13. Sadakichi Hartmann, "A Plea for Straight Photography," *American Amateur Photographer* 16, no. 3 (march 1904), reprinted in *A Photographic Vision*, 166.

14. Abigail Solomon-Godeau, *Photography at the Dock* (Minneapolis: University of Minnesota Press, 1991), 114, 118.

15. Arthur Danto, *Encounters and Reflections* (New York: Farrar Straus and Giroux, 1990), 120.

16. Craig Owens, *Beyond Recognition* (Berkeley: University of California Press, 1992), 84.

17. Paul de Man, *Blindness and Insight* (New York: Oxford University Press, 1971), 23.

18. Wellek and Warren wondered whether the "retention" of the word's "modern association" could be "defended as an enrichment of [the poem's] meanings," as if the crucial question were whether the later associations made the poem better (Rene Wellek and Austin Warren, *Theory of Literature* [New Haven, Conn.: Harcourt, Brace and World, 1956], 177). As I have already begun to suggest, however, and as I argue in some detail later, the question of what different readers (those of the seventeenth century and the twenty-first) are made to think when they read the poem is a question about its effect, not its meaning, and so it's their experience and not the poem's meaning that will be either enriched or impoverished.

19. First published in *Glyph I* in 1977, "The Purloined Ribbon" was reproduced as the concluding chapter of *Allegories of Reading* (New Haven, Conn.: Yale University Press, 1979). The reference to the "illusion of meaning" is on page 298.

20. And there is also, of course, a continuity just as complete between these formal concerns (about what kind of object the work of art is and what kind of subject its beholder must be) and the politics of posthistoricism—the end of the Cold War and the replacement of ideological disagreement by identitarian difference. Indeed, this continuity is explicitly thematized in Don DeLillo's *Underworld* (New York: Simon and Schuster, 1997), which, marking the beginning of the Cold War with the first Soviet explosion of a nuclear device, marks its end with the transformation of the B-52s that "used to carry nuclear bombs" (70) into an "art project," a "landscape painting in which we use the landscape itself." The desert on which the planes are located is "the framing device," which means not exactly that there is no frame but instead that there is nothing outside the frame, that the limits of the work of art are identical to the limits of the beholder's experience. And it is this identification of the experience of the work of art with the beholder's experience as such that, in Tony Smith's words, "makes most painting look pretty pictorial." Furthermore, DeLillo not only identifies the emergence of the beholder's experience with the end of the Cold War but also identifies it with the transformation of the difference between ideologies into the difference between identities. His desert is the site also of a gasoline commercial: two cars, one white, one black, filled with different brands of gas—"First car to get to the Trinity site wins" (530). The ad is meant to identify the competition between the cars with the competition between the United States and the USSR, but the white car's victory sets off a "firestorm of

protest" not from the Soviets but from the NAACP, the Urban League, and the Congress of Racial Equality.

21. Hence the continuity between Fish's very early "affective stylistics" (which claimed that the meaning of the text consisted in the reader's response to it) and his turn to the new "perspective" announced in *Is There a Text in This Class?* (which described the reader as producing rather than responding to the text). On the second account, as we have already seen, readers cannot disagree because they are producing different texts. On the first account, they are responding to the same text, but because their response to the text is their experience of it, they still can't disagree— they can just have different experiences.

22. Richard Rorty, *Philosophy and the Mirror of Nature* (Princeton, N.J.: Princeton University Press, 1979), 298.

23. Of course, it's possible to rescue meaning from illusion (i.e., from the reduction to information) but only through extreme measures, like David Chalmers's panpsychism, where, even though the information (the difference one physical state makes to another) is doing all the work, our sense that we are meaning things and understanding what others mean is preserved by locating it in a parallel and not (or not exactly) physical world. But, as Chalmers himself acknowledges, his effort to preserve consciousness in humans by identifying it as the inevitable accompaniment of information systems requires him to believe that not only humans and other animals have consciousness but that every information system does: since "one can find information states in a rock—when it expands and contracts, for example," the rock must be understood to have "experience" and hence to be conscious (Chalmers, *The Conscious Mind* [Oxford: Oxford University Press, 1996], 297).

24. Which is why it makes sense for Cary Wolfe—arguing in *Animal Rites* (Chicago: University of Chicago Press, 2003) for a critique of "speciesism" that he thinks should follow from what he understands as postmodernism's "posthumanism"—to invoke Derrida and to cite not only his essay "The Animal I Am" but also a passage from "Eating Well" in which he insists that the phenomenon of "the mark in general" (including " 'animal languages,' genetic coding," and "all forms of marking within . . . so-called human language" [73]) makes a clean "cut" between the human and the animal, or even between the linguistic and the nonlinguistic, impossible. Wolfe's point here is not just to claim that some animals (e.g., the "higher" apes) have language but that, following Derrida, we need to rethink our idea of what a language is. And it is certainly true that once the signifier is converted into the mark, or what Derrida calls "the inhuman trace," then our notion of language must be changed, since language has now become information, and not just animals but everything (from computers to thermostats to stones) is involved in exchanging it.

25. "Il n'y a pas de hors texte" is usually understood as something like a declaration of idealist skepticism, and, more generally, nothing is more usual than to identify poststructuralism in particular and postmodernism more generally as a kind of relativism, foregrounding the primacy of the interpreter. But its supposed idealism is really only a by-product of postmodernism's actual materialism. The transformation of sign to mark also transforms interpretation to experience and thus makes the position of the subject relevant, since although the meaning of the sign doesn't change, the subject's experience of the mark certainly does.

26. A parallel claim for posthistoricist avant-garde poetry would be Steve McCaffery's description (in *North of Intention* [New York: Roof Books, 1986]) of the text in Language Writing as "affording both author and reader the possibility of producing endless meanings and relationships" (149). For McCaffery, the recognition that language's "uncontestable graphic, phonic or gestural materiality" is "a necessary condition of, yet insubsumable to, the ideality of meaning" (204) marks the impossibility of what he sometimes calls "absolute" (205) and sometimes calls "unitary" (207) meaning. But the alternative to unitary meaning is not simply multiple meanings, since, as McCaffery recognizes, a text that means, say, four or five things will have just as absolute a meaning as a text that means only one. What's distinctive about Language Writing is, rather, its commitment to "the loss of meaning" (211). And the text that ceases to be a meaningful object of interpretation (McCaffery says it "resists interpretive depth") "comes closer to being an experience" (24) and thus to achieving the "endlessness" that, as we have already seen, is built into experience.

Three: Historicism

1. Malcolm X, *The Autobiography of Malcolm X*, as told to Alex Haley (New York: Grove Press, 1965), 399.

2. As has been widely noted, the great Latino immigration of recent years may pose a serious threat to the American racial system, since Latinos as a group cannot be considered either black or white. To the extent, however, that Latinos can instead be broken down into two groups, the black/white binary might still survive.

3. Art Spiegelman, *Maus II* (New York: Pantheon, 1991), 99. The black dog is a hitchhiker picked up, much to Vladek's horror, by Art's wife, Françoise. The point of the scene is to criticize Jewish exceptionalism of the kind articulated when Vladek, in response to Françoise's charge that he talks about blacks "the way the Nazis talked about Jews," replies, "I thought really you are much more smart than this, Françoise. . . . It's not even to compare, the shvartsers and the Jews." But the iconography of the novel—the fact that American Jews remain mice—reproduces rather than criticizes that exceptionalism.

4. See Hilene Flanzbaum, ed., *The Americanization of the Holocaust* (Baltimore: Johns Hopkins University Press, 1999).

5. In his informative and incisive book *The Holocaust in American Life* (Boston: Houghton Mifflin, 1999), Peter Novick cites this text, remarking that he can "celebrate" his "birthday" and his "Jewish identity" by "learning that on that date in 1298 nineteen Jews were killed in Krautheim, Germany; in 1648 Chmielnicki's men massacred 600 Jews in Ostrog, Ukraine; in 1941 the SS killed 250 in Brianska Gora, Belorussian SSR" (328).

6. Whitley Strieber, *Communion* (New York: Avon, 1987), 123.

7. Greg Bear, *Blood Music* (New York: Ace, 1985), 111–12.

8. Toni Morrison, "The Pain of Being Black," *Time*, May 22, 1989, quoted in Mae G. Henderson, "Toni Morrison's *Beloved*: Re-membering the Body as Historical Text," in *Comparative American Identities: Race, Sex, and Nationality in the Modern Text*, edited, with an introduction by Hortense J. Spillers (New York: Routledge, 1991), 83.

9. Toni Morrison, *Beloved* (New York: Plume, 1987), 13.

10. Valerie Smith, " 'Circling the Subject': History and Narrative in *Beloved*," in *Toni Morrison: Critical Perspectives Past and Present*, ed. Henry Louis Gates Jr. and K. A. Appiah (New York: Amistad, 1993), 345.

11. Which is not, of course, to say that enslavement is the only or, necessarily, the defining racial experience; indeed, Paul Gilroy follows Morrison in claiming that too often slavery "gets forgotten," and he explicitly opposes Morrison's memory of slavery to the memories of Kemet, the "black civilization anterior to modernity" that Afrocentrists sometimes invoke "in its place" (*The Black Atlantic: Modernity and Double Consciousness* [Cambridge, Mass.: Harvard University Press, 1993], 190). The difference matters to Gilroy because he associates the appeal to Kemet with the attempt to "recover hermetically sealed and culturally absolute racial traditions," and he thinks of the appeal to slavery "as a means to figure the inescapability and legitimate value of mutation, hybridity and intermixture" (223). Gilroy prefers hybridity to purity, and so, for the purposes of "identity construction," he would rather remember slavery than Egypt, but from the standpoint of the argument developed here, the questions of which past you choose to remember and of what kind of identity you choose to construct obviously matter less than the commitment to constructing identity by remembering the past in the first place.

12. Smith, " 'Circling the Subject,' " 350.

13. Stephen Greenblatt, *Shakespearean Negotiations: The Circulation of Social Energy in Renaissance England* (Berkeley: University of California Press, 1988), 1.

14. Caroline Rody accurately describes the appeal of *Beloved*'s historicism when she observes that "writing that bears witness to an inherited tragedy approaches

the past with an interest much more urgent than historical curiosity or even political revisionism" and goes on to contrast what she calls an "objective 'prehistory of the present' " to "the subjective, ethnic possession of history understood as the prehistory of the self" (Caroline Rody, "Tony Morrison's *Beloved*: History, 'Rememory,' and a 'Clamor for a Kiss,' " *American Literary History* 7 [1995]: 97). Insofar as to inherit a tragedy involves something more than living with its consequences (as, of course, it must, since everybody is already living with the consequences of past events), it is only through some mechanism of "possession" that any tragedy can count as an inherited one. The sense of urgency, in other words, is entirely dependent on the claim to possession.

15. Cary Nelson, *Manifesto of a Tenured Radical* (New York: New York University Press, 1997), 47.

16. Claude Lanzmann, "An Evening with Claude Lanzmann," May 4, 1986, quoted in Shoshana Felman and Dori Laub, *Testimony: Crises of Witnessing in Literature, Psychoanalysis, and History* (New York: Routledge, 1992), 213–14.

17. Claude Lanzmann, "Seminar on *Shoah*," *Yale French Studies* 79 (1991): 85. Berel Lang makes a slightly different ethical argument against the representation of the Holocaust when he says that any way of representing something suggests the possibility of *other* ways of representing the same thing and thus that representing the Holocaust is inevitably the first step toward misrepresenting it. He recommends that the Holocaust be treated the way that the Exodus is in the Hagadah: "As the Hagadah places every Jew at Sinai, instructed to recount the events of the Exodus as though they had been part of his own life, the presence of all Jews is also fixed within the events of the genocide—those born after it ['you who never was there'] as well as those who died in it or who lived despite it" (Lang, *Act and Idea in the Nazi Genocide* [Chicago: University of Chicago Press, 1990], xiii). But although pretending you are a victim of slavery or the Holocaust might have some identitarian value (might make you feel more black or Jewish), it's hard to see its epistemological utility. Not even the most fervent empiricists think we have more accurate accounts of events we have *pretended* to experience.

18. Claude Lanzmann, "The Obscenity of Understanding: An Evening with Claude Lanzmann," *American Imago* 48 (winter 1991): 481.

19. J. L. Austin, *How to Do Things with Words* (New York: Oxford University Press, 1952), 6.

20. Paul de Man, *Allegories of Reading* (New Haven, Conn.: Yale University Press, 1979).

21. Where Lanzmann privileges a language that cannot be understood by its hearers, Cathy Caruth takes the argument in a more radically de Manian direction by introducing a language than cannot be understood by its speaker. Of Eiji Okada,

the Japanese actor who appeared in *Hiroshima mon amour* and whose character spoke French although he himself did not, Caruth says that he introduces "a specificity and singularity into the film that exceeds what it is able to convey on the level of its representation" (Caruth, *Unclaimed Experience* [Baltimore: Johns Hopkins University Press, 1996, 52). We have already seen how the language a hearer cannot understand may be imagined to convey a *presence* precisely because it does not convey a *meaning*. Here the fact that Okada does not understand the language he himself speaks (he just memorized the French phonemes) is imagined to preserve the "difference" that his French-speaking character has begun to lose. For the "assumption of a foreign language," Caruth writes, involves a "forgetting," "a loss of culture and history." And it is this forgetting that Okada has saved himself from. But not only has he saved himself from being understood (and hence losing his cultural difference), he has saved himself from being understandable. The point, in other words, is not just that other people can't understand what he means; it is instead that he doesn't mean anything: "he does not represent, but rather voices his difference quite literally and untranslatably" (51). The speaker no one understands has not yet succumbed to translation; the speaker who doesn't mean can never succumb to translation. The way to preserve one's specificity, then, is to refuse language, and Caruth's trauma thus provides a psychoanalytic supplement to de Man's deconstructive refusal of meaning and Rorty's pragmatist refusal of understanding. (For a devastating critique of Caruth from a psychoanalytic perspective, however, see Ruth Leys, *Trauma: A Genealogy* [Chicago: University of Chicago Press, 2000].)

22. Geoffrey Hartman, "Introduction: Darkness Visible," in *Holocaust Remembrance: The Shapes of Memory* (Oxford: Oxford University Press, 1994), 7.

23. Michael Krausz, "On Being Jewish," in *Jewish Identity*, ed. David Theo Goldberg and Michael Krausz (Philadephia: Temple University Press, 1993), 272. Subsequent references to this essay and to other essays from this volume are cited in parentheses in the text.

24. One could, of course, claim the Holocaust as part of one's history not because one had oneself experienced it but because one's parents or grandparents had. But to make this claim would be, of course, to relocate one's Jewishness in one's blood, which is to say, in the genetic material that connects you to your relatives. You cannot, in other words, as Anthony Appiah has pointed out, invoke your history to determine your identity because you can't tell which history is yours unless you already know your identity (Appiah, "The Uncompleted Argument: Du Bois and the Illusion of Race," in *"Race," Writing, and Difference*, edited with an introduction by Henry Louis Gates Jr. [Chicago: University of Chicago Press, 1986]).

25. Yisrael Gutman, "On the Character of Nazi Antisemitism," in *Antisemitism through the Ages*, ed. Shmuel Almog (Oxford: Oxford University Press, 1988), 359.

26. This is, of course, different from saying that the *individual* Jew is subsumed by the *group* of Jews. The issue in cultural (as in racial) identity, despite the assertions of polemicists on both sides, has nothing to do with the relative priority of the group over the individual; it has to do instead with the identification of a certain set of beliefs and practices as appropriate for a person or persons in virtue of the fact that those beliefs and practices are his, hers, or theirs. What's wrong with cultural identity, in other words, is not that it privileges the group over the individual but that it (incoherently) derives what you do from what you are.

27. This is, to some extent, implicit in the very idea of genocide, inasmuch as genocide is understood as the extermination of a people rather than as mass murder. In genocide, it is what makes the people a people that is the ultimate object of destruction, so the murder of persons is in a strict sense only incidental to the elimination of the people. If, of course, the people are understood as a race, then genocide will require that they be killed or sterilized; if the people are understood as a culture, then genocide will require only that they be assimilated. From this standpoint, even writers who have not lost sight of the fact that Hitler's goal was physical extermination rather than cultural assimilation may find themselves subordinating the death of persons to the destruction of a people. Thus Berel Lang describes Nazi genocide as worse than cultural genocide because, "Where life remains, as in cultural genocide or ethnocide, the possibility also remains of group revival; but this is not the case where genocide involves physical annihilation" (13). The point here is that physical destruction is the worst kind of genocide because, unlike cultural genocide, it is in principle irreversible. The relevant difference between physical and cultural genocide is not, in other words, the fact that, in cultural genocide, no persons may be killed, which is to say that what's worse about physical genocide is not, on this account, the fact that so many persons must die. For genocide involves the extermination not of persons but of a people. So cultural genocide is less bad than physical genocide not because no persons have been killed but because the people ("the *genos*") may still be revived. It is not less murderous (in both cases, the group dies); it is less irreversibly murderous (in the second case, the group may live again).

28. Ellis makes sure that even when Bateman commits what looks like a truly racial assault—attacking a Japanese delivery boy—the attack has an economic trigger, a "tirade" by one of his friends about the Japanese buying "the Empire State Building and Nell's. *Nell's*, can you believe it?" that "moves something inside me, it sets something off" (180). And when, tearing open "the cartons of Japanese food" to dump their contents on the dying body, Bateman sees that they contain beef chow mein and mushu pork instead of sushi and soba noodles and that he has

"accidentally kill[ed] the wrong kind of Asian" (181), he finds himself apologizing—
"Uh, sorry"—to the corpse; the *Chinese* haven't bought Nell's.

29. Edith Wharton, *Novels* (New York: Library of America, 1985), 1021.

30. Which is also why the only interest it has in culture is in mass culture; the commitment to Phil Collins and Huey Lewis and the News and Whitney Houston is the commitment to a culture that everyone can have whether or not they have any money or any taste. Culture in Ellis is the fantasy of equality produced by the reality of inequality. And it is this persistent economization of culture that links him to Wharton and to Theodore Dreiser rather than to their successors, for whom cultures became expressions of identities.

31. Samuel R. Delany, *Return to Nevèrÿon* (Hanover, N.H.: Wesleyan University Press, 1994), 19.

32. A more plausible candidate for a sexual identity that could be understood on the model of the people would be homosexuals, although homosexuality too—for reasons given in "Autobiography of an Ex-White Man"—cannot finally count as an identity, and, in any event, homosexuality as a distinctive practice doesn't seem to exist in Nevèrÿon, which is to say, no one is much interested in and nothing much follows from whether you sleep with men or women—"It makes a great deal of difference to you now. But I think shortly that you'll find that it seems a less and less important distinction" (175). Masochism, however, *is* marked.

33. Gayle Rubin, "The Leather Menace: Comments on Politics and S/M," in *Coming to Power*, ed. members of SAMOIS (Boston: Alyson Publications, 1987), 220. SAMOIS, named after the estate in *The Story of O*, described itself as a lesbian/feminist S/M organization. One of Pat Califia's contributions to *Coming to Power* ("A Personal View") gives a good account of the context out of which SAMOIS emerged, and Califia is also the author of *Macho Sluts* (Boston: Alyson Publications, 1988), a collection of erotic fiction vividly committed to the pornography of consent.

34. It might, of course, be argued on Kantian grounds that the masochistic contract—the choice of slavery—is no contract at all. No one, according to Kant, "can voluntarily renounce his rights by a contract or legal transaction to the effect that he has no rights but only duties, for such a contract would deprive him of the right to make a contract, and would thus invalidate the one he had already made" (Kant, *Political Writings*, translated by H. B. Nisbet, edited with an introduction and notes by Hans Reiss [Cambridge: Cambridge University Press, 1991], 75). The response to this criticism has been a commitment to the safe words ("And always be sure to agree on some sign to let you know when the game is over: a word, a gesture—that need be all" [175]) that are the hallmark of postmodern masochism. The safe word is in part a protection against someone getting hurt in a way that or to a

degree that they don't want but it is also an effort to rescue rights from duties (i.e. to redescribe duties as rights). What the safe word does is guarantee the continual presence of consent; you can't, in a moment of freedom, give up your future freedom because the safe word guarantees you the opportunity to withdraw your consent. The safe word makes masochism the utopian form of liberalism—all consent all the time

35. Samuel Delany, *Silent Interviews* (Hanover N.H.: Wesleyan University Press, 1994), 137.

36. Robinson, *The Debt*, 13.

37. If we say that black people are people whose ancestors were black, we leave open the question of what made them black; presumably some other physiological marker, which we're now required to name. But if we invoke the basic social construction line—black people are people who are treated as black—then the argument is obviously false. Black people were sometimes treated as less than human; did that make them less than human? For the full version of the argument against race as a social construction, see Michaels, "Autobiography of an Ex-White Man." It may, however, be worth noting here that my point is not that treating people as something can never make them the thing you treat them as; an outcast, for example, is an outcast because he is treated as an outcast.

38. Orson Scott Card, *Pastwatch: The Redemption of Christopher Columbus* (New York: Tom Doherty Associates, 1996), 28.

39. Chorzoi Factory Case, Germany v. Poland, 1928, quoted in Lord Anthony Gifford, "The Legal Basis of the Claims for Reparations" (paper presented at the First Pan-African Conference of Reparations, Abuja, Federal Republic of Nigeria, April 27–29, 1993); reproduced on the Africa Reparations Movement Web site, www.arm.arc.co.uk/home.html.

40. Carolyn Porter, "Are We Being Historical Yet?" *South Atlantic Quarterly* 87 (1988): 783.

41. Reluctant not only because she has to go back and run the risks of life as a black person in antebellum Maryland but because the white ancestor she must, if she is to save herself, rescue is a brutal and deceitful slaveholder.

42. David Horowitz, "Ten Reasons Why Reparations for Blacks Are a Bad Idea for Blacks—and Racist Too," *FrontPageMagazine.com.*, January 3, 2001.

43. The most serious and intelligent critical reading of *Kindred* is the chapter devoted to it in Ashraf H. A. Rushdy's *Remembering Generations* (Chapel Hill: University of North Carolina Press, 2001), but Rushdy is so committed to current orthodoxy about race (its meaning is social rather than biological) that he thinks its heroine, Dana, must be more committed to "symbolically disrelat[ing] herself from

her biological kin" (115) (because they're cruel white slave owners) than she is to the project of stopping people (even black people) from "killing my ancestor" (117) at least until he's forced the black woman who will become Dana's great-grand-mother to sleep with him (*Kindred* [Boston: Beacon Press, 1988]). The "past," Rushdy says, "must be confronted if it is to be altered" (117), but what gives *Kindred* its bite is the requirement that Dana confront the past in order to keep it unaltered and therefore "assure [her] family's survival, [her] own birth" (29).

44. Dinesh D'Souza, *The End of Racism* (New York: Free Press, 1995), 477 and passim.

45. These figures are extrapolated from Table 663, *Money Income of Households—Distribution by Income Level and Selected Characteristics: 1999* of the U.S. Census Bureau's *Statistical Abstract of the United States* (2001).

46. Because the social (but not biological, since the idea of deserving has no place in evolutionary theory) Darwinism invoked by the effort to distinguish between those who do and those who don't deserve their poverty opens up dismaying avenues of justification for every form of inequality, it would be cleaner to insist that no one, no matter how feckless, deserves his or her poverty. But once, of course, one adopts this position—once, that is, one becomes committed to absolute equality—the whole question of reparations becomes irrelevant (since everybody should have as much or as little as everyone else).

47. What exactly equal opportunity is and what the criteria for success might be are, of course, vexed and much discussed questions, absolutely central to post-Rawlsian liberalism. For a useful and extremely influential discussion of these issues, see Amartya Sen's *Inequality Reexamined* (Oxford: Oxford University Press, 1992), and for an excellent survey of contemporary thinking about them, see Alex Callinicos, *Equality* (Cambridge: Cambridge University Press, 2000).

48. Hence the irrelevance also of Ashraf Rushdy's appeal to a distinction between two different ways of understanding responsibility—one that relies on narrative and on the insight that past social practices like slavery have "enduring material effects that significantly determine life chances in contemporary society" (144) and one that insists that it is the present, not the past, that is (in Steven Knapp's words) the "locus of authority" in determining our obligations. This, as I've been arguing, is a false antithesis. It doesn't at all follow from the fact that the past has what Knapp (in *Literary Interest* [Cambridge, Mass.: Harvard University Press, 1993]) calls "explanatory relevance" (116) to the present that anyone in the present can coherently be held responsible for things that they didn't do. Knapp, of course, goes farther and criticizes the idea that they can be held (metaphysically, at least) responsible for things they *did* do.

Coda: Empires of the Senseless

1. Bret Easton Ellis, *Glamorama* (New York: Vintage, 1998), n.p.

2. Don De Lillo, *Mao II* (New York: Penguin, 1991), 123, 129.

3. The obvious exception to these remarks is, of course, those evangelical Christians who might be said, from my point of view, to have their theology wrong but their theory right. As implausible as their beliefs may be, the commitment of, say, the Southern Baptist Convention to converting Jews and Muslims makes it clear that they at least understand what it means to have them. The exact opposite set of implausible but theoretically defensible views is held by the tiny and otherwise insignificant (Eric Rudolph's affiliation with them is their only claim to fame) Christian Identity movement who understand themselves (coherently if incredibly) as belonging to the Christian race and whose religion therefore really is what they say it is, an identity.

4. Or, à la Huntington, like a "civilization." Insofar as commentators regard the post-9/11 world as fulfilling Huntington's predictions, they must regard it also as embodying the posthistoricist fantasy—the clash of civilizations is, as we have already seen, understood as a clash of identities rather than of ideologies. As I suggest later, however, the current discussion tends to convert the valorization of the difference between identities—different ways of being—into the valorization of being as such.

5. It's also why the Bush administration got itself so quickly frozen into support of virtually anything Ariel Sharon did in response to suicide bombings, despite its desire to cultivate the support of Arab nations for the attack on Iraq—as long as the enemy is terrorism, even goals that the administration actually supports (like the establishment of a Palestinian state) must be subordinated to the war against the terrorist means used to achieve those goals. Not only do the ends not justify the means; the means make the ends irrelevant.

6. Michael Hardt and Antonio Negri, *Empire* (Cambridge, Mass.: Harvard University Press, 2000), 13.

7. Richard Powers, *Plowing the Dark* (New York: Farrar, Straus and Giroux, 2000), 215.

8. Kathy Acker, *Empire of the Senseless* (New York: Grove, 1988), 210.

9. Slavoj Žižek, *Welcome to the Desert of the Real!* (London: Verso, 2002), 89.

10. The theoretical apparatus for this commitment to the act is established in one of Žižek's contributions to *Contingency, Hegemony, Universality,* where he argues that the fundamental distinction is between the "authentic" and the "inauthentic" act. The "authentic" (and hence truly revolutionary) act is one that does not "simply express/actualize my inner nature" but "redefine[s] . . . the very core of my identity"

(124); the inauthentic act produces only a "pseudo-change" (125). So the mark of the true revolutionary is (just like it says in *Glamorama*!) that he's not afraid of change.

11. It "makes very little sense to posit an affirmative lower-class identity," John Guillory says in *Cultural Capital*, since "such an identity [has] to be grounded in the experience of deprivation per se" (13). But once the goal of equality is reconfigured as the goal of sainthood, the obstacle ("deprivation per se") becomes an opportunity.

Index

ghosts, function of in New Historicism, 145–46

Gifford, Lord Anthony, on slavery reparations, 161

Gilroy, Paul, *The Black Atlantic*, 204n.11

glance, 94–94, 104

globalization: and the discourse of terrorism, 172–73; emergence of, 20

glossolalia, 82–83, 124

Gordon, Avery F., and Christopher Newfield, *Mapping Multiculturalism*, 50, 151

Gould, Charles, *America, A Family Matter*, 42

Greenberg, Clement, 94–95, 185n.13

Greenblatt, Stephen, 15, 141; and alternative histories, 162; *Shakespearian Negotiations*, 137–41

Guillory, John, *Cultural Capital* on lower-class identity, 212n.11

Habermas, Jürgen, "Richard Rorty's Pragmatic Turn," 188n.16

Haley, Alex, *The Autobiography of Malcolm X*, 129

Haraway, Donna, 15, 64, 69, 119–20, 174; "The Biopolitics of Postmodern Bodies," 36

Hardt, Michael, and Antonio Negri, *Empire*, 171–82

Hartmann, Geoffrey, on Jewish identity, 146

Hartmann, Sadakichi, 96–98

Hawthorne, Nathaniel, *The Scarlet Letter*, 91

heritage, 132; transmission of, 151

hermeneutic circle, 109

Historicism, 15; looms when causes replace reasons, 77; and Morrison's *Beloved*, 137–39; of Robinson's *The Debt*, 166

history, 23, 139, 164; acting as justification for, 78–79; appeal to, 131–32; as a chain of causes, 159; denial of, 151–52; end of history in Fukuyama, 9, 12, 80–81; and equal opportunity, 165; and individual identity, 133, 206n.24; irrelevance of, 166–68; and Jewish identity, 146, 206n.24; as a kind of memory, 135; loss of one's own, 206n.21; masochism's indifference to, 158; and national identity, 192n.35;

opposed to ideology in de Man, 9; and reparations, 161; and remembering, 138; in the shadow of poststructuralism, 140; as speaking for another, 162; transformed into memory, 145; that unites all humanity, 134

Hitler, Adolf, 129–31; and the attempt to destroy Jewishness, 147–48, 207n.27; in Ellis's *Glamorama*, 174

Holocaust, 14, 150; centrality of, 130–31; de Man's relationship to, 143; heritage of, 132; hostility to knowledge of, 141; and Jewish identity, 146–40, 205n.17, 206n.24

hope, preferred to knowingness in Rorty, 74, 77

Horowitz, David, "Ten Reasons Why Reparations for Blacks Are a Bad Idea for Blacks," 163

horror: impossibility of representing, 141; and the performative, 142

Howe, Susan, 1, 17, 104; on indifference to authors, 5; on the materiality of the signifier, 13; on the ontology of texts, 185n.13; and the social control of meaning, 2

Huntington, Samuel, "The Clash of Civilizations," 13, 26, 28, 33–34, 36, 41, 62–63, 66, 78, 211n.4

hybridity, 37, 190n.25, 204n.11

idealism, 89

identification, 38; with the narrative of the Holocaust, 146; and poverty, 181; and pride, 80

identitarianism, 185n.12; of Butler, 179; and cosmoplitanism, 190n.25; and deconstruction, 114; of Huntington and Fukuyama, 63; of the Left, 178; of Morrison and Spiegelman; of the radical Right, 187n.9; of Rorty, 44, 78; of Žižek, 181

identity, 17, 24, 41, 45–47, 78, 149–50; Cold War irrelevance of, 30; critique of, 184; constitution of Jewish, 146–48; and deconstruction, 65–55; and desire, 157, 208n.31; different religions as different, 170, 211n.3; essentialist versus antiessen-